Spending, Saving, and Employment

SPENDING, SAVING, & EMPLOYMENT

BY

H. GORDON HAYES

Professor of Economics at Ohio State University

ALFRED A. KNOPF   *New York*   1945

"It seems that somewhere in the present industrial process there is a factor of retardation which is only occasionally cast out by such a holocaust as war. What is the secret of its casting out, even for the space of three years? If this secret can be discovered, we may indulge the hope of institutionalizing it and adding permanently ten billion dollars to our annual national output. We could then realize the high standard of living of which reformers have dreamed. . . ."

David Friday, *The Journal of Political Economy*, February 1919.

Contents

Acknowledgments

THIS BOOK, like all others, has grown out of the past, for ideas no less than persons have ancestors; also, like most other books, it is a product of the times in which it was written. Certain persons who have thus unwittingly contributed to it are indicated in the text and footnotes, but most of them are, of course, unknown to me and their help can be acknowledged only in this general way. I am indebted also to a large number of persons who in discussion or merely by listening have helped in the clarification of the ideas expressed herein. I thank especially the following friends who have read portions of the manuscript and made helpful suggestions: Viva Boothe, Edison L. Bowers, Benjamin Caplan, John N. Hart, Clifford L. James, Alva M. Tuttle, and the late Virgil Willit, all of Ohio State University, Dudley Dillard of the University of Maryland, Jacob Kamm of Baldwin-Wallace College, and particularly John Fagg Foster, formerly of the University of Texas and now in the United States Army, whose extended assistance and searching criticism were unusually helpful. I gratefully acknowledge, too, the sympathetic co-operation of my wife, and the skillful work of F. Morris Sedgwick in deciphering and typing manuscripts.

My thanks are also due to the following publishers for permission to quote from the books indicated:

The Brookings Institution, *Income and Economic Progress,* by H. G. Moulton (1935), and *Business Leadership in the Large Corporation,* by R. A. Gordon (1945).

Harcourt, Brace & Company, Inc., *The General Theory of Employment, Interest, and Money,* by J. M. Keynes (1936).

Harper & Brothers, *Capitalism, Socialism, and Democracy,* by Joseph A. Schumpeter (1942).

Henry Holt & Company, *Towards Stability,* by Sumner H. Slichter (1934).

Little, Brown & Co., *The Good Society,* by Walter Lippmann (1937), and *A Time for Greatness,* by Herbert Agar (1943).

The Macmillan Company, *Conditions of Peace,* by E. H. Carr (1942).

W. W. Norton & Company, Inc., *Fiscal Policy and Business Cycles,* by Alvin H. Hansen (1941).

The University of North Carolina Press, *The Theory of Economic Progress,* by C. E. Ayres (1944).

Columbus, Ohio   H. G. H.
June 8, 1945

Postscript—Since this book was set in type, what is here said in respect to increasing economic interdependence as a result of technical improvements and in respect to the moral necessity of altering economic, political, and social institutions as a result of technical change has been dramatically high-lighted by the revelation that man has learned to utilize atomic power.

Spending, Saving, and Employment

PART ONE

MARKETS AND EMPLOYMENT

"Who could have thought that it would be easier to produce by toil and skill all the most necessary or desirable commodities than it is to find consumers for them? . . . It is certain that the economic problem with which we are now confronted is not adequately solved, indeed is not solved at all, by the teachings of the text-books, however grand may be their logic, however illustrious may be their authors."

WINSTON CHURCHILL: *Amid These Storms* (1932), pp. 237, 235.

CHAPTER I

Jobs for All

I

JOBS—A JOB FOR EVERY WORKER—this is our problem number one. It is not a problem just now, for we are at war, and war gives us jobs. But when the war is over, jobs will be scarce again. Indeed, this will begin to be true as soon as we start to reduce war production.

The men and women who work for wages have had a hard time finding jobs throughout the whole of our national history, except for a few brief periods. The oldest persons among us can remember only two times of full employment—the first World War and the present one. Not only have we suffered from chronic unemployment; we have had recurring periods of mass unemployment.

It appears probable that we shall be very prosperous as soon as our economy is reconverted to a peace-time basis. Even so, it is not likely that all who wish to work will be able to find jobs. There were some two or three million workers unemployed during the prosperous years of 1928 and 1929. But however well we may do in providing employment in the post-reconversion period, the years of prosperity will be few. We shall presently be floundering in a depression, unless we take the steps that are necessary to keep ourselves at work.

Depressions are an integral part of the economic practices that we have followed and are still following. They have been as much a part of our national history as have periods of prosperity. One can be as certain that another depression is not far off as one can be of anything in the future that depends on human conduct. It is only by altering the practices that breed depressions that they can be avoided, and we are apparently not yet willing to do that, although we are moving in that direction.

[1]

This book, it should be noted, is concerned with only one type of unemployment: namely, depression or chronic unemployment; that is, the condition of there not being jobs for those who want them. Other forms of unemployment are variously designated as "seasonal," "technological," and "frictional." The last of these three terms is often used to include the other two. Such unemployment is an almost inevitable part of a dynamic society, for changes in weather, methods of production, and demand for products cannot but cause certain kinds of work to be stopped, and the "frictions" in the society tend to prevent all workers so affected from immediately getting other jobs. That is, such unemployment results from available workers not having yet found the available jobs, while the unemployment dealt with in this book is that which results when there is a scarcity of jobs relative to available workers.

The absence of jobs, when that condition prevails, is wholly the result of practices that we follow. There is nothing in the physical nature of the universe that makes it necessary to deny some people the right to work. There is nothing in the physics or chemistry of producing and distributing goods that compels unemployment. The difficulties are wholly social—they are entirely of our own and our ancestors' making.

Certainly there were no physical factors that kept our economy running at only half capacity during almost the whole of the 1930's. There were no crop failures—no natural calamities —to cause our trouble. We had the most adequate equipment that the sun had ever shone on, we had plentiful supplies of raw material, we had abundant skills to do the work that waited to be done. Yet millions of our workers and their families rotted and starved in idleness, and distress pervaded the land. Monkeys would not starve in a coconut grove.

The practices that human beings follow are commonly referred to as a "way of life" or as traditions. They are also called folkways, or mores, or "mana and taboo"; a recent writer has used the word "ceremony" for them. But by whatever term we describe them, the practices of men, and back of these the attitudes and notions that they have, are of profound importance. And, for our present purpose, we must note that they are clung to with persistence and tenacity. Men have died of hunger rather than eat food that was under a taboo and have perished of disease because they would not accept remedies that had been proved helpful. Tragic losses have occurred during this war because men in authority were slow to see that old practices had to be given up and new ones adopted. Men may be imprisoned by ideas as firmly as by walls of iron.

We are making progress in respect to our attitude toward unemployment. The belief that a lack of jobs is part of the universe and must be endured is being abandoned as has been a similar long-held view in respect to epidemics of disease, and our attitude toward methods of control in this field is becoming realistic instead of traditional as it did long since in medicine. Soldiers in our armies do not die of typhoid fever today although they died like flies from that disease in some camps during the Spanish-American War, and within the next few decades the scourge of unemployment will undoubtedly be eliminated likewise. We shall do what we must do to accomplish this.

3

Certainly no one who understands these times believes that unemployment can be tolerated much longer. We, and our fathers before us, have been patient in this matter, but the end of the road is in sight. Men will no longer passively accept the humiliation of unemployment, for they have come to understand that the lack of jobs does not come from God's displeasure, but from the rules that men have made.

Perhaps the most important single factor in this change of attitude is the sheer weight of the numbers that are involved today when unemployment is widespread, and the proportion that these represent of the total population. During the whole of the 1800's our population was essentially rural. Recurring unemployment brought suffering, but the nearness of most persons to available land made this endurable for the nation as a whole. Today, with our high degree of urbanization—with half of our entire population living in 6.5 per cent of our 3,000 counties—unemployment has become more and more intolerable.

The whole temper of the times calls for "doing something about it," for not "letting nature take its course." During the past hundred years, and especially during the past fifty, the forces about us have been increasingly subjected to control. The technical revolution in agriculture and industry, the vast gains in all the fields that pertain to health, the spectacular developments during the present war—radar, jet-propelled planes, the life-saving techniques—everywhere we find emphasis on the "know-how." And in all the magazines and on practically every radio program the advertisers of the nation emphasize the controls that have been perfected in manufacturing processes and the ease of modifying one's health, beauty, and personality. This emphasis on control, although confined to physical elements and forces and actuated by a desire to sell goods, cannot but suggest the possibility of control over economic, political, and social relationships.

At any rate, the past few decades, and especially the past few years, have brought a great extension of control in human relations. The regulation of the railroads and other public utilities, controls over food and drugs, the insurance of bank deposits, legislative standards for hours and wages, the social security program—all these and other similar innovations reflect the temper of this age. Besides these expressions of the common will, the rapid growth of trade unionism is another important indication that people are "doing something about it." The broad movement along these various lines in this country not only has its counterpart in most other countries, but has been greatly extended in many places.

The saying "The common people are on the march" is a vivid

portrayal of the dynamism of today. The breaking away from old customs and the adoption of new ways all over the world point toward attempts to create a well-ordered economic life. Specifically, the trade unionists in this country, with experience in making demands and getting what they ask for, together with the men and women who will have been in the armed services, will not accept without protest the humiliation of mass unemployment. The common man will insist increasingly upon security in his job. Such security is as necessary for human dignity today as was the security in the ownership of property a hundred years ago when farms and small-scale businesses were the principal means of livelihood.

This *is* a matter of human dignity—not a matter of starvation. Men no longer starve when they are out of work, and most ironically this increases their suffering, for they have strength to feel the humiliation of being cast aside as useless. Nothing is as bad as unemployment. Disease and accident are misfortunes that can be borne. They are hard luck, but only that. But not having a job means that one does not count—that he is useless—that he is merely a bother, a cipher.

Further, the prevention of depression here in America is a vital part of the conditions necessary for the maintenance of peace. The present war, directly provoked by the aggressions of Germany and Japan, is certainly not unrelated to our depression of the 1930's. A nation such as ours cannot cut its purchases in the markets of the world from over 4 billion dollars per year as in the last five years of the 1920's to 1.33 billion as in 1932 without bringing acute distress throughout the entire world and prompting some people to seek relief through the primitive method of warfare. If in the next few years our foreign purchases amount to 6 or 7 billion dollars per year and then are cut in two because of widespread unemployment here, no one can measure the suffering that will be induced in other nations with economies like ours nor forecast the demagogic plans that will be offered as remedies. The paths of the Mussolinis and Hitlers are made easy when men have nothing to lose but their humiliation.

4

To write a book on the cause and cure of unemployment is to engage in high endeavor. It is a search for the means to a better world, whether or not the search is fruitful. Obviously, I believe that my search has yielded results that I should share with others, or I would not publish them. My answer as to the principal cause of unemployment is simple. Any high-school student can understand it. My major suggestion as to what should be done is also simple and easily understood.

This will discredit the book in the eyes of some men. For some believe that correct answers to economic problems are very involved. This is a complex world, they argue, and its problems and their answers are complex too. Such a notion is very satisfying to certain persons. It pleases them to believe that understanding is reserved to themselves and a few others like them.

Professor C. E. Ayres of the University of Texas in his book *The Theory of Economic Progress* (1944) emphasizes in a heartening way the virtue of simplicity. He says:

[The formulations of the economists who will] elaborate and systematize the economic thinking of our time . . . will be notable for their simplicity. In recent decades economic orthodoxy has become increasingly recondite, and professional economists have barricaded themselves from criticism behind the formidable complexities of their trade. "Oversimplification" has become a mortal sin. This is scholasticism. . . . The progress of science is always in the direction of the simplification of what seemed complex before. [The meaning of our economic activities will be] essentially simple and comprehensible once they are stripped of the half-truths of the past and the humbug of the present. [Pp. 306–7.]

CHAPTER II

Pressure to Sell

I

THE REASON for the scarcity of jobs that is so characteristic of our economy lies in the difficulty in selling the product that has been or might be produced. If buyers were always plentiful, there would never be any unemployment. It is only because the product cannot be sold that business men curtail production and dismiss employees. Customers make jobs.

The question as to why sales are usually difficult and sometimes impossible is the central issue in economics today. It is the major problem that confronts business men as they insist that "free enterprise" can provide jobs. It is, of course, the central problem in this book. I shall attempt to show why markets fail—why they cannot but fail periodically under our present practices.

2

Before we begin our analysis of the market problem, it may be well to emphasize the difficulty that producers have in selling their products. This is perhaps the most conspicuous feature of our economy. We all feel the pressure to sell whenever we turn on the radio, open a newspaper or magazine, or go into a store. Buy, buy, buy is a constant refrain. Every business establishment has a group of very alert and able men and women who devote themselves continually to the problem of disposing of the firm's product. Selling is a major activity of our economy. "Who could have thought," as Churchill has said, "that it would be easier to produce by toil and skill all the most necessary or desirable commodities than it is to find customers for them?" *

It is difficult to estimate what portion of the total economic effort of the nation is devoted merely to selling. Census data do not help as much as we might expect. Sellers are not distinguished from fabricators in manufacturing, or from those who

* See p. xiii above.

"produce" in mining, fishing, publishing, and other fields, and many who are listed in the wholesale and retail trades are not engaged in selling, but in assembling, classifying, and otherwise making goods available for potential users. The annual bill for advertising alone is estimated to have amounted to almost 2 billion dollars during the latter part of the 1930's. The total net income receipts of persons in wholesale and retail trades in the pre-war year 1939, according to the Department of Commerce,* amounted to almost 11 billion dollars out of a total net national income of approximately 71 billion dollars. This was more than twice the amount of the net income received in agriculture and almost two thirds that in manufacturing. But a portion of this, as noted above, was for what should properly be called non-selling services.

Despite the lack of exact figures, we all know that great effort is devoted to inducing people to buy. Thousands of able men and women spend their entire lives analyzing consumer interests and overcoming buyer resistance. The more successful of these are paid very handsomely, because of the great value that is set upon getting rid of goods.

One seldom, even in the course of a whole lifetime, importunes a seller, unless a war or other occurrence reduces the supply of goods or increases the supply of money. It is practically always a matter of indifference to the buyer whether he makes a particular purchase since other sellers stand ready to serve. As a result of this sellers are sometimes treated brusquely by buyers, but they always turn the other cheek. They flatter the customer, thank him for his patronage, and urge him to come again. If later he is dissatisfied, adjustments are made to please him.

It is also of note that stores are almost always well stocked. Normally one can find in any city practically anything that anyone might possibly wish to purchase. Yesterday's supply is never wholly sold—shelves are never cleared. How strange it would seem to one of us to be dropped down into a society

* *Survey of Current Business*, April 1944, p. 15, table 16.

where, aside from periods of emergency, goods were sold as soon as they came on the market and buyers importuned sellers and gave them presents and kind words.

Selling is not, however, just a matter among us as citizens; it is also a matter of national policy in relation to persons outside our borders. As a nation we normally spend a great amount of effort getting foreigners to buy our goods and then an almost equal amount of energy keeping them from paying for their purchases with other goods. Our pressure to sell has as its necessary counterpart a resistance against buying from abroad.

This constant pressure to sell is an expression of our chronic inability to distribute what we are able to produce. It is here that we must look for the retarding element in our economy which is the basic cause of unemployment. The holocaust of war has temporarily given us a market for all that is or might be produced and has accordingly given jobs to all, including the "unemployable" of a few years ago. But the return of peace will find our markets clogged again and men hunting vainly for jobs, if the usual practices are continued.

3

It may be contended that the difficulty in selling can be easily explained and that there is no need to think of it as being especially significant. For, it may be said, selling is made difficult by the mere fact that sellers always tend to overreach the market. By trying to get as much as possible, it may be argued, sellers make it difficult for customers to buy.

This is an important point. Selling for profit almost necessarily makes sales "slow." But this cannot explain the matter of a lack of markets. There must be another element in the situation. While certain firms may destroy their chance to sell and to provide employment by demanding too high prices, this cannot be the reason for a general failure in markets. Business men as a whole are not so shortsighted as to bring on a depression such as that of the 1930's by refusing to sell at fair prices. There must be something else that destroys the market.

It may also be said that our attitude as a nation toward foreign trade comes from the attempt of producers to limit competition, and is hence merely part of a system of private enterprise. But here again this does not appear to be sufficient to explain the attitude of a nation decade after decade. The selfish interests of a relatively few producers could hardly be expected to determine national policy indefinitely. There must be another factor in the situation, and it is reasonable to believe that it is merely the basic difficulty that we have of selling the product of the nation to the persons who together produce it.

The analysis in the following pages attempts to explain why it is that we have so much difficulty in selling what we produce. The argument is, in brief, that there tends to be a chronic shortage of buying power in our markets because of the amount of money that is withheld from use. The difficulty, it will be contended, is not that there is not enough money disbursed by producers, since the total money receipts from the productive process—wages, interest, rent, and profits—are necessarily equal to the value of the product. But, obviously, any withholdal of money from use in purchase or investment means that the money used would be less than the value of the product and hence that it would then be difficult or impossible to sell the total product even if it were offered at cost—even if there were no overreaching by sellers. It will be argued, further, that the process of saving as we practice it almost necessarily means that some of our money savings are not used in investment, and, particularly, that this is practically inevitable periodically. This, it is contended, is the crux of our difficulty in distributing our product and maintaining employment.

It will be pointed out that we have developed several devices or expedients that permit us to overcome this difficulty and enjoy periods of prosperity, but it will be shown that certain of these are necessarily limited in duration, and that depressions appear to be inevitable under our present practices.

CHAPTER III

If Savings Are Uninvested

I

WE TURN NOW to a consideration of the consequence of saving money, if the money saved is not invested. This involves, in other words, a consideration of the results that flow from the hoarding of money. For money that is not spent but saved and then not invested is of necessity hoarded. It is not used; it is held idle.

Money that is held idle does not take any goods or services off the market. It does not provide any employment; it induces unemployment. This is so simple and obvious that to state it seems to be a reflection on the intelligence of the reader. But it is of such prime importance in respect to employment, and has been neglected over such a long period of time, that it must be set down and, indeed, emphasized.

An economy of specialists, such as ours, depends on the exchange of products. And when, as with us, money is used in the exchange process, the work of the various specialists can be carried on only if their products are bought and paid for. That is, workers can be employed only if others will buy what they produce. The flow of money in an economic system such as ours is as vital to its health and life as is the flow of blood to the health and life of a human body.

The non-use, or the hoarding, of money applies, obviously, only to money that is saved. It could not apply to money that is spent. Thus the problem of hoarding money brings us back to the matter of saving money, not spending it, and after saving it, then not investing it.

The word "spending," as it is used here, means the use of money in consumption. It means buying food, clothing, entertainment, transportation, hair-cuts, and so on. It carries the connotation that the buying power involved is gone, exhausted, spent, as is one's strength after a hard race. The word "investing" means the use of money with a view to maintaining or increasing one's wealth. This normally means the securing—or the attempt to secure—a recurring income while maintaining the principal sum of money value that is used. It means buying a bond, a share of stock, a factory, or other property of this sort.

The line between spending and investing is often indistinct, as is the line between boys and men, but the general difference is clear and important. These two ways of using money may also be characterized as the purchase of consumer goods and services and the purchase of producer goods. Here, too, there may be doubt whether certain purchases belong in one or the other category, but there can be no question of the validity of the broad classification.

The investing of money means, then, usually that it is used to employ labor in the construction of factories, mills, office buildings, residences, or other forms of income-yielding property. One may "invest" in property that has already been constructed or in the paper claims—stocks, bonds, or mortgages—to such property. Such an investment does not provide employment. The question of employment in such a case is then transferred to the seller of the investment property. Does he spend the money received for consumption goods or does he save it? If he saves it, does he invest it or hoard it?

Even the purchase of consumption goods does not necessarily provide employment. The merchant may not replace them—he may hoard the money. But usually the spending of money—using it to purchase consumption goods and services—does give employment. And similarly investing it—buying stocks, bonds, or other commercial paper, or business property, or loaning it directly to business men—generally puts people to work. We shall accordingly assume that the investment of savings provides employment while their non-investment does not.

It should be noted, however, that even when savings are

invested the time interval between the receipt of money and its use in hiring labor tends to be longer, perhaps considerably longer, than when money receipts are used in consumption. The accumulation of funds by individuals, their collection by lending institutions, the demands for funds by business men, and the blueprint stage of planning may delay the utilization of money funds. To be sure, a series of steps such as these might become so routinized that the flow of funds from the saver to the investor-user would be comparable to putting water in one end of a long pipe and immediately getting water from the other end. That, however, is not actually the case. The steps that money takes from saving to use in investment not only are of a halting nature but vary from case to case. The time lag is important. Nevertheless, in general, the investment of savings means that the money saved is used to put people to work.

Just when should we say that savings are not invested? That is, when is money hoarded? Certainly every dollar is not, and could not, be passed on immediately upon its receipt. Each week's wages are not spent the instant they are received. A time interval is required for spending or for investing the money that one gets, which is roughly the time between pay days. Any holding of money or delay in writing checks against one's bank balance beyond such a period tends to cause unemployment.

It is sometimes said that money held idle is in "use" just as is a fire-extinguisher that hangs undisturbed year after year. It is being kept available for purchase when prices of either consumption or investment goods fall low enough to suit the canny holder of the money. But as the illustration suggests, the "use" to which it is being put permits prices to fall and unemployment to increase. Certainly for the purpose of maintaining employment and an ordinary degree of health in the economy such funds are not in use. They are unused, uninvested, hoarded.

There are conditions under which the hoarding of money does not create unemployment. This is the case when sufficient new money is being created and used to equal the amount being hoarded. During the present war, for example, the government is borrowing so much money at the banks—is exchanging its bonds for such large amounts of newly created checkbook money—that this more than offsets any amount of hoarding that may be taking place. Further, the government expenditures become buying power to the recipients, but what they produce consists of goods that are not for sale—planes and tanks—so buying power runs ahead of available civilian goods. Even after taxes and war-bond purchases there is a big excess of money as compared with the output of civilian goods at current prices. This is called an "inflation gap" and makes it necessary to ration goods and control prices. This compels people to hoard money or buy war bonds. Either of these is a patriotic act.

Hoarding may also be offset by the creation of check-book money by the banks as loans are made to business men. But usually when loans to business men are increasing, hoarding is not taking place. Hoarding normally is not offset by the creation of additional buying power. The hoarded funds constitute a "deflation gap." They mean falling prices and unemployment.

2

There is apparently no difference of opinion in respect to this. Economists, journalists, business men—all who discuss the problem of employment today—stress the need of having investments equal to the volume of money savings.

It has long been common knowledge among students of business fluctuations that employment and construction rise and fall together. But it is only recently that this has been related to the volume of savings. John Maynard Keynes, now Lord Keynes, deserves great credit for clarifying our thinking in this matter. His major contribution is contained in his book

The General Theory of Employment, Interest, and Money,
published in 1936. More detailed consideration will be given
to Keynes in Chapter xii. Suffice it to say in this place that he
developed the point that if the people of a nation have a given
"propensity to consume," which means also a given "propensity
to save," the volume of investment will determine the degree
of employment that is provided. He accordingly recommended
policies to encourage investment, and, failing that, the spending of government funds to put the unemployed at work.

Professor Alvin H. Hansen has also been very influential in
teaching the public the relation between saving and investment.
There has, properly, been an element of pessimism in his analysis, as he feels that our economy is so "mature" that there will
not be sufficient investment by business to provide full, or even
high, employment in the years that lie ahead. Hence he sees
need for "investment" by the government. But however that
may be, Hansen has emphasized the importance of investments
equaling savings if all of us are to be employed. Apparently
there is no difference on this score among economists. Savings
must be invested if all of us are to be permitted to work.

This simple and now obvious point is made repeatedly in
the journals that deal with economic problems. The *United
States News,* for example, spoke in a recent issue (December
17, 1943, p. 7) of "the problem of finding investment outlets
for all savings." *Fortune,* in discussing the possibility of producing 165 billion dollars' worth of goods per year in the postwar period, said in its January 1944 issue:

. . . if what people want to save . . . plus what corporations retain as undistributed profits is not offset by borrowing and spending
for new machinery, houses, equipment, then we shall not have $165
billion of production. Instead we shall have something less. This is
not theory but arithmetic. [P. 192.]

The leading business men use the same language. Sloan of
General Motors said in a widely circulated address (*Post-War
Jobs,* The Economic Club of Detroit, October 11, 1943, p. 27)

The disposition of the savings of business and individuals raises an important economic problem—one little appreciated. It is essential that we reinvest our savings promptly and productively. They must not remain static. An economic formula tells us that production is equal to consumption plus savings. To the degree that we freeze our savings we reduce our ability to produce by just that much; hence, we contract job opportunities.

There is apparently no remaining opposition to the idea that investments must equal savings if employment is to be maintained. This part of the terrain has evidently been completely won and occupied.

3

The present view of the disastrous consequences of having uninvested savings—unused or hoarded money—is in the sharpest possible contrast to that which prevailed among economists for the past one hundred and fifty years or so. A glance at this may contribute to the argument presented here.

This problem has been one of the economist's blind spots. He has looked over or around or through it without seeing it. It has not concerned him. When the idea of hoarded money did occur to him he dismissed it as did David Ricardo (1772–1823) when he said: "If ten thousand pounds were given to a man having £100,000 per annum, he would not lock it up in a chest" (*Principles,* Chapter xxi); or as did Boehm-Bawerk (1851–1914), who observed simply "an economically advanced people does not hoard" (*Positive Theory,* Book II, Chapter v).

There is apparently no discussion of the matter anywhere in orthodox economic literature. The word "hoarding" seldom appears in the indexes of the books published after the inclusion of an index became the custom. Taussig's comprehensive two-volume work is something of an exception in this regard. He says: "Saving may take the form of simple hoarding" (Vol. I, p. 73), but his discussion pertains to misers, to conditions when "property is insecure," or to persons as in India who hoard from habit. There is no reference to the relation of hoarding and unemployment.

Lest these references seem captious, I must observe that there is not a word about this matter in a general text on economics that I published in 1928. It is only in what Keynes calls the "underworld of economics"—made up of those outside the respectable academic circles—that this problem was considered before the decade of the 1930's.

From the beginning of modern economics, however, attention has been given to a "store of value" as one of the three or four functions of money. Perhaps no economist who ever wrote about money or talked about it—and that must include almost every one of us—failed to mention that one can "store value" by keeping money. We thus talked about hoarding money, but we never called it that and never discussed the economic consequences that flow from that practice.

Our blind spot is also evident when we note what we did with the well-known equation of exchange, $MV = PT$. This equation means, in the simplest view of it, that the money paid by buyers equals the money received by sellers. The volume of money, M, that is used multiplied by the number of times it is used—that is, by its velocity, V—is the amount spent and invested during a given period, say one year. The volume of trade, T, multiplied by the average price received, P, is the amount of money received by sellers during the same period. In its expanded form bank deposits, M', multiplied by their rate of turnover, V', was included, giving us $MV + M'V' = PT$.

This equation, which every economist used during the past several decades, was kept wholly in the field of prices. The analysis concerned the effect of changes in the volume of the primary money and bank-check money or changes in their velocities on the level of prices. Prices were the focal point in the use of the equation. Prosperity and depression were brought into the analysis only as the conditions of business were influenced by rising or falling prices. Unemployment was never mentioned as the result of a slowing down of the promptness with which money was spent or invested.

The man in the street has always had a clear understanding of the importance of "putting money in circulation." He has emphasized the benefit that flows from "free spending" and from the spending occasioned by accidents and calamities. The economists, however, had great sport lampooning him for his nonsense. Did not everyone know that money is always in circulation and that if it does not have to be used to repair damage it will be used to add to our stock of goods? Or that if it is not used to provide trivial employment, it will be used to provide wholesome employment? The fool may now laugh at his detractors.

We know now that money does not automatically stay in circulation. We know, indeed, that large sums of money are likely to be hoarded, particularly after a few years of prosperity. We know too that when money is hoarded accidents, calamities or wars that call the hoards into use or lead to the creation of new money do provide employment. We know from our experience during this war that waste on a grand scale may enable the people of a nation to live better than ever before. We are learning.

4

There are perhaps four principal reasons for the failure of economists until recently to understand the problem of hoarded money or uninvested savings. First modern economics developed in the latter part of the eighteenth century, and the first part of the nineteenth and had to fight its way against the philosophy of Mercantilism. One of the tenets of that school was that it is very important to have a large supply of money coin or bullion within a country and that public policy should be directed to induce an inward flow of money metal and to prevent it from flowing out again. The economists attacked this notion and in doing so were easily led to play down the importance of money. John Stuart Mill, for example, writing in the middle of the 1800's, said: "The difference between a country with money, and a country altogether without it, would be only one of convenience; a saving of time and trouble, like grinding corn by water instead of by hand, or (to use Adam Smith's illustration) like the benefit derived from roads." * The tragedy of this lies in the failure of Mill and others to realize that when a country is adjusted to the use of a given quantity of money, hoarding any appreciable amount of it is comparable to blocking the roads that people have come to depend on in the conduct of commerce.

In the second place, the great value that was placed by the early economists on competition as a force that transmutes all economic behavior into good no doubt made them conclude, if they thought about the matter at all, that any tendency to withhold money from use would lead to such a prompt adjustment of prices that the money hoards would be by-passed, and that the economy would go on its way as if such funds of idle money did not exist. Today, however, it is increasingly evident that trade is so hedged about and limited that less can be expected of competition than was expected of it when classical economics was being formulated. Anyway, however "perfect" competition may be, the baneful effects of letting money lie unused cannot thereby be overcome, as we shall see later.

Thirdly, the neat, equilibrium analysis, which was part of the economists' general theory of competition, led them to the conclusion that the volume of savings was dependent upon the prevailing rate of interest. Hence any failure to secure the going rate would cause money to be spent that would otherwise have been saved. The rate of interest demanded by the savers who were on the margin of spending and received by them as the price of saving, was available as well to the non-marginal savers. There was no place in this doctrine for uninvested savings. We know now, of course, that the disposition to save is

* *Principles of Political Economy* (1848), Preliminary Remarks, 5th London edition, p. 23. See also the reference to J. B. Say, in Chapter xiii of this book.

not dependent on the receipt of interest. Savers welcome the gain from interest, but if they cannot get the rate that they want with what appears to be reasonable safety, they continue to save and hold their money idle despite the social devastation that their conduct produces.

A fourth factor in the neglect by economists of the consequences of hoarding money is that the problem of unemployment was far less serious during the 1800's and the early 1900's than it is now. The relative importance of self-sufficient agriculture made the lack of jobs in cities more endurable then, and, in part because of this, but little attention was given to unemployment by the leaders of thought. Depressions were regarded as aberations from normal economic conditions. The economic forces, it was maintained, tended to prevent the occurrence of depressions, and, even more, tended to restore prosperity whenever hard times appeared. Part of all this was the dominant fact of vigorous capital expansion throughout this period, which led rather promptly to recovery from depression. The economists reflected the optimism of the period, but in doing so they failed to observe a most important factor in economic behavior.

5

Since the hoarding of money largely takes the form of not drawing checks against bank deposits, some consideration must be given to this phase of the problem. It is a common opinion that if a person does not use his bank deposit, the bank itself will use it. Thus according to this view hoarding cannot take the form of holding bank balances idle.

In answer to this it may be noted, in the first place, that bankers as well as depositors may not be able to find attractive investments. When such a situation occurs bankers, obviously, would not use their depositors' money, even if they could. Secondly, deposits are invested by being transferred by check, and if the general opportunities are such that savers prefer to wait rather than to invest at once, such delay does not in any way give banks an opportunity to use their depositors' funds.

In further illustration of this point, it may be observed that if the account of A in bank 1 is increased by his depositing a check from B drawn on this same bank, the bank does not come into possession of additional funds and has nothing to use if A refrains indefinitely from drawing checks against his deposit. Similarly for the banking system as a whole, transfers from one bank to another, or failure to make such transfers, do not alter the volume of deposits held by the banks as a group or the power of the banks to make investments.

If C increases his account in bank 1 by depositing a check from D on bank 2, and if there are no offsetting transactions between the two banks, bank 2 will have to pay cash to bank 1. Let us assume that the bank pays in currency and that the amount involved is $1,000. Bank 1 must use a portion of this deposit to enlarge its reserve at the central bank, and it will have to set aside a small portion of the currency received as additional till money. If the legal reserve requirement is twenty per cent, as is true now for almost all banks that are members of the Federal Reserve System, and if the bank keeps till money equal to three per cent of its deposits, it will be able to invest for its own account $770 out of the deposit of $1,000. Bank 2, it should be noted, must disinvest by this amount. Hence there is no net increase in investment. If now, C, the receiver of the additional deposit of $1,000, hoards this "money"—if he refrains from drawing checks against this deposit—the bank is in no way able to invest the funds in his stead.

A minor exception to this conclusion should be noted. The hoarding of funds in the form of bank deposits—keeping savings in this form—does make it possible for banks to increase their investments since the slowing down in the volume of checks reduces the withdrawals of cash and thus makes it unnecessary for banks to keep as large a volume of till money as formerly. But as till money normally represents a very small portion of demand deposits, three per cent or less, any reduction in the volume of till money will be of no appreciable significance in altering the total volume of investments. Finally, it may be observed that the practice of encouraging depositors to maintain large balances does not come from a bank's desire to use the deposits, but from a desire not to pay cash to another bank to whom checks may go when deposits are reduced. In general, then, the failure of bank depositors to invest the funds that they save in banks is not offset by any investment of the unused funds by the banks.

6

Certain followers of Keynes may object to the expression "savings in excess of investment" or "uninvested savings" on the ground that savings and investment are equal. As Keynes says, however, they are only equal as aggregates for society as a whole. Further, it is more strictly accurate and Keynesian to say that they *become* equal rather than that they *are* equal. Failure to invest savings reduces incomes, and this decreases money savings on the next round. This continues until savings fall to the amount that is invested. Keynes also makes the point, as will appear later,* that the saving of an individual does not necessarily bring into existence a corresponding investment. His quip that his great discovery was that the persons who save are not the ones who invest makes sense only in terms of money savings not being invested.

7

The making of investments—the construction of new plants and new equipment—is in line with the best American tradition. This has always been extolled. For in this way the output of goods was enlarged and the scale of living was raised decade by decade. The new tools always served well—better than had their predecessors. Capital building enlarged consumption.

This view of the need for more and better equipment sharp-

---

* Chapter xii.

ened the scorn of our fathers for anyone who proposed that the government "make work" in order to provide employment, or, what amounted to the same thing, who argued that the nation "oversaves" or "underconsumes" and hence creates unemployment. The need for more capital, it was insisted in all respectable quarters, meant that there could not be too much saving or any occasion for "making work."

We now see that these views were inaccurate, but they carried the point that investments were desired because consumption would thereby be enlarged. The emphasis on investment today is, in contrast, based largely on employment. This is certainly the meaning of the statements concerning this matter that are made almost daily. The main idea is that investments will put or keep people at work. It is essentially a "make-work" idea.

Occasionally, in connection with the clamor for investments, a reference is made to the flow of consumer goods that will thereby be made possible. But such expressions usually sound like afterthoughts. They seem to be apologies for having been caught fraternizing with the "make-work fallacy" of the nineteenth century. Certainly no one can deny that Keynes, Hansen, and all their academic followers, and all the business men and other good citizens who stress the need for investment in order to maintain employment, have in the fore-front of their minds the idea of "making work."

Business investments must pay, or must be expected to pay, or they will not be made. Thus there is always at least a latent notion of a flow of consumer goods and services. But this tends to be submerged. The vital idea is to provide jobs constructing equipment. Investments have thus taken on something of the character of "boondoggling." They are more respectable than leaf-raking, but serve the same immediate purpose as did that maligned activity in 1933–4.

Wherever thoughtful and respectable men gathered at any time during the early 1930's, one heard the cry that investments were needed to make us prosperous. Yet during these years there was perhaps not a city in the nation that did not have acres of well-equipped factories standing idle. The real need was to put the unemployed to work in these idle factories. But the only way open to us was to build new factories. That was the only way that we could put the idle men and the idle factories to work. For that was the only way that we could, or would, put our idle money to work.

There is thus a most unfortunate element in the insistence on providing investments. No notice is taken of social needs— of whether it would be better to make more shoes in the factories that we already have or to build more shoe factories. Certainly there are situations in which it is better to use an axe to cut firewood rather than to make more axes.

These considerations suggest that the current emphasis on investment will prove to be ephemeral. After all, we are creatures of intelligence and we must expect that our conduct will not long continue to be irrational. We will surely continue to attempt to direct our energies to the most important tasks. Folkways are persistent, but when they become antisocial they can be modified.

But however unjustifiable it may be to build more equipment rather than use what we already have, the point remains that, under our present rules, investments must balance savings if employment is to be maintained. Or more generally, the income generated at any given level of employment must be used promptly in consumption or investment if that level of employment is to be maintained. Every dollar of a given national income must be used if the yearly income is not to fall by the unused amount multiplied by its annual velocity, except as new money is added to the system.

8

Three frequently expressed notions as to why we have so much difficulty in selling our product and maintaining employment must now be considered. They are, namely: (1) there is not enough money; (2) the poor have too little income; and (3) profit-making creates a deficiency in buying power.

Contrary to the first of these, there is always enough money to buy the product, since the amount of money disbursed by firms and retained as profit and depreciation is necessarily the same in amount as the value of the product. The value of the product and the money involved are merely two sides of the same coin, but it does not follow from this that there is always enough money to buy the product at formerly prevailing prices.

Indeed, this cannot be true if the productivity per worker or the number of workers is increasing, unless the quantity of money is increased to correspond with the increase in production. Hence with no increase in money the product would have to be sold at a decrease in price and this would tend to make sales "slow," or impossible for the entire quantity if sellers refused to cut prices. This was apparently the condition experienced by our economy following the Civil War until the middle of the 1890's, at which time an increase in the production of gold augmented annually the supply of money beyond the increase in the production of goods and services.

The establishment of the Federal Reserve Banking System has made it possible apparently for the supply of money—check-book money—to increase as the volume of production increases. The use of bank credit, it should be noted, is sharply different, for this purpose, from the use of consumer credit. The limit to bank credit lies in the volume of business done, except when a fixed reserve of gold imposes a limit, but the possible volume of consumer credit depends on the incomes of buyers.

In general, then, the supply of money may not be adequate to permit sales except at a reduced price if the volume of trade is increasing, although the possibility of expanding bank credit in this country has made this of but little moment to us. But if the supply of money is sufficient to permit sales at no reduction in price, the amount used will be inadequate if any is saved and not invested. Lack of an adequate supply of money is thus at most only contributory to the difficulty that comes from saving. Failure to invest all that is saved is the basic difficulty.

The second point, that the failure to sell comes from a lack of buying power on the part of the poorest sections of the population, is not sound except as a more equal division of income would so reduce savings that they would all be invested.

If the poorer half of the population can buy only twenty per cent of the total national product, then, obviously, the richer half can buy the remaining eighty per cent. If there is no hoarding of money, all that is produced can be sold. Hence it is not poverty as such that impedes sales, but failure of the more well-to-do groups to use all of their money funds.

Further, the total elimination of poverty would not solve the problem. Indeed, it would make it worse. If, for example, every family in the United States received at least three thousand dollars per year, the difficulty from saving would be augmented. If a chronic depression did not result from the added savings, at least any suggestion that business might decline and workers lose their jobs would cause such a nation-wide saving for the expected "rainy day" that a storm of great intensity would be induced. The poorer we are, the better we can do in maintaining employment. Blessed are the poor.

(Furthermore, our economy becomes more unstable as we make our products more durable, because this increases the likelihood of postponing replacement purchases whenever coming events take on a dark aspect. Similarly, any accumulation of stocks of goods also contributes to economic instability. The better we do for ourselves, the more precarious our position becomes.)

Nevertheless, our present national income would give more continuous employment if it were divided so that there were less inequality. The transference of, say, one third of the total amount of money received by the upper economic half of the population to the lower half would undoubtedly reduce unemployment, for it would increase the share of the total income that is spent and reduce the portion that is saved.

The third of these beliefs—that the profit-making nature of our economy prevents sales from being made—is also invalid. It is said, for example, that if a firm pays out 90 units of money as wages, interest, and other outlays, it cannot sell its product at 100 and make a profit of 10 without robbing some other seller of a market. This appears valid at first glance, but it is not sound. The error comes from considering one firm as typical of all firms taken together. If there were only one firm in an economy, it could not pay out 90 and get back 100, but since there are many firms the profits of one or more may be used in purchasing goods and services from the others.

Consider thirty firms, for example, and assume that each one markets its product on a different day of the month. Certainly, then, each one could pay out 90 units and sell its product for 100, if the 10 units of profit made by each one is used in purchasing from the others, or even in the case of just one firm it could pay out 90, get back 90, and retain 10 units of product as profit. There is nothing in our economy to prevent enterprise from being rewarded, as well as labor and capital. Making profit does not lead to unemployment except as the money receipts may be hoarded rather than spent or invested. It is the non-use of money funds—the non-investment of money savings—that causes the difficulty. Profits, however, are very likely to be an important source of such funds.

9.

We turn now to a consideration of the question whether it is possible to invest our savings continuously. Keynes and almost every other person who discusses this problem talk as if it is possible. If the economy expands sufficiently, they say, investments can be kept equal to savings. But can the economy continue to expand? Particularly can it do this without breaks—without depressions? Does the savings process itself prevent investments from being made continuously? Is it inevitable that we shall have uninvested savings at least periodically?

CHAPTER IV

Uninvested Savings Inevitable

I

THE SAVINGS-INVESTMENT PROCESS as we practice it leads inevitably to unemployment. It prevents the sale of consumer goods from being sufficient to utilize present producer goods and thus destroys the demand for further investment. This is true because (1) investment results in an increased output of consumer goods and (2) investors refuse to buy the share of these goods to which their incomes entitle them, since they wish to increase their savings.

These two propositions hardly need defense, but misunderstanding may be avoided by a hasty survey. In respect to the first one, it is certainly true that both from the point of view of national welfare and of money return to investors, business investments are justified only as they result in an enlargement of the output of consumer goods and services. To be sure, certain investment goods turn out other investment goods—some factories produce machine tools—but this is merely a step toward the production of things to be sold to consumers. It is only when consumers will buy that there is justification in producing intermediate goods.

Further, some investments merely replace previous investments—are of the nature of "repairs and maintenance" and hence do not enlarge output. Similarly some investments are purchases of already existing equipment, as noted earlier, and so do not augment the flow of consumer goods. Investments of these sorts, however, do not contribute to the growth of the national plant. They are very far from what is typically American and are not what anyone has in mind in charting our course. In short, investments must be assumed to enlarge the consumer product.

It should be noted in passing that some savings are invested

[28]

in the bonds of government units and result in school buildings, roads, and so on, which yield a product that is not sold on the market. We are limiting the discussion at this point, however, to business investments.

The second of the two propositions also expresses a typically American practice—getting ahead. We wish as individuals to grow in wealth. We wish to save, and to save the income from our previous savings. That is, we wish to enjoy the fruits of compound interest.

There are exceptions, of course. Large numbers of persons have incomes that are too small to permit saving and some others simply do not wish to save, but certainly our savers as a class have never reached the limit of their desire to accumulate wealth. Nothing is more a part of the capitalist process than the quest for compound interest.

The argument of this book is then, briefly, that the desire to save prevents the purchase of the consumption goods and services that must be sold if employment is to be maintained. The market impasse to which the savings-investment process brings us may be postponed or avoided during certain lucky periods by the use of various expedients such as sales on credit, exports in excess of imports (net exports), and fortunate inventions. We shall consider these in the following chapter. Suffice it to observe here that all of these expedients merely postpone the market impasse. They cannot enable us to avoid it.

2

Let us assume a "free enterprise" economy such as ours, but small enough so that the relationships that we are considering can be readily seen. We assume an absence of consumer credit either in the form of sales on credit or of loans at financial institutions and an absence of foreign trade. We also assume that there are no monopolies, no trade unions, no taxes and no politics. There is nothing to hamper business except such conditions as are inherent in business. Let us see what happens.

All of the savings in this community, other than those devoted to repairs and maintenance (which some persons would not call savings), are made, let us assume, by one man, a Mr. Z. His available savings at the beginning of the first year of our observation amount to $2,000 and he loans this sum to a business man who uses it to improve his equipment. The new equipment permits the regular labor force to increase the yearly output by an amount of goods valued at $100. This extra product, plus the customary product, cannot be sold at the usual prices if the amount of money available is not increased. Hence to make the use of the savings as little disturbing as possible, let us assume that a bank extends $100 of credit to the business man on the security of the extra product valued at $100. The business man pays this sum to Z as interest at 5 per cent on the loan of $2,000.

Note that the only changes that take place in this community during this first year as a result of the savings and investment are that the output of goods is increased by the amount of $100 and that Z's money income increases by $100. All other things remain as before. Workmen are not displaced as a result of the new equipment—they merely have better things with which to work. In terms of strict productivity theory Z produces the extra output valued at $100. He might have used his $2.000 in consumption, but chose instead, in effect, to use it to employ labor to produce new equipment and then to use that equipment in turning out an extra product. Z is the only one who has come into possession of extra money, and this is his due.

Thus Z, and only Z, can buy the extra product that has been created, if the customary product that has been produced as usual is to be sold as formerly. If Z will buy the extra product to which he has the money tickets, or will buy an equal quantity of the customary product and let others buy the increment that we are designating as the extra product, all will be well, employment will be maintained.

We may, if you like, think of the product of this community

as consisting of a single kind of good, and hence that the only change made is that the product is enlarged by $100 worth of additional but identical units. The significant point is still the same: that Z, and Z alone, has the money with which to buy the addition that has been made to the product as a result of his investment.

Let us assume that Z continues to save $2,000 each year, that this is invested so as to increase output by $100 each year, that Z gets $100 additional income each year as interest, and extends his consumption annually by $100 worth of goods. Z, obviously, consumes an ever larger portion of the total output of the society, but this is merely his reward for abstaining from the consumption of the amount that he saves each year. The significant point is that employment is maintained. Z buys and consumes, or invests in, the share of the total product to which his share of the total income entitles him. All is well in respect to employment.

Suppose now that Z hears about the magic of compound interest and decides to save the income from his savings. He wishes to save during the ensuing year not only $2,000 as formerly but the additional $100 which he receives during that year. Certainly $100 worth of product cannot then be sold. The only man who has the money to buy it refuses to do so. He wants to save that sum of money. A market glut will have been created.

But, it will be said, if Z could save $2,000 each year without disrupting the economy, surely he can save $2,100 without disrupting it. He could if the business men could count on his then buying the product from the enlarged saving. Business men will not, and cannot, go on piling up equipment if they cannot sell the product. And the product must eventually consist of consumption goods. Failure to buy them as in Z's case creates a market glut. This will mean that the community will have "overproduced." Supply will have outrun demand. Business men will then "take in sail"; they will attempt to get in a liquid position; they will dismiss employees; a depression will settle over the community.

Please note that the many things that are frequently cited as explanations of unemployment are not involved here. There are no "sticky" prices, no exorbitant demands by workers, no taxes that penalize investment, no administration that destroys confidence. Nothing at all has happened to bring sorrow into this garden except an attempt to save at compound interest —a refusal to consume the fruits of previous saving.

If a group of people in the United States build 10 billion dollars' worth of new industrial equipment during a given year and receive a half billion dollars as interest, is it not clear that if this extra income is used to buy the goods and services that are added to the yearly output by the new equipment, or a similar amount of the customary goods, the total enlarged output can be sold, but that if the interest is saved, goods will be left unsold?

Let me state this once again. If a nation has an annual product of 100 units and a national income of 100 units, and if 80 units of the money income are spent and 20 units saved, then a division of the product into 80 units of consumer goods and 20 units of producer goods will permit the market to be cleared and employment to be maintained. In the second year the total output will amount to 101, assuming 5 per cent gain on the 20 units saved and invested the first year. This extra unit of product will normally consist of consumer goods. Thus the product will be divided 81:20 as between the two categories of goods. But the extra unit of money income will accrue as interest to the savers, and they will normally wish to save it. Money income will then be divided 80:21 as between spending and savings, while the corresponding goods are divided 81:20. One unit of goods will not be sold; one unit of money income will not be used. A market impasse will be created—workers will be dismissed.

3

The trouble arises not just because Z or any group of persons attempts to save at compound interest, but because the people of the nation as a whole attempt to augment their money savings. If additions to money savings were made by an entirely new group of persons each year, the result would be the same as if a given group compound their money savings.

The pioneer farmers could accumulate savings without disturbing the economy. They could grow in wealth without injuring others, for they took their savings in the form of barns, orchards, and livestock. But their descendants are not so fortunate. We cannot save today the food, clothing, and entertainment that we shall want a decade or so hence. If we could do that, we could save without embarrassing one another. But our savings, with minor exceptions, must take the form of money claims, and as I have shown this leads to hoarding and unemployment. To put this in another way, there are limits to the extent to which money will be, or can be, borrowed at interest and invested, since the amount that is borrowed reduces the amount left with which to buy the products to be produced with the borrowed money.

If out of a personal income of 100 or a national income of 100 billion, 20 are saved, 80 remain with which to buy consumption goods. If 30 are saved, only 70 remain for consumption; if 40 are saved, 60 remain, and so on. Further, the more that is saved, the larger will be the supply of equipment if the savings are invested. Thus savings cut the profitability of investment with a two-edged sword. They increase the output of consumption goods and reduce the funds available for their purchase. Since the profitability of investments depends solely on the sale of consumption goods and services that are produced with the equipment in which the investment is made, any increase in savings and investment tends to destroy the profitability of investment.

How could there be a more fantastic notion than that the profitability of investment is without limit? America may not be "mature." There may be big opportunities for investment in the years that lie ahead, but these are not unlimited. Aside from the very important factor of the accident of inventions and discoveries, the return from investment depends inversely on the volume of savings and tends to disappear as savings increase. There can be no escape from this. If we all decided to save money by reducing our purchases of clothing to one outfit every three years, what business man would borrow our savings and hire men to make additional looms and sewing machines? Persons already working at such tasks would be dismissed, and in addition most of those engaged in making materials and fabricating finished garments would lose their jobs. Consumption is the key to employment.

To pursue this a little further, how possibly could all of us remain employed at present wages and for present hours if national consumption were reduced 10, 20, or 50 per cent? How, possibly, could we maintain a national income of 120 billion dollars per year and consume only 60 billion dollars' worth of the product? That is, how could we invest half of our national income? How could our business men find it profitable to employ half of all of us workers year after year making equipment with which to produce consumption goods if each of us, on the average, is willing to spend only half of his income on consumption? How, to neglect other items in income, could business men year by year pay out 120 billion dollars in wages, get back only 60 billion by sales of consumption goods, and then see any profit whatever in borrowing the other 60 billion at interest for the purpose of producing more consumption goods?

Business men cannot borrow money and invest beyond the point at which the resulting output of consumer goods can be sold. And who can doubt that any saving reduces the possibility of selling? That is its essence.

Everything in our economy may be made satisfactory to the business men—taxes, labor relations, government personnel, everything, yet they will not be able to maintain employment as they so earnestly desire to do if we save persistently. Men may declare that private enterprise "can and will provide jobs for all who want them," but the savings-investment process will have its way as inexorably as would the coming of winter in the face of similar incantations that "there can and will be warm weather."

The main idea here is old doctrine to economists. They have always held that so much *could* be saved that the rate of return would fall to zero, but they have thought that this will not happen because they felt that the failure to get a return on savings would cause would-be savers to turn spenders, and thus prevent "oversaving." But as argued in the preceding chapter, this view is no longer acceptable. Every economist today apparently believes that savings *can* outrun investment and lie unused. The argument of this book is that that necessarily happens as savers attempt to augment their savings.

Business men despite their earnest desire to do so have never been able to provide reasonably full employment for more than a few years. Various excuses have always been made for the collapse of prosperity, even when, as in 1929 to 1933, the political climate was and had been all that business men desired. We have steadfastly resisted the conclusion that there is anything inherently wrong in our marketing process. Much of the current talk about postwar employment indicates no appreciation of the difficulty. We may have to learn the hard way.

4

The market congestion that results from the savings-investment process is accelerated by the necessity of making some investment in "working" capital. In all of the discussions of this problem, investments are spoken of, as in the above pages, as if they took the form solely of steel mills, railway engines, or similar tools of production that are converted into consumer goods only over a long period of time. But, obviously, as soon as a capital good enters, or is about to enter, on its work of production it must be supplemented by investments of "working" or "circulating" capital. This fact has been a standard part of economic literature from the beginning of modern economics, but it has apparently not been related to the savings-investment problem. Clearly, investments of this sort turn into consumer goods within a very short time, and that is very important.

The saver in such a case, in effect, invests in consumer goods. The goods are his in the same sense that a factory building that has been built with his savings is his. By investing in the factory building, by taking title to it or taking a mortgage on it, he, in effect, takes it off the market; he takes it from the contractor who built it. Employment is in no way impeded by this process; it is facilitated. If the saver followed a similar course when he contributes working capital, similar results would follow in respect to employment. But the saver will not "hold" the consumer goods in which, in effect, he invests in such a case. He sells them, or attempts to sell them, or the business firm concerned does this, or attempts to do this, for him. But there is no money with which to purchase them if the goods that have customarily been sold are to find a market.

This matter may be illustrated as follows: Let us assume an economy similar to ours and that, following a depression, new discoveries and inventions make it appear profitable to build an extensive series of new mills, factories, and other equipment. This capital building will, we assume, provide full employment, will require several years for completion, and will utilize 20 per cent of the economic effort of the community.

If we let 100 represent the total economic effort, then 80 units are devoted to providing consumption goods and services and 20 units are devoted to providing production goods. This will mean that if the total money income of the community amounts to 100 units, 80 units are spent for consumer goods and services and 20 units are saved and invested in producer goods. That is, each month, or each year, 80 per cent of the money income of this community is used to buy the consumer goods and services that are produced and 20 per cent is used to finance the producer, or investment, goods. The markets are kept clear of consumer goods and services and also of production equipment. Full employment is maintained.

Let us assume that it takes five years to get these new capital goods ready for use, and in order to throw the point at issue into strong relief, let us assume that all of them are finished at the close of the fifth year. At the beginning of the sixth year, then, the business firms that have been using their yearly savings to produce equipment for their own use will now use their current savings to operate the new equipment, and, similarly, the annual savings of individuals that have been borrowed during the preceding five years to build equipment will now be borrowed to operate it. The same men who have been employed in getting out raw material and building the factories, let us assume, will now be employed to produce raw material and fabricate it within the factories. Everything remains the same as during the preceding five years except that the men who have been in effect employed by the savers in producing capital goods are now employed by the savers in producing consumer goods; investment this year takes the form of consumer goods. There is still full employment and there is no change in the total national income, but trouble impends.

At the close of this sixth year the division of the money income between spending and saving will remain, let us assume, unchanged from the preceding year—20 units are saved and 80 units are spent. The total product this year, however, consists of consumer goods. There are 100 units of them, but only 80 units of such goods will be purchased. An impasse will have been created. Twenty per cent of the year's product cannot be sold.

No one would suggest that the buyers of consumer goods,

with their 80 units of money, could have purchased annually the total produce of the community during the five years when 80 units of consumer and 20 units of producer goods were being produced, but this is just what we expect them to do in the sixth year when the savers have invested their annual savings of 20 units, not in the production of producer goods, but in the production of consumer goods, and have that quantity of such goods for sale.

To be sure, the savers in this case may increase their consumption by curtailing their saving and purchasing some of these additional consumer goods, but unless they cease saving entirely in the sixth year the market cannot be cleared. In view of the customary practices of savers we cannot expect these persons to cease saving altogether. A market impasse cannot be escaped.

It will be noted that in this illustration the volume of savings, contrary to experience, is held constant. Any increase in savings, as from interest earnings, would augment the market problem.

5

The bizarre condition that inevitably occurs when we attempt, as we do, to augment our savings by saving the income from our savings, may also be stated in terms of compound interest. This is a finite world, and any compounding will in time reach astronomical proportions. If the population of this country should double only four times, we should have more people than there are now in the entire world. Beginning with only one couple in the year one of the Christian era, a doubling of population every twenty-five years, or only seventy-seven times, would by 1925 have brought the population of the world to 189,000,000 persons for every square foot of the land area, including swamps and mountain peaks. Whether we consider people, hummingbirds, elephants, orchids, wheat, or any other living form, procreation, within rather narrow limits, must be offset by death. The one requires the other.

Similarly, the offspring from money or wealth in the form of interest must be almost equally matched by economic death —losses and bankruptcy. Compound interest over a considerable period of time is as impossible as is geometric progression among plants and animals. One cent compounded yearly at six per cent from the year one A.D. to the end of 1944 would have amounted to approximately $156,531,000,000,000,000,000,000,-000,000,000,000,000,000,000,000. To put this—shall we say?—in more understandable terms, this sum of money is equivalent to the value of balls of pure gold the size of the earth to the number of more than 6,000,000,000,000,000,000 (6 billion billion). If a rate of 5 per cent is used the number of balls of pure gold the size of the earth required to equal the value reached would amount only to a little over 64 billion. These figures would be increased by one tenth if standard gold rather than pure gold were used.*

How impossible it would be for even just one family to compound its savings for very many generations! How ridiculous it is to talk, as some men do, of the possibility of our all becoming rich if we would only save at compound interest! How inevitable depressions are when even only a small portion of the population attempts to save at compound interest! Yet in spite of the absurdity of it we base our economy on the principle of compound interest and expect the observance of the Ten Commandments to save us from the consequences of our folly.

Practically, the limit to the compounding of interest by any group of persons depends on the particular circumstances that prevail. One group can succeed only as the losses of others permit its holdings to grow. If losses were sufficiently regular and did not alarm savers and deter them from investing, employment could be maintained continuously, however wasteful the process. A period of prosperity prevails when the various expedients to which we resort, together with possible lucky acci-

* I am indebted to my colleague Alva M. Tuttle for making this computation. He used Glover's interest tables and assumed pure gold to have a specific gravity of 19.3 and the earth to be a sphere with a radius of 4,000 miles.

dents, cut down losses and encourage investment. But the checking of economic death makes it necessary that presently there shall be an epidemic, which we call a depression, to destroy enough savings so that the process of compounding can begin once more.

As one of my colleagues * has suggested, we have here what may be called a Malthusian theory of investments. Thomas R. Malthus, it will be recalled, developed the well-known theory of population to the effect that the finite nature of the earth and the instinct to procreate tend to result in a population of such size that only bare subsistence is possible. He advocated the exercise of moral restraints, by which he meant the postponement of marriage and sexual continence, as a means of limiting numbers and attaining a good standard of living. He pointed to wars, pestilence, and other calamities as means by which numbers were reduced when they became excessive. Somewhat similarly, the finite nature of the earth and the urge to save and marry the savings to investment, and then save the offspring for another mating, finally result in such a flood of goods that the returns in interest from savings fall to bare subsistence or less. A pestilence is then generated and savings are killed off in sufficient volume so that, when all other things become propitious, the wedding bells may ring once more.

6

The above discussion is based almost wholly on the assumption that savings are enlarged year by year during a period of prosperity as a result of saving the income from previous saving. The case is, however, much stronger than this. Every form of income received by the upper economic group tends to be enlarged when times are good. Payments for personal services (salaries, fees, bonuses, and commissions) and profits usually show pronounced increases. Rents and royalties also increase. To be sure, the wage-earner group normally gets more income

* L. Edwin Smart.

during such a period, but this tends to be very moderate as compared with the increases enjoyed by the owner-manager-professional group. Indeed, average wage rates may show no increase at all, the gain to the group coming wholly from the absorption of the unemployed. Since additions to moderate and large incomes tend to be saved rather than spent, a period of prosperity augments savings far beyond the volume that would result from the compounding of income from savings already made. This, as already argued, enlarges the product and at the same time makes it increasingly difficult to dispose of it. The increase that takes place in wage payments facilitates sales and adds its mite to the forces making for the maintenance of prosperity, but this tends on balance to be of but little effect. The effort to accumulate money checks the flow of money and stalls the wheels of industry.

The data for the 1920's, as shown in Chapter x, confirm this analysis. They show marked gains in incomes other than those accruing to wage-earners, and that the percentage of the total income that went to persons in the upper brackets was very high in 1929 and apparently much higher than in the earlier years of the decade.

The course of events during a period of prosperity and the beginning of a depression may be put in terms of financial incentives. Business men insist, as everyone knows, that they must be permitted to make money if they are to go forward. No one can deny them this point. The very nature of a private-enterprise economy means that rewards are necessary to induce effort. Most unfortunately, however, these essential incentives to business tend to destroy business incentives. What they give with one hand they take away with the other. For the money gains that spur business men to increase output mean that relatively less is available for the purchase of the output, since such additions to business incomes are largely saved.

There was, for example, perhaps never a time in the history of this country when the incentives to business endeavor were more pronounced than during the 1920's. The administrations of Harding, Coolidge, and Hoover encouraged business in every possible way. President Coolidge expressed the dominant political sentiment of this decade in the terse statement: "The business of the country is business." But the collapse in 1929 and the subsequent long decline showed that the encouragement of business can destroy business. Indeed, the general rule is that business destroys itself. The incentives to business destroy the basic incentive to business—the chance to sell the product of business. Business men must be allowed to win marbles in order to induce them to play, but presently they have so many of the marbles that the game must stop.

7

The limit to which we thus come periodically in the building of capital goods is not related to *need*. A simple, matter-of-fact, common-sense attitude leads one to believe that as long as the yearly output of goods can be increased by the use of available equipment, it will be installed. Thus the London *Economist* emphasizes the need for additional capital equipment in England, citing two significant facts: (1) that the productivity of the average worker in British industry before the war was lower than in Germany or the United States, and (2) that the British worker received a higher share of the total receipts of industry than either the German or the American (December 11, 1943). The *Economist* says: "Until the degree of mechanization in British industry is raised to the American level, it is ridiculous to say that there is no advantage in increased Investment."

This is true enough if the economy of Britain operated in a simple common-sense fashion, but as it is in Britain, and in the United States, the limit of profitability to investors may be reached long before workers have all of the equipment that would best serve them. Certainly we did not stop building equipment in 1929 because the bottom economic third, or even the bottom two thirds, had all of the equipment that they ideally needed with which to produce the goods that they wanted. After we have had a short run of constructing equipment, we cannot build more, however much the general welfare would benefit thereby, until we have in great travail digested the new batch of capital goods. The whole matter turns on the profitability to savers, not to workmen.

It must be accounted a great fault of our process of saving and investment that we cannot as a nation determine the advisability of allocating economic effort between the production of consumption goods and services and the production of equipment with which to enlarge the output of consumption goods and services. We are dependent on the accidental distribution of the income stream into spendings and savings and on the opportunities that happen to prevail for profitable returns from the savings that are made. We may be oversupplied or undersupplied with equipment.

Certainly nothing could prove this any better than the case that the *Economist* cites. Welfare in England would be served by having better equipment, yet for a hundred years the ability of the upper income groups in England to save—to supply capital—has not been exceeded anywhere. Why has the equipment not been provided? Could it be that too much of the national income went to the few and that too little of it was available to the many as buying power? It could be.

8

The above analysis has been carried on in terms of savings as the source of investment. No mention has been made of the use of bank credit in directing economic factors to the construction of industrial equipment, and this is an important source of such funds. But certainly the argument is strengthened when it is related to bank credit, for banks, obviously, do not wish to consume the product which is the equivalent of the money income that they receive from investments. If banks alone furnished investment funds, and if these were wholly created by the banks, the difficulty of operating our economy would be increased, for some individual savers do consume some of the product to which their income from saving gives them claim. Banks are compounders *par excellence*.

9

This argument is not in accord with the opinion of the best-known writers who have discussed these matters recently, nor with that of the public generally. The Keynesian analysis runs in terms of constant additions to investments being the remedy for unemployment. This is apparently the prevailing view among economists and is certainly the view of business men and their spokesmen.

One may grant that if we could have a constantly expanding economy we should have no trouble in respect to unemployment. Similarly one could accept the proposition that if people never got sick there would be no difficulty in having adequate medical service. The *if* in respect to a constantly expanding economy puts us in a never-never land.

The only possibility of continuous investment without a depression break is that losses shall equal accumulations—that losses shall keep the output of consumption goods and services at levels low enough to permit sales. If old firms are driven out of business and their plants closed, and if enough new investments turn out to be of the nature of dry oil wells or of new office buildings that stand empty, we might continue a period of prosperity indefinitely. But all this depends upon happy accidents. New inventions and discoveries and new consumer styles must make it appear profitable to produce new equipment. Further competitors must be put at such a disadvantage that they close their plants. This calls for the outmoding of their products, not simply making a given product more cheaply. It calls for railroads to displace canal boats; for electric lights to displace kerosene lamps. For if a product is merely produced at a lower cost, old firms may continue in business even when producing at a loss, since the value of their equipment is destroyed whether they close shop or continue to produce. They may retain something if they stay in business. But this clogs the consumer markets and prevents new firms from prospering. Further, to permit prosperity the losses to new investors must not be so numerous or of such a nature as to discourage continued investment. All in all, there can be no assurance that these forces will permit continuous capital building. As Professor Samuelson has said, this feature of our economy is "sporadic, volatile, and capricious." *

Many writers, including Keynes, have laid great stress upon a low rate of interest as a factor in promoting investment. The payment of interest is, of course, a cost of production and hence any reduction in rates tends to encourage enterprise. The tendency will become an actuality, however, only if all other factors are favorable. A zero rate of interest, if the principal must be repaid, will not encourage investment if the market conditions do not warrant a belief that the product can be sold advantageously. Even a negative rate of interest—a provision that, say, only 90 dollars must be repaid for every 100 borrowed —would not encourage investment if people are saving so much that they have but little left with which to buy consumer goods and services.

Not only does analysis lead us to this conclusion, but our history is replete with illustrations. We have never had continuous investment of our savings. We have had depressions. They have been as normal in our experience as have the reasonably good times that have been intertwined with them.

This appears, too, to be the real opinion of the writers who stress the matter of investments. They seem to believe that investments cannot be made continuously, for they provide in their argument, almost without exception, that when private

* Paul A. Samuelson: "Full Employment after the War," in *Postwar Economic Problems* (1943), ed. S. E. Harris, p. 41.

investment fails, the government shall take over and provide opportunities for the use of savings, or by-pass the idle savings with newly created money. The reed is a slender one even in the eyes of those who ask us to lean upon it.

10

It is interesting to note that Professor Hansen by a different chain of reasoning and by the use of different terminology comes to essentially the same conclusions that we have reached in this chapter. He says:

. . . every boom * eventually dies a natural death. Available outlets of capital expansion have been temporarily exhausted.

The boom is a period in which we exploit to the full all the available new developments which the progress of science and technology, together with the growth of the population, have up to that point made economically possible. . . . [Finally] there remains little that can profitably be done except to maintain the capital plant already constructed. When this point is reached the boom dies a natural death.

This is essentially what happened in 1929. Nearly all over the world, England excepted, there had been going on for some years a gigantic construction boom. . . . It is not difficult to see that if we had kept on constructing office buildings, apartments, hotels, houses, commercial and industrial structures, and the like, at the rate they were being constructed in the late twenties, we should very soon have bankrupted all the owners of old property. For a time there was no room left for further plant expansion or for other new capital outlays.†

But while expansion cannot be continuous—while we must stop being prosperous after a few years and cast ourselves into the slough of depression—there are no precise points at which this must occur. Our economy is extremely complex. The multitude of forces of which it is composed, the accidents to which it is subject, and the degree to which in any period of prosperity

---

* "Every period of prosperity" in the terms used above.
† *Fiscal Policy and Business Cycles* (1941), pp. 344-5.

we utilize the various expedients that we have devised to overcome the inherent defect of our economy, make it impossible to forecast accurately the termination of good times. These and related topics will be the subject matter of the following chapter. We can, however, be certain that any period of prosperity will be brought to a close. Arithmetic is not mocked.

CHAPTER V

Postponing a Market Impasse

I

THE DISCUSSION in the preceding chapter shows that the sale of all that we could produce with customary employment tends to become impossible as soon as the consumer product is enlarged as a result of new productive business investments. Failure to sell all that is produced, or the anticipation that what could be produced cannot be sold, naturally and inevitably leads to the dismissal of workers. It was also shown that under certain conditions capital building may prolong a period of prosperity, but it was emphasized that such capital building tends to be narrowly limited in time as indicated by our history and also by the analysis of the forces that operate in our economy.

Most readers will feel that the picture was painted too black. Our economy cannot be as bad as this, they will say. If it were, how could we have reached the high level of well-being that has been achieved? Yes, the picture was made unduly dark. As was mentioned several times in the course of that chapter, certain methods that are normally employed to prolong a period of prosperity were omitted, as the purpose of the chapter was to show the fundamental factor that operates in our economy to cause unemployment. We must now supply the omitted parts.

Before proceeding with the discussion, it may be pertinent to observe that periods of prosperity are much shorter than they are commonly believed to be. If one examines a chart such as General Ayres of the Cleveland Trust Company has prepared showing the ups and downs of business since 1790, one is struck with the extreme shortness of the periods of prosperity. Further, one is impressed with the dips that are found in even a few years of good times. In terms of employment the chart can be interpreted as showing that the times of fullest employment are "peaks"—periods of extremely short duration, only one or two months at the most. This chart shows that since the close of the depression of the 1870's the longest period of prosperity covered about four years—from the latter part of 1879 to the middle of 1883—but was very uneven throughout that time. The period marked on the chart as "Coolidge Prosperity" covers only three uneven years, falling between the sharp recession of 1924 and the milder recession in 1927. The "Bull Market Boom" covers only parts of 1928 and of 1929. Our economic course is a very jagged one. We never have full employment except during a major war, and the periods when we do reasonably well in supplying jobs are of extremely short duration.

We return now to the discussion of the prolongation of periods of reasonably full employment. The method that is of prime importance in this regard is the sale of goods on credit. The consumer goods which must be sold if employment is to be maintained can be purchased on a cash basis only by the receivers of money income from the investments that have produced these goods, assuming that the customary consumer goods are to be sold. But anyone can buy them if the sellers will accept I O U's. The goods that Z would not buy in the above illustration can be sold on credit. The bottom two thirds of the population on the income scale with one third of the total national income, as in 1935–6, can buy one half of the total national product if permitted to buy on credit. Credit sales may be made, of course, on open book account and on installment plans. Sales for cash that has been borrowed from finance institutions are essentially credit sales and are meant to be included in this discussion.

The use of credit is of the greatest possible importance in extending periods of prosperity. If it were not for this device, the usual period of prosperity that follows a depression would be brought to a rather prompt close as the fruits of the new investments that brought employment were offered for sale. For, to repeat, the desire to save prevents the receivers of income from buying the goods that are produced by aid of the investments. The other factors to which attention will be called presently might, in some cases, permit the extension of a period of prosperity without the use of credit, but credit is the major life-line.

The record in this particular during the 1920's is especially impressive. Outstanding consumer credit increased by more than 5.5 billion dollars from 1922 to 1929 inclusive.* This means that on the average we sold approximately 60 million dollars' worth of goods each month for 96 months to persons who were not able to pay for them and had not paid for them when the depression began in 1929. Certainly this was an important factor in giving us eight years of reasonably good times, including two or three years of prosperity. Besides this the sale of residences in part on credit was also an important element in the general prosperity from 1922 to 1929.

It must be admitted, of course, that the use of credit may be abused. So much credit may be extended that prices are forced up unduly and a speculative boom engendered. Some observers have concluded, on the basis of such observations, that we would never have depressions if it were not for a credit boom and its inevitable collapse.† But the fact that credit may be unduly extended and result in severe derangements in our economy does not warrant the conclusion that if we operated our economy wholly on a cash basis we should not have depressions. Rather it is only because we use credit that we can have periods of prosperity. If we attempted to conduct business for cash only, the persistent refusal of savers to buy the share of the consumer product that their incomes entitle them alone to buy would keep us perpetually in the quagmire of depression. Our system has been saved to date only by the use of credit.

There are obvious limits, however, to the extent to which

* Mordecai Ezekiel: "Savings, Consumption, and Investment," *American Economic Review*, June 1942, p. 275.

† Alfred Marshall, for example, says: ". . . the only effective remedy for unemployment is . . . that reckless inflations of credit—the chief cause of all economic malaise—may be kept within narrower limits." *Principles of Economics*, 5th edition, p. 710. See also S. H. Slichter: *Toward Stability* (1934), Chapter i, Section viii.

credit may be extended to consumers. As increasing numbers of persons pledge their future incomes for the payment of goods, prudent business men become increasingly reluctant to expand the scope of their operations even though outstanding consumer credit is still increasing. Further, prudent buyers become reluctant to continue easy purchase plans as their debts increase. The market impasse cannot be avoided by this means.

2

Another method of postponing unemployment is to sell goods abroad in excess of the goods purchased from abroad. Net exports, obviously, lessen the congestion of goods in the home market and to that extent permit production to go forward. Selling goods and taking pay in gold or in credit instruments of some sort—bonds, mortgages, shares of stock, or bank balances—is manna from heaven. It permits us to export our unemployment. That is, like sales on credit it takes goods off the market and hence gives us employment. In each case the savers, in effect, invest in the credit instruments that are used in payment, or if gold is paid in the case of exports, the savers, in effect, invest in the paper that the importing banks get for the gold when it is turned over to a Federal Reserve bank for transfer to the government.

Our sales of goods and services abroad, minus purchases, for the eight years 1922–9 amounted to almost 6 billion dollars,* or an average of approximately 60 million dollars every month for 96 months. How fortunate we were to get rid of this vast quantity of produce in exchange for gold and pieces of paper! †

If we add the figure for net exports during these years to the net increase in short-term consumer debt, we get the astounding total of 120 million dollars as the measure by which we relieved

---

* Net exports of goods totaled approximately 5.69 billion and net exports of "invisible items" about 170 million. *The United States in the World Economy,* Economic Series No. 23, Department of Commerce (1943), table facing p. 216.

† The source just quoted shows net gold imports for these eight years of 420 million and "capital claims" increase of 4.4 billion, leaving a little more than 1 billion "unexplained."

the pressure on our markets every month for 96 months. A total for these eight years following the sharp depression of 1921 of 11.5 billion dollars! If one wishes an explanation in small compass of the relatively good times of the latter part of the 1920's one can find it here.

Sales abroad are somewhat fortuitous. The policies of other nations in respect to importation change from time to time. Likewise the amount of available foreign investments for which we exchange goods depends upon a number of circumstances. The extent to which we travel abroad as compared with that of foreigners visiting here is also a factor in determining the ability of our producers to get rid of goods abroad. The net gain from this will depend upon how much is spent abroad as compared with what our travelers would have spent if they had stayed at home. If they spend money abroad that they would have saved if they had not gone, the amount spent is obviously increased, thus permitting our producers to sell more abroad in settlement for our tourists' expenditures than they would have been able to sell at home if these persons had not gone traveling. The amount of gold that happens to be produced abroad is another variable, as is the price that we pay for it. If all of these elements are favorable to us, a period of prosperity may be considerably enhanced and extended by foreign sales. And by a parity of reasoning, as conditions become unfavorable to exports, sales drop off and unemployment results.

3

Any reduction in the prices of commodities and services during a period of prosperity will encourage the prolongation of good times if profit margins are left adequate to encourage investment. Such a policy does two important things at the same time. It facilitates the purchase of the product and it lessens the probable volume of savings by reducing profits, assuming that the price reductions are carried far enough to reduce profits. The reduction in the wholesale prices of non-agricultural goods by almost ten per cent from 1926 to 1929 undoubtedly contributed to the prosperity of that period.

It is a serious error, however, to believe that prices might be cut sufficiently to permit a period of prosperity to continue indefinitely. The most vigorous price-cutting cannot make the savings-investment process bear only sweet fruit. The market impasse that developed in the illustrations in the previous chapter could not have been resolved by price reductions. Prices in these illustrations were assumed to be at cost. Hence any cutting of prices would have resulted in losses and in the curtailment of operations and the dismissal of workers.

Certainly if savings are being hoarded producers as a group are not getting back as much money as they pay out, and price-cutting cannot put them in a better position. If they pay out 100 and if 20 is saved and kept uninvested, only 80 will be returned to producers and 20 units of product will not be sold if prices are maintained. If prices are cut so that the entire product is sold for 80, the producers will suffer losses of 20. If now the 80 units of money received back are paid out as income and if 15 are saved, the product must be sold for 65. The situation will get worse continually. Industry cannot stand this.

If we assume an absence of hoarding—assume that savings can be invested continuously—we have a condition of continuous transfer of economic factors to the making of producer goods, with the final consequence that we will all be making plows and will perish for the want of corn. Price reductions could not improve such a situation.

Price-cutting is the remedy that many economists advance for almost any ill that besets our economy. It is part of the competitive process that always works for good, according to one school of thought. Certainly our economy functions the more smoothly the closer prices are kept to costs. That, indeed, is implicit in the argument presented in this book. Nevertheless, the general beneficial effects of price reductions do not justify us in believing that even the keenest of price competition can prevent a market impasse when business men and citizens generally act as capitalists must act.

Price-cutting, to repeat, can clear the market of a given volume of produce, but it cannot at the same time encourage the continuation of that production that is necessary to maintain employment. Nevertheless, and this is the major point in this section, price-cutting would tend to postpone a market impasse. It would make it easier for consumers to buy. Business men, however, do not usually encourage this method of facilitating sales, as witness "fair trade" and "price maintenance" laws and trade association pressure.

4

The above general line of reasoning leads to the conclusion that increases in wages, if investment is not thereby discouraged, also tend to prolong a period of good times. For shifting a portion of the national income away from profits to wages will tend to encourage consumption and lessen the volume of savings. The failure of wages in manufacturing to increase beyond 600 million dollars per year from 1923 through 1929, while the value added by manufacturing increased by more than 6 billion dollars per year, or 10 times as much,* must have been an important factor in bringing the prosperity of those years to a close. A strong trade union movement may thus be an effective agency in prolonging a period of full employment. There is danger, however, that unions may be so aggressive that investment will be discouraged.

Just the opposite line of reasoning is often employed. Thus it is argued that the reason for shut-downs and unemployment is to be found in the disappearance of profit margins as a result of increased costs, including labor costs. Hence wage cuts would prolong periods of prosperity. This is an essential part of a well-known presentation of business-cycle theory by Wesley Clair Mitchell. This view obviously neglects wages as a source

---

* See footnote p. 112.

of buying power. The conclusion seems to be inescapable that wage increases, not the opposite, would tend to prevent prosperity from turning into depression.

5

In the preceding chapter it was argued that a low rate of interest, even a zero rate, will not permit investments to be made continuously. Is it possible, however, to prolong a period of prosperity by lowering the rate of interest? There is some reason to believe that this would be helpful. The demand for houses and durable goods purchased in part on credit would tend to be increased by any reduction in the rate used in financing the unpaid portions of the purchase price. Likewise business firms would be encouraged to invest more than they otherwise would if rates of interest were cut. But the best that we can hope for here is a postponement of a business collapse.

There is apparently no reason to believe that a lowering of the rate will have a favorable effect on investment if a market impasse has already been reached. If the consumer market cannot be further expanded, any downward trend in the rate of interest would tend to be of no effect. Business men do not borrow money and throw it away when the charge for borrowing is low. The rate of interest is perhaps usually one of the least important of the items considered by business men when they are contemplating a business venture. The outstanding factor is the state of the market for the contemplated product. In general this means the state of the consumer market. This is the *sine qua non.*

It is also to be noted that while a drop in the rate of interest, if other conditions are favorable, will encourage business borrowing, it may at the same time discourage lending. For any rise in the interest rate tends to reduce the principal value of an investment. For example, if the rate of interest is 1 per cent, a bond that pays 1 dollar per year in perpetuity will be worth 100 dollars, but if the rate were 2 per cent, the price of this bond would be 50 dollars. Hence to invest when the rate of interest is so low that a rise of considerable proportions is likely to occur involves the risk of a loss in principal that might easily outweigh the amount of interest that would be secured over a very long period. Thus low rates tend to encourage hoarding, and afford another reason for not expecting a declining trend in interest rates to result in the continuous building of capital goods.

A declining interest rate has a favorable effect on employment, however, by tending to reduce the volume of savings. But the effect here is limited, because the return on investments already made will not be influenced by a decline in the rate of interest. In general, however, a falling rate tends to cut down the receipts of income from previous savings and thus reduce the volume of money savings. Again, this cannot save the day. Prosperity must turn into depression.

It may be added, somewhat parenthetically to the purpose of this chapter, that if the rate of interest behaved, and if men behaved in respect to it, as the classical school of economists thought, the savings-investment problem would never have arisen. That is, if the rate of interest fell as the demand for funds decreased, and if every fall in the rate turned savings into spendings, all would be well. As markets became congested, both increased consumption and decreased investment would relieve the situation. Savings would never be hoarded. But savers do not obey this law of the old text-books. They save and they wait their opportunity to invest, though bread-lines lengthen.

6

It is also to be noted that any alteration in the equipment used in production will tend to prolong periods of prosperity. The almost continuous change in the character of our equipment during the past hundred and fifty years has been of great importance in furnishing us employment. Certainly if there were no changes in the techniques of production, nor changes in consumption that call for new equipment, we should soon have all of the equipment that we could possibly use. With the total produced wealth of the nation estimated to amount to only some two or three times one year's product, it is evident that we could deluge ourselves with equipment if new kinds were never available. It is reasonable to believe that the people of England in, say, the year 1700 had all of the equipment that they could possibly use. Spinning wheels, looms, plows, forges, hammers, saws, and axes were undoubtedly about as numerous as the people available to use them.

During the highly dynamic decades of our national history the cessation of industrial change at any date—1900, for example—would have made our economic institutions intolerable because of a lack of opportunities for investment. A drastic redistribution of income so as to cut down savings would have been imperative unless the persons with large incomes had enlarged their consumption so as to provide employment. The large incomes would have had to be used or given up. There would have been, and is, no escape from that.

The rate of obsolescence throughout our history has been high. Some of it has been sheer waste, but it has furnished something for our saved dollars to do and hence has furnished employment for workers. It has in general, of course, been of great gain to us as a nation in terms of wholesome living. We need to encourage research both for the gain that may come as a result of new and better products and for the employment that may be furnished. We need the added opportunities for employment during periods of prosperity so that they may be prolonged and during depressions so that they may be shortened.

The growing size of industrial units apparently both encourages and discourages investments as a result of research. The big units make it possible to provide almost unlimited funds for research, but the degree of control exercised over an entire industry may prevent the utilization of new inventions or discoveries if they involve the scrapping of expensive equipment and the building of new. The conduct of research by government units on a more extensive scale than at present might be very helpful.

7

Another element that may delay the inevitable market impasse is the tendency of some persons to "dissave" while others are saving. Some persons of the less frugal type may sell their houses, bonds, or other property to those who wish to save and may spend the money received. Thus the total volume of funds kept out of the consumer markets may be greatly reduced as compared with what it would have been without this dissaving. Here again one cannot be certain just what will happen at any particular point in the flow and ebb of business. As days of prosperity follow one another, the feeling of security may lead many persons to turn their protection against the future into means for gratification today. At the same time the increased flow of income will make possible better provision for the future without the sacrifice of present consumption standards. But clearly dissaving may make an important contribution to the prolongation of a period of well-being.

8

We come now to the final element to be considered in this catalogue of devices that may by design or by chance help to postpone the congestion of the market and thus permit a period of prosperity to be more prolonged than would otherwise be possible. If the government undertakes large expenditures at such a time and secures the funds by taxing away sums that would otherwise be saved or by borrowing savings, a marked contribution to the continuation of prosperity may be made. Savings will thereby be converted into employment and the market for consumer goods will be enhanced. Further, and this is very important, the investments made by the government in the building of schoolhouses, roads, parks, and other public projects will not result in an augmentation of goods and services for sale. Thus at the same time that saved funds, or those that might have been saved if they had not been paid as taxes, are converted to consumer buying power, the volume of product to be sold is kept below what it would have been if the savings had gone into business investment. Construction of public works during a period of prosperity is contrary to what is usually recommended as a feature of public policy. We are commonly told that public works should be delayed to periods of depression and used to relieve unemployment, but certainly it would be better to use them in prevention rather than in the cure of unemployment.

Our survey indicates that there are many elements that may contribute to a postponement of an impasse in consumer markets. Hence there is no definite limit to periods of prosperity. But none of the factors surveyed give any promise of being able to do more than postpone for a time an economic collapse. A recurring market impasse is an inseparable aspect of the savings-investment process as we practice it.

CHAPTER VI

Consuming the Product

I

THE ARGUMENT of the three preceding chapters amounts to this: unemployment occurs because we do not consume the product that we produce or might produce. If we, the people of the United States, could and would consume as the means available permit, we should never need to stop working. It is as simple as that. We stop and stand idle because our institutional arrangements will not permit us to use the fruits of our labor. We cannot distribute what we could produce.

Robinson Crusoe had no difficulty on this score. As he increased his supply of food he ate more or consumed more fully in other ways, as by taking more leisure. He planned his work with consumption in mind. Pioneer farmers followed this same pattern. They planted orchards that they might eat apples, and raised sheep that they might have wool clothes. Similarly when we serve our wants through the instrumentality of the government we are equally forthright. We build schoolhouses because we want to use them; we construct roads because we wish to travel on them, and build bridges because we wish to cross rivers.

When we engage in war we produce the tanks and bombs and other matériel according to the plan of our need. Likewise in an economy in which collective ownership of factories, mills, and other instruments of production prevails, as in Russia, the consumption of the product is the goal of production, as it is with us in our limited application of the collective principle. Shoes, overalls, dresses, and bread are the lure that induces the Russians to construct the equipment needed to produce them.

A private enterprise system proceeds on a different basis. Savers do not lend their money for the construction of shoe factories so that they may have shoes, nor so that they may get shoes to swap for coats or potatoes. No, they let their money be used in building shoe factories so that shoes may be sold and they may make money and save it and make still more money.

The business man who undertakes the enterprise is likely to have in mind the getting of shoes or other articles of consumption as part of the reward for his enterprise, but he will count such returns as wages—as payment for his labor. He will want the interest and the profit on the money that he invests, not in the form of consumables, but in money with which to make more money. It is thus that he will get ahead. It is thus that business men before him have got ahead.

Certainly this effort of savers to make money and not consume the goods that they and other savers produce cannot but fail to be self-defeating. If each of 100 men on an economic island should determine not to consume more than half of what he could produce, or its equivalent, then surely after they got their houses built and their cellars full they could have profitable employment only half time. Failure of some persons to buy the share of the product to which their money incomes entitle them is the only conceivable reason for the dismissal of workers and the closing down of plants. It is the refusal to use an adequate amount of income in consumption that prevents sales being made and compels the laying off of workers.

That this simple fact should have for so long escaped our ablest economists, editors of bank bulletins, and public men generally is certainly one of the strange phenomena of human thought. But the sun is well up on a new day. Note this refreshing bit which appears as a footnote to the article in *Fortune* to which attention was called in an earlier chapter. We assert "that American business will turn out all of the goods for which there is a market and that the limits on production in the thirties, for example, were the limits imposed by an insufficient market, i.e., insufficient spending" (January 1944, p. 192).

It is not because the wants of all of us are satiated that we fail to consume the product that is, or might be, available. At least a third of the population are always underfed and shabbily clothed, except during a major war, and always poorly housed. Another third are far from having their desires for the necessities and comforts of life satisfied and know practically nothing of luxuries. The catch is, obviously, that the lowest two thirds of the population on the economic scale cannot buy the available consumable product and that the top one third will not buy their money share of it because of their already adequate consumption and because of their desire to save. As Malthus put it more than a century ago, those who have the will to buy do not have the means, and those who have the means do not have the will.

But strange as it may be, some economists, including men who are unusually familiar with the income data for the people of the nation, continually point to the poverty of the masses as a source of markets. Professor W. I. King, for example, says: "As long as the modal family income is under $1000, there is certainly no need to conjure up wants for new and untried products or to establish new industries in order to find a market for far more goods than our present industries can produce." *
True enough, if need were a coin men could buy with, but as every teacher of economics, including Professor King one may be sure, has told successive groups of students year after year, buying power as well as desire is essential to market demand. One had better say: As long as the modal family income is under $1,000, there is certainly no need to conjure up dreams of a market large enough to purchase what our present industries can produce.

The explanation of the attitude that finds expression in statements such as that by Professor King must lie in an inarticulated major premise that our economy is a communal one. An idea akin to this is often expressed. Thus it is said that our economy is essentially co-operative—that specialization is the counterpart of co-operation—that as specialists we all co-oper-

* *Journal of Political Economy*, October 1939, p. 617.

ate to make a living for the entire nation. There is realism in this view, but there is only mysticism in the notion that this gives us communism in consumption. Product is distributed only in exchange for money. Production can be continued only if sales can be made.

If the poorest third of the population receives, as the National Resources Committee estimated was the case in the twelve months from the summer of 1935 to the summer of 1936,* only 10 per cent of the total income, or 5.9 billion dollars, then their purchases are limited to that percentage of the total and to that absolute sum, except as they may increase their scanty debts somewhat during the period. And if the top third, as reported by that study, receives 66 per cent of the total, they and only they can buy that portion of the total. And if they refuse to use some of their income except in the purchase of goods, or liens on goods, that promise to yield an annual return of 4 per cent or better, and if such goods are not to be had because inventors have failed to be sufficiently ingenious and consumers sufficiently prodigal, then their money will lie idle and the poorest third will be still poorer the following year for lack of employment.

2

If there is any doubt as to the dependence of employment on consumption, it should be dispelled by the experience of war. War is a veritable orgy of consumption. It is collective consumption, not individual consumption, and hence it does not depend on the buying power of individuals but on the productive power of the entire nation. As Mr. Baruch said of our experience during the first World War, "Through application of the principle of priorities, the processes of manufacture and trade were made to move in response to a national purpose rather than in response to the wills of those who had money to buy." †

* The total national income in that period was estimated at 59 billion dollars. For 1943 the estimate is 150 billion dollars and for 1944, 160 billion.

† B. Baruch: *Taking the Profits out of War*, p. 29. Quoted by E. H. Carr: *Conditions of Peace* (1942), p. 76.

And Mr. Churchill spoke similarly of the British experience at that time. During the war, he said, a requisition "for half a million houses would not have seemed more difficult to comply with than those we were already in process of executing for a hundred thousand aeroplanes, or twenty thousand guns. . . . But a new set of conditions began to rule from eleven o'clock onwards. The money-cost . . . asserted a claim to priority from the moment the fighting stopped." *

The ritual of finance, the ability to recover costs—to find persons who both desire to buy and have the means with which to buy—is paramount to production during peace, but when bombs begin dropping, the nation follows a more simple and a more common-sense ritual; it decides what it needs to consume on the battlefield and at home and proceeds in a forthright manner to produce those things.

The appetite of the modern war machine is insatiable; feeding it and producing for essential civilian needs permit everyone to work and to feel significant and to eat regularly. The result is a flood of goods that astonishes everyone and that may permit a nation not only to win a war but to provide a better living for the bottom economic half of its population than either before or after the conflict. Our war experience will be commented on further in Chapter ix.

3

To anyone who wishes to solve problems by direction rather than by indirection it cannot but appear regrettable that, under our present rules, we must approach the problem of employment through the door of investment rather than that of consumption. We cannot set to work to produce what we want to consume and incidentally produce such tools as we may need to get the job done. We must forever build more plant. We can never be prosperous—never fully employed—with the equip-

* Winston Churchill: *The Aftermath* (1929), p. 19.

ment that we have, however good and however plentiful it may be. We must build, build, build.

But it may not be profitable to build. Business men cannot go on making ovens continuously if savers will not stop saving and buy cake. Being frugal and thrifty, the savers want only additional mortgages on still more ovens and, failing these, they wait and hold their money even without interest. Construction workers lose the privilege of making more ovens and can no longer buy bread from the ovens that we already have. Fires are drawn and bakers walk the street. Ovens stay cold because we are not building more ovens.

This makes our economy appear to be less common sense and matter of fact than we like to believe it to be. It reminds us too much of Gilbert and Sullivan's billiard game:

> On a cloth untrue,
> With a twisted cue
> And elliptical billiard balls!

Indeed, our dislike of thinking of our practices as being other than highly rational may have been an important factor all these years in keeping us from seeing the relationships that really prevail.

Thus, to retrace ground that we have already covered, if the population is in great need of consumer goods and if we are possessed of more than adequate equipment and raw materials, as during the 1930's, we cannot proceed straightway to the supplying of our needs. We cannot use the factories that we have unless we are constructing more; and we cannot construct more unless the new ones promise to be enough better than the present ones to permit the investors to make a satisfactory rate of interest.

There has been much talk during the war of the tremendous efficiency shown by private enterprise. The privately managed plants have done a magnificent job, but they have not been operating within the confines of the capitalist system. They have not generated the buying power for which they sell their products. That has come from society acting collectively through the government.

How impossible it would be to fight a modern war on the basis of private enterprise! We should not be able to make guns in the plants that we already had unless it was profitable to build new gun factories. The weapons that we could turn out might be more than adequate to our needs by being far superior to any that the enemy had, yet our production of them would have to wait upon the inventors' making new equipment profitable to the savers, either by inventing new guns that would call for new equipment or by inventing new equipment for the production of the old types of gun. While we were waiting for the inventors, the welkin would no doubt ring with calls to have faith in our way of life. We would be assured that there were new frontiers of war manufacture to be conquered— that the future of America lies ahead!

4

Not only does our investment process put the cart of building new plant before the horse of using what we already have; it is, as I have argued above, subject to self-defeat. Investment can go forward only as savers are willing to consume the fruits of their investments. They and they alone have the means, barring the use of expedients of some sort, to consume the product of their investments. But the ideology of capitalism entices them to save; and the ideology of democracy forbids them to consume as extravagantly as would be necessary if they were to consume the fruits of their investments.

Keynes's frequent reference in his *General Theory of Employment, Interest, and Money* to the "low propensity to consume" may suggest to some that he believes that it would be well if the propensity of the saving class to consume were greater. The proper inference, however, is that he is stating a fact, not that he is complaining about the low consumption of the more well-to-do group. Indeed, his suggestion as to changing the propensity to consume is that this be done by "redistributing incomes or otherwise" (pp. 321, 324). As the distribution of income stood in the pre-war years, the bulk of the savings were made by the upper three or four per cent on the income scale, who in this country in 1929 got from one quarter to one third of the total national income before taxes, and an even larger portion after taxes.*

The postwar distribution of income after taxes may be less unequal than formerly, but it is reasonable to believe that it will not be greatly altered from that of 1929. Certainly the top 3 to 5 per cent of our income-receivers and their families cannot consume, after small savings for which there is always likely to be a demand, some 20 per cent of the total income. To do so would mean that they would have to adopt a scale of living and burial that would make the rajahs of India and the ancient Pharaohs of Egypt seem like penny-pinching misers. This would be intolerable today. "White parasols and elephants mad with pride" are not for this day and generation. We must eliminate unemployment, but our employment must be socially significant. We must consume the produce that we could turn out with full employment, but we must produce and consume according to social need.

5

The dependence of the whole process of our economy on the consumption of the product that we turn out or might turn out appears to be so obvious that it seems strange to find opinion to the contrary. Yet many eminent men have taken that position. They minimize the matter of consumer spending in providing employment. They point to the fact that a decline

* Data given by the Brookings Institution in *America's Capacity to Consume* (1934) show the top 3 per cent of the income-receivers to have received a little over 33 per cent of the total income in 1929. The Brookings study does not consider the matter of taxes, but clearly the top 3 per cent did not pay one third of the taxes in 1929.

in business investments usually precedes a decline in sales to consumers when a slump occurs, and that the decline in the one is usually far more pronounced than in the other. Hence they conclude that the problem of consumer spending power is of but little, if any, significance.

One would have thought that the only reason why business men build shoe factories or factories to manufacture shoemaking machines is that they believe that people will buy shoes. And analogously one would have thought that the only reason for cutting down on the manufacture of shoemaking equipment would be an actual or an expected decline in the sale of shoes. Evidently not!

This brushing aside of the consumer market is so suggestive of comic opera that one almost expects to hear a burst of song:

> The people who spend their money,
> Tra la,
> Have nothing to do with the case.

Thus Professor Slichter says "the over-expansion" of "consumer-goods industries" "does not seem to be the usual cause for depressions. If it were, depressions would begin with weakness in the demand and prices for consumers' goods rather than capital goods. As a matter of fact, the curve of retail sales is usually among the last to turn downward and the first signs of trouble appears in the capital-goods industries." *

Why should there be trouble in the capital-goods industries? What business reason could there be for a decline in capital building other than an anticipated failure to sell the consumer goods that new equipment would help to produce? In this rational age business men do not curtail expansion because of what oracles tell them after looking at the entrails of birds. They act on the basis of what their analysts say after looking at their charts. If it appears that limits are being reached in sales on credit and in net exports, the construction of additional facilities will be curtailed. Consumer sales may be making new

* *Toward Stability* (1934), p. 19.

highs every month and no price weakness may be manifest, yet prudent business men may halt expansion because of anticipated difficulty in being able to continue to expand sales to consumers. Not only *may* such forecasts result in a curtailment of capital building, but one is at a loss to imagine any reason in the normal course of business for checking additions to equipment other than the anticipation of difficulty in selling the product.

General Ayres, a vice-president of the Cleveland Trust Company, in a pamphlet entitled *The Chief Cause of This and Other Depressions*, published in 1935, discusses the theory of the "shortage of consumer purchasing power" along with others (p. 17). "The fact is," he says, "that a condition of depression is not due to deficient spending by consumers nearly so much as it is by deficient spending by business, which always restricts its spending when the prospects of profit appear doubtful." He then points to the great decline in business spending —"largely durable goods"—as compared with the smaller decline in consumer spending during the early 1930's.

The comment is: "Of course." Business investment stops, as Ayres says, "when the prospects of profit appear doubtful." But what would cause the prospects of profits to appear doubtful? A demand for still more consumer goods? Or a belief that consumer sales could not be increased much further?

Ayres goes on to speak of "the huge federal expenditures, designed to increase consumer purchasing power." These were, he said, "passing into the hands of business men and then piling up in the banks as demand deposits, without producing any important increase in business activity." Business men it seems, according to Ayres, were completely discouraged by selling goods to consumers for money derived from federal expenditures.

They used their receipts "in part to pay down indebtedness, in part to sustain slow-speed business operations, and in large measure to build up bank balances." Business men, according to Ayres, would evidently have been much happier if they had not had to sell the goods that they disposed of as a result of government spending. "We have tried on a vast scale," he concludes, "a great economic experiment based on the consumer purchasing power theory of business cycles, and it is failing because the theory on which it is based is not valid."

This is baffling. To find a banker playing down—or practically tossing aside—the role of consumer buying power is strange indeed. When General Ayres is considering the advisability of making a loan to a business man does he neglect the question of whether or not consumers can and will buy the goods that the prospective borrower expects to produce? Does he, after the experience of this war, still believe that business men will not restock their shelves if they sell as a result of federal expenditures?

General Ayres's doctrine is of a piece with the statement so often made during the 1930's: "We can't spend our way to prosperity." As a matter of fact, it is only by spending that we can have prosperity. It is not because we are prosperous as a nation that we ride in automobiles; we are prosperous because we ride in automobiles. Our war experience has taught those who care to learn that government spending, if there is a lack of private spending, can make us prosperous, however unfortunate it may be to create a big government debt. This experience emphasizes Keynes's point that war is the only activity on which we are willing to spend enough to provide full employment. How can there be any question that consumer markets are the nerve center of our economy? How can we explain the attitude of people who deny this? The answer appears to be: folklore.

6

We think and act as producers, not as consumers. We destroy crops and meat animals, or hold back their production, not because all of us have had too much to eat but because limitation of output will add to the incomes of producers; we beggar ourselves as a nation by subsidizing exports, imposing tariff duties on imports, and devising other policies that will prevent us from importing as many goods as we export, in order that producers may gain; we follow policies in respect to patents, the purchase of silver, the use of the radio, and most other aspects of our economic life that will benefit producers.*

Occasionally a bow is made to the consumer, as by Mr. Hoover in his campaign for the Presidency in 1928, when, goaded by the interest aroused by the first Five-Year Plan of the Soviet Union, he declared that we, too, had a plan and gave a long list of things that we were to have, which was popularly summarized as "a chicken in every pot and two automobiles in every garage." But a few months later Mr. Hoover as President had to admit, to his own soul at least, that our economy was geared to producers, not consumers, and that garages and even cooking pots would be empty unless the state of the consumer markets happened to make it possible for producers to produce at a profit.

The emphasis on production is also evidenced in the frequent expressions heard during periods of unemployment that what we need to do is to produce. Working men are told in effect to get to work. If they would only begin producing there would be no unemployment. But since the only unfilled money demand during such a time is for capital goods that have not yet been invented, it seems somewhat unfair to scold the unemployed workmen for not producing them.

7

In further emphasis on the disturbance that comes to our economy from the increased flow of consumer goods as a result of investment and from the refusal of the investors to buy them, when they alone have the money funds to purchase them or their equivalent, attention may be called to comments on this subject by Professor Hansen. Messrs. Foster and Catchings in

* For an interesting treatment of this point, see E. H. Carr: *Conditions of Peace* (1942), Chapter iv.

their book *Profits,* published in 1926, emphasized the significance of the addition made to the supply of consumer goods as a result of new producer goods. Professor Hansen in discussing this says:

They have, in fact, omitted leading factors of economic dynamics—inventions, discoveries, and improvements . . . these factors are constantly upsetting the economic equilibrium.*

The inference is, apparently: so why worry about the disturbances caused by additional consumption goods flowing from new capital instruments?

Two points are to be made in reference to this. First, even if there are other factors that disturb the equilibrium, this one is not to be brushed aside simply for that reason. Secondly, the other factors mentioned by Hansen need not, and normally do not, create a market impasse. That is, they may disturb price and production relationships without making a market glut. Suppose that a supply of wild fruit is discovered adjacent to a small economy organized along the lines of ours, and that the finder brings it to market and buys other goods with the money that he receives from the fruit. The prices of the goods that he buys will tend to rise while the prices of fruit will tend to decline. Capital and labor will be shifted from customary into new lines of enterprise and a new equilibrium will be established, but a market impasse will not be created. The reason for this is that the finder of the fruit, in effect, exchanges it for other things. He extends his consumption. It is this that prevents the market from being congested. No discovery or invention will glut the market if consumption is extended by the amount of the added product.

In his recent book on fiscal policy Hansen discusses this matter further. He says:

It has sometimes been argued, especially from the standpoint of the under-consumption theory of the cycle, that the boom comes to an

* *Business Cycle Theory* (1927), p. 172.

end because of a deficiency of consumption *in the boom years*. According to this view, there is something wrong with the ratio of consumption to investment during the boom. The ratio is said to be too low. But this position is, I think, not defensible. . . . If consumption is increased, the investment needed to supply the flow of consumption goods will increase also. . . . Thus, if you increase consumption, you will also increase investment. The ratio of consumption to induced investment will not be altered. Thus the boom will be magnified if consumption is stimulated, and, if spontaneous investment is strong, such a process may even engender some considerable price inflation. [P. 297.]

This position, it seems to me, is definitely wrong. A Crusoe does not have to make more fishnets because he eats more fish as a result of having made a net. The relationship is the other way about. When new factories are built we must consume more, if employment is to be maintained, but this increase in consumption does not mean that "the investment needed to supply the [increased] flow of consumption will increase also." The consumption of the goods flowing from the newly completed plants does not call for the building of new plants. The plants are adequate, obviously, for the extra consumption that they make possible. To be sure, speculative building of plant with newly created credit may be encouraged if plants are used to capacity, and this might engender price inflation that would disturb the equilibrium of the economy at full employment; but if newly built plants are not used because of the failure to extend consumption, the equilibrium is already disturbed in the opposite direction.

The notion that the difficulty "lies in the periodic outbursts of investment activity," which results in the capital-goods industries being "overbuilt for continuous operation," * is also erroneous. The capital-building spurt gives us the only prosperity that we can have under the present rules, other than that occasioned by war or other outside circumstances, and it certainly cannot be said to be the reason for the appearance of

* D. M. Wright: *The Creation of Purchasing Power* (1942), p. 92.

depression. It is in the failure to make use of the new capital goods by extending consumption that the difficulty lies. This is the reason that we cannot have continuous operation of what we build; this is why our industries are chronically cursed by "excess capacity." Regardless of how much or how little capital building we have had, industry is always "overbuilt for continuous operation." It could not be otherwise when those with money title to the added product refuse to consume it.

Dr. H. G. Moulton, president of the Brookings Institution, put this matter well in a statement that deserves far more attention than it has received.

Our capacity to produce consumer goods has been chronically in excess of the amount which consumers are able, or willing, to take off the markets; and this situation is attributable to the increasing proportion of the total income which is diverted to savings channels. The result is a chronic inability—despite such devices as high pressure salesmanship, installment credits, and loans to facilitate foreign purchases—to find market outlets adequate to absorb our full productive capacity.*

* *Income and Economic Progress* (1935), p. 46.

CHAPTER VII

Depression and Recovery

I

THE COURSE TAKEN by business as the economy moves from the stage of recession into depression further illustrates the problem of markets as related to savings. At such a time there is not only a series of uninvested savings, month by month, but also a continuous stream of disinvestment. The latter provides an extra force that adds to the downward pressure on the course of business.

The decline is marked initially by uninvested savings, which comes about, in Keynesian language, from an increase in "liquidity preference." Business firms and well-to-do individuals attempt to get into a cash, or a liquid, position. The making of additions to factories, mills, transportation equipment, apartment houses, and other capital goods is curtailed, and also perhaps the making of repairs. Production for inventory is reduced and sales are made increasingly from stocks on hand. Loans are called, credit is restricted, debts are paid, and cash balances are accumulated.

Families follow a similar policy of "wait and see." Additions to houses that would otherwise have been made are postponed, automobiles that would have been customarily replaced are retained, purchases of furniture, household equipment, clothing, and luxury items are delayed. Public officials follow suit and curtail public building and government expenses generally. They say: "In times like these government as well as individuals must cut down expenses." "Economy, economy," becomes the slogan of business men, statesmen, and heads of families. "Thrift, thrift," it is repeated, "has made the nation great." We then see what we expected to see and what we bring about: business failures, bankruptcies, unemployment, bread-lines.

We are then likely to push ourselves further into the abyss

by levying or increasing consumption taxes when public revenue is needed to replace the loss from customary channels. Such taxes bring but little complaint, whereas taxes that fell upon the savings that are being frantically accumulated against a still rainier day would bring vigorous protests from that portion of the community which is the most vocal and at the same time a very powerful political group.

This series of events does not take place within a few weeks. Many months may elapse while the pattern is being woven. Both among business firms and among families the impact of the decline is felt at different times. Many may attempt to carry on as usual, hoping that a turn will come, only to succumb to a mood of pessimism eventually or to the hard reality of a decline in income. The important point is that the forces making for a decline tend to be cumulative. Curtailment both of investment and of spending tend to produce unemployment; this further reduces buying power in the markets; this curtails production still further and increases unemployment; incomes fall still lower and the course of the economic tragedy continues.

Although the well-to-do group, including the managers of business firms, are as a whole responsible for a business decline, one could not well advise any member of the group at such a time to follow a course other than that of hoarding all the money he can save. Certainly no one family or business firm could stem the tide by a liberal policy of spending all of its available money above what it invests. All will not stand together, so the rule of every one for himself and the devil take the hindmost almost necessarily comes into play. This is far from the general rule formulated by Adam Smith that an invisible hand guides the individual to do what is best for himself and at the same time what is best for society as a whole. The members of the upper economic group are increasingly in a dilemma in such a time. They need to provide continuous employment if they are not to jeopardize their position, but each can maintain his own position only by scrambling to accumulate cash, and this intensifies an unemployment crisis. The capitalists themselves pull down the temple of private enterprise.

In general the society will suffer to the extent that it is already possessed of durable goods that can be used for an extended period without being replaced and to the extent that goods have been accumulated by business firms and by households. This is another unpleasant fact about our economy that many persons dislike to believe. The better provision we make for ourselves as individuals and firms, the worse it is for the nation as a whole. An unwillingness to accept this fact does not cause it to disappear.

The reversal of our practice in respect to credit is another item in the calamitous chain of events that pulls us further down when a decline begins. We not only cease to extend credit, or to desire it in many cases, but press for payment, and to pay. Thus instead of the economy's adding to its buying power by creating debts, it now subtracts from buying power by the process of debt payment. Since the payment of debt merely transfers money funds from one person to another, thus leaving the total the same, it might seem that this would not decrease buying power. Creditors, however, generally wish to save, and thus the funds paid on debts are likely not to be spent. Certainly at such a time it is not probable that such funds will be invested. To hoard them would be bad enough, but the chances are that they will be used to reduce bank debts which the creditors incurred as a basis for their extensions of credit.

The reduction of bank loans will mean the equivalent reduction of bank deposits, our chief form of money, and hence a cancellation of buying power. To be sure, if customers of banks are holding their deposits idle, the situation is already essentially the same as it will be if they pay off their bank loans and reduce their deposits. Yet if persons and firms have bank deposits, they are more likely to use them than they are to contract loans in order to create deposits for a similar use. The reduction in bank loans tends to worsen the situation. Unemployment will be further increased and aggregate incomes will be reduced still more. Sales of both consumer and producer goods will then be further curtailed and unemployment will sweep still more workers into its net.

Bad as this is, it is not all. The debts generally cannot be paid. Only a relatively few creditors will be able to collect. Bankruptcy and resulting business disorganization will take their toll. For the chain of events that is set in motion when the general limit of credit extension is reached will so reduce aggregate income that debts cannot be paid. This is part of the social catharsis that is necessary after every period of prosperity.*

As the decline proceeds, savings are reduced. The distress that comes is not borne by the unemployed workers alone. Incomes generally decline and as a result savings decline. We can as a society, as Keynes has taught us, save only as much in the aggregate as we invest. As we fail to invest—as we fail to use the money that is saved—incomes fall and the amount that we choose to save, or can save, falls likewise. There is no stopping place until we get so poor that the amount that we save is down to the point where it will be invested. Or, turning this about, the decline continues until the amount that we wish to invest is equal to the amount that is being saved. Fortuitous circumstances, such as the accident of a new invention that makes it appear profitable to invest in new industrial equipment, or the sudden need to prepare for war, may interrupt a decline in business. Without some such occurrence, the decline goes on until the society as a whole is starved down to the point that savings and investments are equal. This point will not be reached until stocks on hand are exhausted and durable goods are badly worn.

* See H. P. Fairchild: *Profits or Prosperity?* (1932), pp. 60–2 for a discussion of debt payment.

2

What happens to the economy when the decline is halted? Does the stage of depression in its turn blossom into the stage of recovery? There is an interesting point in economic theory here. The general view among economists has been that business fluctuations constitute a *cycle*—that prosperity, recession, depression, and recovery are tied together causally. Professor Mitchell propounded this idea several years ago, and since that time many cycle theories have been advanced, including one set forth by Keynes.* He argues that economic forces "wane and give place to their opposites," thus producing a causally connected series of stages that can properly be called a *cycle*.

There is a growing school of thought that holds a contrary view; namely, that the fluctuations of business do not make a true cycle, that, as Irving Fisher said twenty-five years ago, they merely show a fluctuation around their own mean, as is true of the weather or of Monte Carlo luck. This view, in other words, is that there is not a business cycle in the sense that each stage of business has within itself forces that generate the next stage.

The principal point of difference comes in respect to whether the economic forces that are operative during a depression tend to produce recovery. It may be contended that Keynes cannot logically hold that cyclical forces impel the economy upward from depression since he has demonstrated the possibility of equilibrium at less than full employment. That is, if the economy may be in equilibrium (the economic forces having no tendency to cause any changes to be made in the volume of employment) when there is unemployment, it may logically be in equilibrium after several years of decline. Or, again, if the forces within the economy do work in a cyclical fashion, they will not permit equilibrium to be reached as long as unemployment prevails.

* *The General Theory,* Chapter xxii.

The principal contention in this book does not depend upon the truth or validity of either of these notions in respect to recovery from depression. Our position is that prosperity itself induces recession, and that recession goes on into depression. There are causal relationships that far, and that is the significant point in this book. It does seem to me, however, that the analysis of economic forces leads to the conclusion that they cannot, without outside aid in some form, bring about a business recovery.

Keynes lays considerable stress upon the exhaustion of stocks and the wearing out of durable goods as a force making for recovery. At first glance this appears valid. If the demand for certain goods amounts to 100 per month and is being filled from stocks on hand, it seems that the exhaustion of these stocks would call for the production of such goods to the extent of 100 per month and hence would absorb some of the unemployment. A similar point can be made in respect to the wearing out of automobiles. When replacements must be made, savers will use funds to purchase cars, and employment will be provided. The additions to employment will give added buying power, will lead to increased demand and more employment, and thus cumulatively promote a business revival.

But is there not a fatal weakness in this analysis? The sale of goods from inventory clearly contributes to the business decline. The 100 in money that is received each month is saved and held idle. If it is not held idle—if disinvestment does not take place—unemployment is not increased. Thus the argument that using from stocks increases unemployment depends on the money receipts from sales being held idle. Finally stocks are exhausted and the goods that are sold must be replaced. This, however, will not increase employment; it will merely check the decrease in employment that has been going on as the society lived off its stock of goods. The decline is stopped, but no upward pressure is exerted. Similarly, a person who has been hoarding his savings instead of buying a new automobile has contributed to the decline. When he uses his income (not his savings) to buy a new car, he helps to check the decline to which he has been contributing. But his purchase does nothing to bring about a revival; it merely helps to stop the decline.

Putting this matter differently, the use of current income merely maintains employment. Or, more broadly, using income to replace what is consumed—stocks from stores, automobiles, or anything else—maintains but does not augment income. The goods and services that comprise the national product—potatoes, lipsticks, dental services, and the thousand and one other items—can be increased only by additions. Similarly, and equally obvious, the money income of the nation can be increased only by addition, not by merely being maintained. To employ the unemployed workers, money additions must be made to the national income by using hoards, creating new bank-check money, or using more frequently the money that we already have.

In short, then, we cannot recover from a depression—we cannot put the unemployed at work in an economy such as ours—unless we use additional money. And, to press the point in respect to the cycle, there is nothing in the economic forces as such that will cause that to be done. Historically, we always have recovered from depressions, but this has been because forces outside the economy created conditions that made it appear profitable to use not merely current income, but also the money that had been hoarded and additional funds that the banks were willing to create because the operations that the would-be borrowers had in mind appeared to promise a sufficient yield to make the loan safe.

It is possible that the replacement of depleted stocks and the repair and replacement of worn-out equipment might call out hoarded funds or lead to borrowing from the banks. In so far as this does happen, there is a force here making for recovery, and the position that I have taken above must be modified. Perhaps certain groups of persons who spend practically all of their incomes do borrow to replace automobiles and similar goods when they wear out, and others use saved hoards for this purpose. This would definitely exert an upward pressure, but it might be more than offset by additional continued hoarding by savers. The exhaustion of inventories, however, would not necessarily lead to any borrowing or use of hoarded funds. Replacements there could be made from current sales. On balance there appears but little reason to expect recovery merely as part of a cyclical process.

3

The new and outside forces that have taken us out of depressions have been in the form of new inventions—the railroad, trolley-car, automobile, structural steel, continuous-strip steel mills, and dozens of other items that have created employment. Or an increase in population has called for much public building and the construction of residences, all of which have seemed worthy of loans. Gold mining has been another outside force that has helped to rock the economy off dead center, and wars and preparation for war have played heroic parts in stimulating employment.

Along with these opportunities to make profit by new ventures it is highly important in our economy that the political climate be favorable to business if revival is to take place. If business men are suspicious of the party in power—if they fear heavy taxation, or encouragement of trade unions, or harassment under the anti-trust laws—conditions that might otherwise induce them to undertake new enterprises may leave them sulking in their tents. The liberal relief policies and other features of the New Deal were said repeatedly during the closing years of the 1930's to be deterrents to enterprise. This view cannot well be challenged, but at the same time the policies followed cannot easily be condemned. For some such policies were apparently necessary to relieve distress and perhaps to prevent revolts. Thus we have the anomalous condition that government activity may be necessary to prevent calamity and yet may postpone recovery.

A political climate that is highly favorable to business is not in itself sufficient to bring recovery, as the experience during President Hoover's administration amply demonstrates. What is needed is investment. And, to repeat, recovery will not take place if investments are only equal to current savings. That will merely keep us from getting worse.

We must have investments in excess of current savings—capital goods constructed by the use of money funds saved during an earlier period or newly created. This is why gold used to be such a help during hard times, when gold really counted as money. The unemployed to some extent turned to digging gold. The money supply was increased; demand increased; and additional goods were produced, thereby providing employment. Keynes makes a clever observation that the same results could be obtained now if we would put newly printed paper money in bottles, place the bottles in abandoned coal mines, fill in the pits, and then mine the paper money when times get hard, if "political and practical difficulties" prevent our using other methods (p. 129).

Within the framework of our customary procedure, what is needed is new investment. This is attested to by the piteous cries during the 1930's for new capital building despite a plethora of equipment in all of our industrial centers. The prosperity that President Hoover so pathetically announced from time to time as just around the corner failed to appear because some new industry hungry for money and labor was not still nearer to the corner. Equipment that was not yet invented, or the product not yet invented that would require new equipment, was our crying need.

The editor of the National City Bank *Bulletin* (New York) in the issue of August 1940, expressed the matter well:

During the past ten years many of our people . . . have searched eagerly for signs of some new industry capable of absorbing large amounts of capital and labor. It appears now that such an industry is in the making—the manufacture of armaments.

The editor regretted, of course, that armament building was the new industry that was to save us from continued unemployment, but he was shrewd enough to see that it would provide us with work to do. And what a job it has done!

CHAPTER VIII

The Postwar Period

I

THE MARKET CONDITIONS that will prevail during the first half-dozen years, more or less, following the reconversion of our economy to the ways of peace will furnish interesting illustrations of the conclusions that have been reached in the preceding chapters. The reconversion period itself will not be without its special interest in respect to employment. The cessation of the war will greatly disarrange the market for goods and services and cannot but result in unemployment. The number out of work will depend on a variety of factors. If we are wise we will ease the shock that will come from the loss of the war market. But however this may be, the problem of demobilization is a highly special one and is outside the scope of this book.

In the post-reconversion period one set of factors or conditions will contribute to an active market and to employment. These conditions will all be related to the war, but nevertheless illustrate by their unusualness the difficulty that normally confronts us. But along with these postwar factors that will contribute to employment the persistent tendency to save so much that employment is impeded will, it seems reasonable to believe, be unusually pronounced, because output per worker will be greater than ever before during peace. The effect of this general propensity to save—that is, the refusal to consume enough to maintain employment—will be further heightened, we may be sure, by the large accumulation of stocks of goods that we shall have in the postwar period. Our marked success in increasing our productivity will greatly aggravate our chronic malady of "oversavingitis."

In general our ability to find jobs will depend on the balance struck between the group of new forces on the one hand and the usual but augmented tendency to save on the other.

2

The factors growing out of the war that will contribute to an active market and high employment may be put into five groups: deferred demand; liquid savings; low consumer debts; opportunity to export; and public works and industrial construction.

Large numbers of persons are no doubt anxiously awaiting the opportunity to make purchases when the war ends. A demand is being built up for such things as automobiles, furniture, and houses, and perhaps also for less durable goods such as clothing and house decorations, and for a "good time," including travel. Many observers have no doubt overrated the volume of this deferred demand, but there can be no question that sales for the first few years of the postwar period will be appreciably increased as a result of our not having bought as extensively as we should have liked during the war.

The urge to buy when the war ends will be greatly augmented by the supply of monetary buying power that we shall possess. The total savings by individuals and unincorporated business units during the war amounted to about 115 billion dollars by the end of 1944. Some 22 per cent of these savings were in the form of houses, life insurance, debt reduction, and similar items, and 78 per cent in the form of currency, bank deposits, and government bonds.* A portion of the currency, bank deposits and war-bonds savings will differ sharply from those that we have been discussing in the preceding pages. They will have been made not because of a desire to save but because of a lack of opportunity to buy plus a patriotic reluc-

---

* Department of Commerce data, *Survey of Current Business,* September 1944, p. 8. Professor Slichter has estimated the total liquid savings as probably amounting to 106.6 billion dollars by the end of 1944; 135.6 billion by the end of 1945; and 157.7 billion by the close of 1946, depending, of course, upon when the war ends. He divides these into "hot" and "warm" savings, meaning those that are particularly sensitive to a disposition to spend and those that are moderately sensitive to such influences. He estimates the "hot" savings as being about 40 per cent of the total in 1944, a little less than that in 1945 and about one third in 1946. *Present Savings and Postwar Markets* (1943), p. 56.

tance not to buy during the war. Such savings are, in effect, deferred spending power, and will be used in consumption when that becomes possible.

No one knows what portion of the total liquid savings will be used in purchases. The portion of these savings that is held by unincorporated business units will presumably not be used in consumer purchases. This amounted to some 20 billion dollars as of July 1, 1944, leaving as of that time, according to the Department of Commerce, 60 billion dollars "which could serve as demand for consumer goods." * But only some of this will be "hot." The urge to guard against the hazard of unemployment may be a strong retarding influence, but some of these funds will be spent, in part as a result of unemployment. However slowly they may be utilized, they will represent a net addition to consumer buying power and will contribute to the maintenance of employment. Further, in so far as these savings are retained it is reasonable to believe that this will lead to less saving—to more prompt spending—from current income than would otherwise take place.

The method by which the funds are secured to redeem the war bonds that owners will wish to use in purchasing goods will determine the total effect upon our markets of redeeming bonds and using the funds in purchase. If the money used in redeeming the bonds should be secured by taxes upon consumption, or from persons who would have used it in consumption, no net gain in market expenditure will be realized. If the funds are derived from taxes that bring in money that would otherwise be saved, a net addition will be made to sales. This is particularly true if the money that would otherwise have been saved would not have been invested; but even if it should be invested, the flow of consumer goods might be so increased thereby that a market impasse would be created. It is to be hoped that our tax revenue in the postwar period will

* Ibid.

come almost wholly from progressive income taxes. This will tend to mean that the redemption of bonds for consumer purchasing will be wholly advantageous to our economy.

Certainly capitalism has never before during peace-time faced a situation in which its market was subsidized as that of the postwar period promises to be. If the accumulated deferred buying power results in an extra expenditure of 10 billion dollars per year, this will be equivalent to employing Santa Claus full time to hand out 30 million dollars every day for people to buy with. The sale of goods and the maintenance of employment will also be helped in the postwar period by the sale of goods on credit. The market for houses will be considerably facilitated, as is customary, by purchases on mortgage. Some 2 billion dollars' worth of single and two-family dwellings may be purchased each year for six or seven years, of which more than half the value may be financed by mortgage.* Other dwelling units, including apartment houses, may also be financed with mortgages, but this may be regarded as part of the usual process of joint ownership by capitalists of productive equipment. Single dwelling units, and to some extent "doubles," are in a different category. They are purchases by consumers and so far as credit is used they permit purchasers, as do installment sales, to buy beyond their immediate means.

Besides house sales on mortgage we may be able to sell some 8 or 9 billion dollars' worth of consumer goods in the first six or seven postwar years to persons who do not have enough money to pay for them within that period. Outstanding short-term consumer credit fell during the depression to less than 3.5 billion dollars by March 1933 and then rose to an all-time high of almost 10 billion dollars in September 1941. Since that time it fell to a little less than 5 billion dollars by the summer of 1943 and has since changed but little.† If a gross

---

* In 1940 we produced one-family dwellings of permit valuation of a little more than 1 billion dollars, and two-family dwellings of permit valuation of 71 million dollars, in 2,397 cities of population of 50,000 or more in 1930. *Statistical Abstract of the United States* (1941), p. 949.

† *The Survey of Current Business*, November 1942 and later issues.

national product of 120 billion dollars, as in 1941, permitted the short-term consumer debts to rise to almost 10 billion dollars, a gross national product of, say, 160 billion dollars should allow this form of debt to rise to 13 billion or to a somewhat higher figure.

The fear of unemployment may retard requests for credit or restrict its being granted both for purchases of houses and for consumer goods, but it will be increased, and by that amount the sale of goods will be facilitated and the national product will be increased up to the point of full employment.

The volume of net exports during the years that will immediately follow the war is also problematical. Our net exports of merchandise in 1919, immediately following the first World War, amounted to over 4 billion dollars, or almost one third above those for 1918. For the first three postwar years, 1919–21, our net exports were more than five times those for the three pre-war years, 1911–13.

We may not be so fortunate this time in getting rid of goods. Our sales abroad may be unusually large for a short time, but the high productivity in agriculture in foreign countries, as well as manufacturing, may greatly reduce the demand in our markets as soon as readjustments to peace have been made. As an offset on this score, we shall perhaps be even more resourceful than before in preventing goods from being imported in payment. We will certainly not permit goods to be sent to us in return for Lend-Lease materials. Nor, of course, will we ask for any indemnities from our defeated enemies as compensation for the losses that we shall have suffered. We well know that if we take in goods we shall suffer unemployment as a result, and that the consequent decrease in national product might easily exceed the volume of goods imported.

We shall undoubtedly inaugurate an extensive public works program at the close of hostilities to bridge the way back to the reconversion of war industries, and this program may continue beyond the time that the economy has been readjusted to peace-time work. If so, this will give us an additional stimulus to full employment. Not only will work be provided, but there will not be additional products added to the market supply.

Further, the building of plant and equipment that will almost of necessity be carried forward by industrial concerns, public utilities, railways, and so forth, together with the probable extensive construction of residences, will contribute to employment and resulting well-being.

There can be no denying that these forces will facilitate the sale of goods and help to maintain employment during the period under review. For once, other than during a war, we may be able to sell all that we can produce. This condition might, especially if we do not retain our war-time controls, generate a disastrous boom with a tragic aftermath. But if we keep the forces in order, they will contribute greatly to our well-being. After a few years, however, the extra grease will have vanished and our economy will have to get along with the buying power that it currently generates. Sellers will again be struggling with one another for the relatively scarce dollars left for buying after savings have been made.

3

Even with the supplementary buying power that we shall have in the post-reconversion period, we shall nevertheless have a formidable problem of consuming the product necessary to a reasonably high degree of employment. The maintenance of the employment and hours of work of the war period would require that, in addition to present consumption, we consume a volume of goods and services approximately equal to those now devoted to war. This would require that consumption be approximately doubled, since about half of our current product consists of war goods and services. The magnitude of the consumption required to maintain war-time employment and hours of work may also be indicated by noting that consumption during 1943 and 1944 is estimated to have been one sixth higher than that for 1939, after making allowance for price changes.*

It is unfortunate that we have to phrase this matter in terms of the "consumption required to provide employment," as if we consumed in order to work rather than the other way about. In part we do just that. Work is an end as well as is consumption, but long hours of arduous toil are not so regarded. Much of our work is still a means, not an end. But under our rules one cannot avoid the phrasing that consumption makes employment possible. The consumption of the middle and upper economic classes is requisite to the employment of the lower economic groups. The upper economic groups must consume lavishly, and more lavishly now than ever before, if the poorer groups are to consume at all, except by charity.

The question is, then, will the consumption of the upper economic groups be sufficient to maintain employment in the post-reconstruction period? Will they keep their savings sufficiently low and their spending sufficiently high to permit the entire national product to be sold? Will they make it possible to sell the product even if production is reduced substantially as a result of shorter hours and the withdrawal of some married women and other workers from the number of "gainfully employed"?

In considering these questions we need to keep in mind that the temporary liquid savings of the war period, plus the possible expansion of consumer debts and plus net exports, may, for a few years, more than offset uninvested savings. The question asked really concerns the period that will begin some three, four, or five years after reconversion to peace work has been accomplished. Can we keep ourselves at work then? The answer is that we cannot, barring unusually fortunate occurrences. Our habits of saving will throw us into a depression.

One change in our economy that would help us to keep going would be an alteration in the division of our income in

* See p. 98.

the direction of less inequality. Obviously, if a larger proportion of the total income were received by the poorest third or the poorest two thirds of the population, spending would be increased relatively to saving and the total product could more nearly be sold. But we are not likely to do much along this line. During the war we have applied very heavy taxes to the higher incomes and have thus reduced the inequality in the distribution of the national income, but all indications now point toward a downward revision of these taxes and a retention of the various sales taxes that fall heavily on the poor. The upper economic half of the population will no doubt get about 80 per cent of the total income in the period under consideration, as in 1935-6, leaving the lower half with 20 per cent. More especially, the upper 4 per cent of the income-receivers will doubtless get about 25 per cent of the total income after taxes. These figures point as straight as figures can to the inability of the nation as a whole to buy the national product, our spending and savings habits being what they are.

These projected figures are the storm signals of a depression as clearly as the data published by the Brookings Institution for 1929* indicate the basic reason for the depression of the 1930's. Those data show that the top three per cent of our income-receivers got more than one third of the total money income in 1929, and that 36,000 families at the top of the economic ladder, each getting $75,000 or more, got as many dollars (about ten billion) as did the poorest 11,653,000 families with incomes below $1,500. Given our propensity to save a depression was inevitable with such a distribution of income, after the usual expedients to keep us going had been exhausted. As well expect water-wheels to turn at their accustomed speed when the streams get low as to expect business men to continue to produce when the buying power that has been flowing to them is impounded in stagnant pools.

The Department of Commerce estimated in the spring of

* *America's Capacity to Consume* (1934). See p. 67 above.

1943 (*Markets after the War*) that we could produce as much in 1946 after reducing hours as we did in 1940 and have 19 million workers unemployed, or about one third of our working population. This means that full employment would require 50 per cent more consumption than in 1940. This may be considered a minimum estimate. Gains in efficiency during the past two years have reduced still further the number of workers now required to produce the 1940 output. Perhaps even with reduced hours and some loss of workers we shall need to consume in, say, 1950 from 60 to 75 per cent more than in 1940 if we are all to have jobs.

To stress again the obvious point, we could as a nation gladly and joyfully increase our consumption by that amount or more, but the distribution of income and our habits of saving will not permit such an increase. Even if all of the families of the nation got an increase of no more than 25 per cent in income over 1940, the upper economic groups would not increase their consumption so that such an income could be maintained.

More specifically, how much may be saved in the post-reconversion period and how much could be invested? The Department of Commerce estimates that in 1944 the gross product of the country amounted to approximately 200 billion dollars and the net income (the gross product minus depreciation, depletion, and business taxes) to 160 billion dollars.* If we assume somewhat arbitrarily a reduction of each of these figures by one fifth, we would have a gross product of 160 billion dollars and a national income of a little less than 130 billion. Could this be maintained after the war savings had been spent and consumer debts increased to their approximate limit? Our savings in a "normal" year are estimated as being about 20 per cent of the total income. This would give us 26 billion dollars of savings. If we assume that savings will amount to only 15 per cent of the national income, that would give us 20 billion. How much could we invest, if only for a few years?

---

* *Survey of Current Business*, February 1945, p. 5.

When it is remembered that total new construction of all kinds in 1939—houses, roads, public utilities, industrial, and all other—amounted to only a little over 6 billion dollars, the high since 1931, and to only 10.5 billion dollars in 1929,* it seems as if it would be impossible to provide profitable investments for anything like the volume of savings that we are likely to have.

Let us put it this way: Suppose that we should cut our production to one fifth below that for 1944, could we maintain it? Would we buy enough of it for consumption so that money savings would amount to only enough to equal the value of the production goods necessary to maintain that flow of consumption goods? There appears to be no escape from a negative answer.

4

Conditions that are now wholly unforeseen, especially by the present writer, may make the spending-saving ratio more favorable to employment, or may make the consequences of the present ratio less disastrous in the early 1950's than now appears probable, but on the basis of present conditions it seems clear that in the post-reconversion period we shall be able to produce goods and services in such almost unlimited amounts that our economic institutions more than ever before will prevent our consuming enough and investing enough (even though the poorest third of the population is in dire need) so that all of us who wish to work will be able to find jobs. It is to this pass that our amazing success in production and our failure in distribution will have brought us.

Dr. Julius Hirsch says on this point:

We will have no difficulty in creating very great production. It is the active consumption power to absorb that production which will be the problem. . . . I deny that our rapidly, progressively increasing additional production is automatically converted into corresponding additional consumption or investment. I deny that

* Ibid., January 1944, p. 11.

any theory or practice except war or similar compulsory production has yet found the way to this conversion.*

5

When the turn from prosperity comes, conditions will tend to get cumulatively worse. Unemployment will increase. The national administration at that time will face a perplexing dilemma. It will no doubt have gone into office on a double pledge of balancing the budget and maintaining "free enterprise." Yet as the number of the unemployed increases, something will have to be done. It is unlikely that the national administration could permit the number out of work to rise to 15 million or more as in the winter of 1932-3. Perhaps 7 or 8 million might prove to be the limit of toleration next time, particularly in view of the promises of employment that are now being made and that will no doubt be repeated. What will be done?

Broadly there will be two alternatives: (1) the unemployed may be provided with money tickets with which to buy consumption goods, or (2) the government may take over the idle factories and put the idle men and women to work. The first of these will involve the troublesome problem of finance. If traditional methods are followed, this will call for an increase in the government debt and it may already be too high. New methods of finance could be used,† but our traditions would oppose using them, as they would oppose also the second of the two alternatives. A vast W.P.A. financed by the sale of government bonds is the course that we are most likely to follow. We could set our house in order and avoid the tragedy that a do-nothing policy will create within the next dozen years, and we may do so. Contrariwise, we may have to suffer another depression before we repair our house.

* "Facts and Fantasies Concerning Full Employment," *American Economic Review, Supplement,* March 1944, pp. 126, 127.
† See Chapter xvi, section 8.

CHAPTER IX

Gain through Waste

I

THE PRECEDING ANALYSIS has indicated that our economy may gain by wasting assets, including labor power. Several references have been made to this, as in noting the economic advantage that may come from war or from using economic resources to drill dry oil wells or to produce other investment goods that prove to be worthless. The references to the gain to us as a nation in getting rid of goods and in refusing to take goods in payment also illustrate gain through waste. This is such a glaring and regrettable feature of our economy and is so closely related to the saving-investment process as we practice it that further consideration of this aspect of our problem appears to be justified.

I hasten to remark that waste can be helpful only within limits, and then only because our economic customs do not permit us to be fully employed at useful tasks. Waste is defensible only as a means of circulating or compensating for idle funds and inducing employment. The limit of its usefulness is marked by the extent of such idleness. Granting the impossibility of otherwise putting idle money and idle men to work, the employment of some of the unemployed workers at carrying water from one side of a lake to the other may set in operation forces that will lead to the employment of many others who are out of work and thus considerably augment the total economic product. Or, if our markets are becoming congested and widespread depression unemployment is about to occur, failure of newly produced investment goods to turn out added consumption goods as a result of imperfect engineering or other wasteful process may permit the economy as a whole to continue at a high level of productivity. Total output would obviously be less than full productivity in such cases, but it might well be far above the level that would otherwise obtain.

2

Perhaps the most striking illustration of this operational aspect of our economy is the effect of war, or of preparation for war. Wars may be so destructive as to be wholly wasteful, but they may so increase the product of a nation as to contribute markedly to total welfare. This is especially likely to be true during the preparation stage, if such activities are kept within moderate limits. This is vividly shown in our economy during the year 1941. Our preparations for war began in the summer of 1940 when the Germans conquered France, the Low Countries, and Norway and threatened England, and by the close of that year it had begun to have a decidedly stimulating effect on our economy. The unemployed—there were about 8 million in the summer and fall of 1940—were finding jobs and the general tempo of our economic activity was increasing.

During the calendar year 1941 we produced some 13.3 billion dollars' worth of war goods and services and Lend-Lease materials and inducted about 1.5 million men into the armed services, and at the same time we produced more peace-time goods than ever before in our history, despite there still being an average of 5 million workers unemployed. With over 10 per cent of the total economic effort expended that year devoted to war, we finished the year better fed, better clothed, better supplied with transportation, entertainment, books, tobacco, candy, and Christmas presents than ever before. If it had not been necessary to increase our war effort we could, verily, have produced our way into the economic heaven of plenty if only the war lasted long enough.*

Our record of production during the war years 1943 and 1944 is still more striking. For in addition to the tremendous effort

* Data cited are from the *Survey of Current Business,* February 1945. An auxiliary factor that helped us to be prosperous during 1941 was the accumulation of inventories by manufacturers, wholesalers, and retailers, as a result of increased business and an anticipation of price increases and material shortages. The Department of Commerce estimates that inventories increased from more than 21 billion to a little more than 27 billion during that year. Perhaps a third of this increase in inventory may be attributed to a rise in prices, but even so, the volume withheld from the market is significant. Ibid., June 1942.

applied to war—amounting each year to almost as much in current dollars as did the total output of our economy in 1939 * —the total consumption of the civilian population is estimated to have exceeded that of 1939 by at least one sixth for each of these years, after adjustment for price changes.† It is, obviously, difficult to make accurate computations of this sort, but there is apparently no question that the bottom half of the population on an income scale, if not the lower three fourths, lived better during these two years than ever before. No one would have imagined that we could wage war on such a vast scale with so little, if any, reduction in our total consumption. Raising, training, equipping, and provisioning an army and navy of 11,000,-000 men, transporting almost half of them and their equipment across the oceans, and providing our allies with vast quantities of material has been, practically, merely an appetizer to our economy.

Our production during the first World War was also spectacular. The Columbia University Commission, which included five men who have been president of the American Economic Association, in its report in 1934 entitled *Economic Reconstruction* says, in discussing our inability to use our equipment at anything like its capacity:

What happened during the War, when the volume of goods, taking war and peace products together, increased at the very time that millions of the younger and more vigorous workers were withdrawn from productive functions, is an indication, highly peculiar though conditions then were, of the manner in which potential productivity lies unutilized in normal times [p. 9].

David Friday, writing in the *Journal of Political Economy,* December 1918, said:

---

* Gross national product, 1939, 88.6 billion dollars. War expenditures by federal government, 1943, 83.7 billion dollars; 1944, 89.2 billion. *Survey of Current Business,* January 1944, p. 2, and January 1945, pp. S–17.

† *Consumer Expenditures for Goods and Services*

	1939	1943	1944
Total (current dollars)	61.7	91.0	96.5
Total (1939 dollars)	61.7	70.8	73.6

Survey of Current Business, December 1944, p. 2.

A careful study of the physical product during 1917 as compared with the pre-war period shows that this increase in physical output was at least 25 per cent and possibly as high as 33⅓ per cent [p. 958].

This was accomplished, he said, in the February 1919 issue of the same journal, "through the complete utilization of our natural resources, our plant and machinery, and our labor" (p. 117). But, one may add, without the services of the men under arms.

In the second article referred to, which was called "Maintaining Productive Output—A Problem in Reconstruction," Mr. Friday said:

If production is allowed to return to the pre-war level output will slump off by 20 per cent. This would mean a corresponding waste of productive resources and a decrease of $14,000,000,000 per annum in our national income as measured by the present price level; even if prices should fall by 30 per cent the decrease would still be approximately $10,000,000,000. In view of the magnitude of this waste the government can well afford to spend several billion dollars per annum if necessary to maintain the level of productive output. The essence of the process would be that we would waste two billion dollars of our productive capacity in order to keep ten to fourteen billion dollars' worth of resources from running to waste because of unemployment. [P. 117.]

Indicating bafflement at the idea that fighting a war helps us to provide ourselves with shoes, Mr. Friday then makes the statement, quoted at the beginning of this book, that there seems to be "in the present industrial process . . . a factor of retardation which is only occasionally cast out by such a holocaust as war," and that if we could discover "the secret of its casting out" and "institutionalize it," we "could then realize the high standard of living of which reformers have dreamed." (It is my hope, obviously, that this book reveals this secret and shows how to institutionalize it.)

Similar high productivity and increased consumption were experienced in the North during the Civil War. References to this will be found in Chapter xii in the quotation from Crocker. The point is, of course, that a war solves the market problem which has normally been beyond our power to solve. The expenditures of the government for goods that do not enter the market gives buying power that is more than adequate, after taxes and savings, for all consumer goods and services that are available. Since there is a market for all that is or can be produced, no one is unemployed and no laborer or business man need "go slow."

It is also to be noted that calamities in general, such as fires, floods, and storms, may provide a stimulus to production and bring the total enough above the amount needed for repairs and replacements to leave a society better provisioned than before the loss occurred. This depends, of course, upon workers being unemployed or upon the economy "going slow" for lack of a sufficient market, but as such a condition usually prevails the assumption of gain from moderate calamities is not unwarranted.

3

The waste of a nation's resources by selling abroad more than will be taken in return, or by refusing to accept goods in payment of debts or war indemnities, may also result in considerable gain to a nation. We are especially happy, as commercial nations have always been, when we have "a favorable balance of trade"—that is, net exports. As noted in Chapter v, our excess of exports of goods and services over imports during the eight years 1922–9 was an important factor in the prosperity of that period. Just now there are great expectations of big sales of goods to China, Russia, and other underdeveloped countries in the postwar period. If we can get rid of enough goods that can be eaten, worn, or ridden about in, and take our pay in gold that we can bury or paper that will not come due for many years, we shall have more goods to eat, wear, and ride about in than we would otherwise have. We can export our cake and have it too. Or, more strictly, by exporting some of our cake we can have still more cake.

Consider, too, our attitude toward the debts owed to us after the close of World War I. We, the people of the United States, were entitled to receive 14 billion dollars in goods from our former allies and other creditor countries without the expenditure of a penny. Did we facilitate the importation of such goods? No, on the contrary we raised our tariffs temporarily in 1921 and permanently in 1922 and again in 1930. We did a great deal of table-pounding as we demanded that our debtors pay, but we kept the door locked so that they could not do so. We were wise in this, for if we had accepted 2 or 3 billion dollars in goods each year for a few years, the added congestion in our markets might have resulted in such a volume of unemployment that goods available for use might have been far below what we had without the payments. The depression that began in 1929 might have set in four or five years earlier if we had permitted ourselves to be paid.*

This indicates how very fortunate we are that someone, perhaps President Roosevelt, early in this war hit on the idea of Lend-Lease.† We have thus been able to furnish goods to our allies and so increase our effectiveness in the war without jeopardizing our economy by the threat of payment after the war. The term "Lend-Lease" does imply that we will be paid and this eases our commercial conscience, but no one thinks for a moment that steel and trucks and food will be sent to us. We will not permit that to happen. One may be sure that we will not even permit any used trucks or jeeps to be sent back. We shall, of course, as a nation in which the Yankee tradition is strong, insist on payment, but we will take our pay in military

* England paid a little over 2 billion dollars on her debt of almost 6 billion, and all of the other nations together paid about 725 million dollars on their combined debt of about 8 billion.

† "There can be little doubt that the concept itself came from the active imagination of Franklin Roosevelt himself."—George Fort Milton, *The Use of Presidential Power, 1789–1943*, p. 294.

bases, concessions, goodwill, or some other commodity that will not add to our imports.

Experience with war indemnities illustrates the same point. They appear to benefit the nation that pays and to injure the nation that receives. The payment of high indemnities by France to Germany at the close of the Franco-Prussian War of 1870 is often cited as having benefited France and injured Germany.* And the indemnities levied on Germany by her neighbor nations at the end of World War I were allowed to fall into abeyance because of the difficulties produced in the receiving countries. Penalties should apparently be in the form of compelling the defeated nation to accept without payment the goods of the victorious nation.

There has not, it is to be noted, been the slightest suggestion during this war that indemnities will be demanded of Germany by this country or Great Britain, despite the extensive discussion of punishing the Germans and keeping them from rearming. In contrast to the attitude of these two nations, the U.S.S.R. is insisting on large payments from Germany in goods. The Russians would welcome a continuous flow of goods from Germany of the largest possible amount. The explanation is that the Russians have no difficulty in distributing all that they produce or might produce. Additions to their economy do not amount to subtractions.

The conservative *United States News* edited by David Lawrence, puts this matter as follows in its issue of December 10, 1943.

It is Germany's hard luck that Russia's socialist setup enables her to import unlimited quantities of German goods, regardless of price or of no price without worrying about competition with domestic industry. U. S.—Britain cannot do that. They can't put Germany to work for them without bringing complaint from their own businessmen, who have trouble distributing all they can produce.

* See Chapter xii.

Reparations in World War I broke down when Allies balked at taking German goods. . . .*

4

The tariff policies which we and other commercial nations have followed are also expressions of this general concern not to import, but to export. To be sure, almost every nation wishes to import certain commodities, but the general desire is that these be considerably exceeded by exports. Also, it is to be noted, as observed in the second chapter of this book, that the immediate self-interest of many business groups causes them to encourage a national policy of extending exports and curtailing imports, but the greed of a few does not seem to be an adequate explanation of the increase of tariff barriers decade by decade. It appears to be particularly inadequate in the light of analysis, such as is presented here, showing the chronic congestion of markets and the consequent unemployment that our economic practices induce.

Practical men, including politicians, have followed their own lights in defending tariff policies, since the weight of the economists has been almost wholly against them. The economists have regarded commerce among nations as identical with trade between neighbors. Each promotes specialization and hence enlarges the total product and thus promotes economic welfare. The economists' lack of concern with unemployment—indeed, their position has been that there is no involuntary unemployment—has prevented them from seeing what now appears to be obvious.†

The argument here is not that unemployment will be less under high tariffs, long after they have been imposed, than with low tariffs, or with free trade. Perhaps there is no difference in the long run in respect to the volume of employment. If this is true, one should expect a generally higher standard of living

---

* Newsgram section, pp. 7, 8. Underscoring as in original.

† I confess to myopia for some three decades in respect to this point as a result of thorough indoctrination in the "sound" theory of the orthodox school.

with low tariffs than with high. The point is that any policy that will increase the net exports of a capitalist nation during a given period will, for that time and to the extent of the net exports, provide employment. And since we live in "short runs," there is a steady pressure to raise tariffs and against lowering them. For raising them tends to curtail imports at once while not immediately reducing exports. Practically we are forced to choose between an increase in international specialization and relief from congestion in the home market.

This process is highly competitive among the capitalist nations. They cannot all have net exports, particularly so far as they trade with each other. And the possibility of retaliation necessarily imposes some restraint on each, but the fact that all cannot win in the constant struggle of each to export its unemployment to the others does not keep each one from trying to improve its position. The race is to the strong and crafty. Furthermore gains to employment from an increase in tariffs are soon brought to an end, but sufficient unto the day is the employment thereof.

Great Britain's long policy of free trade may be cited to controvert this argument, but it does not. She had such a start over the other nations in industrial development and in colonization that she was able to have net exports without a tariff. As soon, however, as the other nations sufficiently caught up with Britain to endanger her ability to get rid of goods, she adopted a tariff policy. Britain's net exports have been euphemistically called an "export of capital," as if the British were graciously sharing their surplus of capital with less progressive nations. The "surplus" was, of course, merely goods, including textiles, that the rich people in Britain would not buy and the poor could not buy.

The whole new cluster of devices in the field of foreign trade, such as monopoly control by a nation through its central bank of all transactions in foreign exchange running to or from that nation, the imposition of import quotas, special arrangements to prevent dumping, and the depreciation of a nation's currency to foreign buyers, are cut from the same cloth as the old protective tariffs. They are the latest tricks by which capitalist nations carry on the old struggle of each attempting to force more goods on the others than it takes in return.

5

It is interesting to note the frank manner in which practical men have advocated the policy of getting rid of goods in order to have goods. They have boldly insisted that by subtracting from the national store we add to it. Thus Senator Albert J. Beveridge of Indiana, following the Spanish-American War, defended our new relations with Hawaii, Puerto Rico, the Philippines, and Cuba by saying:

> . . . we are raising more than we can consume . . . we are making more than we can use . . . there are more workers than there is work . . . more capital than there is investment . . . we need . . . more employment . . . we must find new markets for our produce, new occupations for our capital, new work for our labor.
>
> [Sales to] these islands . . . will set every reaper in this republic singing, every spindle whirling, every furnace spouting the flames of industry.*

Cecil Rhodes, the British Empire-builder, said, also in the closing years of the nineteenth century:

> In order to save 40,000,000 inhabitants of the United Kingdom from a bloody civil war, we colonial statesmen must take possession of new lands . . . where we shall be able to find new markets for the goods produced in our factories and mines.†

Herbert Hoover, a generation later, insisted that we were producing goods "much in excess of our needs" and "to insure continuous employment . . . we must find a profitable [foreign] market for these surpluses." ‡

* "The March of the Flag," *Modern Eloquence,* Vol. XI, pp. 235–6.
† Lenin: *Imperialism—The State and Revolution* (1926), p. 62.
‡ Speech at Boston, October 1928.

Sir George Paish in discussing the condition in this country during the 1930's said:

> . . . one has to realize . . . that America is developed. . . . Her need is not the continuance of the rapid increase of the productive power of the past century, but markets in which to sell her existing output. [She must sell a] vast quantity of cotton, food, metals, machinery, vehicles and other goods . . . in order to utilize her existing productive powers . . . the American people themselves cannot consume anything like enough to absorb all that they can produce, and . . . unless they can find foreign purchasers for their products they cannot maintain the prosperity to which they have become accustomed.*

What the program that these men have argued for, and that we have followed, amounts to is the delegating of the labor of a portion of our population to the production of goods for the use of foreign peoples. We in return are then able to be more fully employed than otherwise and are likely to have a larger product to consume than we would otherwise permit ourselves to have. Granted our saving-investment process, such a policy is the part of wisdom.

It is true, of course, that by burning a large quantity of goods each year, or sinking them in the ocean, we could contribute to our prosperity equally as well as by net exports, but such conduct would be abhorrent to us, as was the destruction of agricultural goods a few years ago, because we have not yet formulated a ritual to justify it. Net exports have ritualistic justification.

6

By way of further emphasizing our need to subtract in order to add, attention may be called again to the lack of this need in the U.S.S.R. The Russians having succeeded in solving the problem of unemployment, they derive no gain from waste. War does not add to their consumption and the termination of war does not frighten them. Similarly they have no fear of im-

* The London *Statist*, March 26, 1938.

ports—it is exports that they dislike. They export only to import, as economists have erroneously said was the reason for any country's exporting.

This indicates a complementary relation between capitalism and socialism that Marx, Lenin, and Trotsky entirely overlooked. The one type of economy desires net exports, the other net imports; the one wishes to export goods and take pay in gold and pieces of paper, and the other wishes to import goods and pay for them with gold and paper. This should be a factor of importance in the maintenance of peace in the period that lies ahead. It indicates that we should not expect the Russians to desire to extend the "economic revolution." The prevalence of capitalism here and in Britain as well as on the continent of Europe is worth many millions of rubles annually to the Russians. They may, of course, let ideology triumph over economics, but it appears unlikely that they will.

CHAPTER X

The Record: The 1920's and 1930's

I

SOME OF THE DATA used in this chapter have been used earlier in this book but are repeated here to make the chapter more nearly complete than if they were omitted. Following the severe depression from the middle of 1920 to the middle of 1921, the economy made a very rapid recovery. We were fortunately very short of housing relative to the effective demand, and the resulting building of residences gave a great fillip to the economy. There had been but little house-building during the war, or in 1919 or 1920. The index of residential construction contracts as compiled by the Federal Reserve Board was 44 for the year 1919 and 30 for the year 1920, the average for the years 1923-5 being counted as 100. The index in 1924 was 95, showing more than three times as much construction of residences as in 1920, and in 1925 the index reached 124, or four times the 1920 volume, and remained at approximately this level through 1928. The index of general construction rose from 63 in each of the two years 1919 and 1920 to more than twice this in 1926. The rise continued through 1928, at which time the index stood at 135.

In terms of dollar outlay, data published by Mordecai Ezekiel in both the March and June 1942 numbers of the *American Economic Review* show expenditures for houses to have been 2.3 and 3.8 billion dollars in 1921 and 1922 respectively, 4.8 billion dollars in 1923, and more than 5 billion dollars in each of the next five years.

We were fortunate in this, for house-building is an especially happy form of capital construction. It uses savings and thus provides employment, but does not result in consumption goods coming on the market later, as does the building of factories. House services do come on the market, obviously, but whether or not the houses are rented, employment is not affected as when factory products are not sold. In both cases, of course, subsequent production is affected by lack of sale.

We also were lucky in not having as good or as much industrial equipment as it was profitable to have in view of the available buying power and the technical improvements that had recently been made. Ezekiel's data show expenditures for plant and equipment to have been each roughly the same in amount as the expenditures for housing for the years indicated. The high for each of these two items, however, was reached in 1929, while the high for housing came in 1928. The construction of this equipment together with the building of houses created additional income which made it possible for persons who would otherwise have been unemployed to demand goods and services that furnished employment and created income for still other workers who would otherwise not have had anything to do.

The total output of manufacturing and mining products in 1919, 1920, and 1921, according to the Federal Reserve Board, amounted to 72, 75, and 58 per cent, respectively, of the average output in 1935–9, and then rose each year, except in 1924 and in 1927, until a peak of 110 was reached in 1929. According to these data, we produced 60 per cent more manufacturing and mining goods in 1929 than we produced on the average during the three years 1919–21.

Selling was facilitated by an increase in consumer credit, and by sales abroad in excess of purchases from abroad, as shown in Chapter v above. By these two methods of disposing of goods, to repeat the figure given, we relieved the pressure on our home market by the huge amount of 120 million dollars a month on an average for the eight-year period 1922–9 inclusive, amounting in all to 11.5 billion dollars.

The Ezekiel data are not compiled to show money savings that were unused because of a lack of opportunity for profitable investment as a result of the difficulty of selling consumer goods. They show savings that took the form of equipment, plant, housing, consumers' credit, net foreign balance, inventories, and net contribution by government. Therefore they cannot be used to show the amount of income that was held idle, saved and not invested, during that period.

The data do show a sharp yearly increase in savings utilized during the three years 1921-3. The national income in 1923 was 17 per cent above that for 1921, but utilized savings were almost twice as large in 1923 as in 1921. The former was up 11 billion dollars and the latter 7.4 billion. That is, out of 11 billion dollars increase in the national income, 7.4 billion dollars were used in investments. In 1924 the utilized savings decreased, then rose sharply in 1925, decreased again in 1926 and 1927 and then rose in 1928 and 1929.

There were three periods in which savings were pyramided during this decade, but there is nothing to show that the savers did not attempt to pyramid their savings each year. It is, indeed, almost a truism that this is the desire of savers. One of the Keynesian postulates is that the percentage of savings to income increases as income increases. This is certainly borne out by common observation and is confirmed by Ezekiel's conclusion, after elaborate statistical work with the data, that "Savings is a function of the current level of income, increasing as the level of income increases, but at a higher rate."

It is also important to note certain other adverse market factors that were operating during this period of expanding prosperity. For one thing, the increase in income that resulted from the increase in production went largely into the hands of the upper income receivers and thus increased the amount of money saved each year and reduced, relatively, the amount available for the purchase of goods and services in the consumption market.

From 1925 to 1929, during which time there were no changes in the provisions for filing income tax statements, the net income reported for taxation increased by 2.9 billion dollars, or 13.3 per cent, but the income reported by those getting less than

$5,000 decreased by 1 billion dollars, or 11 per cent. This means that the incomes reported for taxation by those getting $5,000 or more increased by 3.9 billion dollars, a gain of 30 per cent. This does not mean that those persons who got less than $5,000 in 1925 got still less in 1929. Many of them simply moved over this line. The point is that more persons got large incomes and that the large incomes were increased. Indeed, more than half of the increase in income above $5,000 per person was reported by persons getting $100,000 or above, and more than a quarter of it (1.13 billion dollars) by those getting $500,000 or more. The amount of income reported by this last-mentioned group was 150 per cent more in 1929 than in 1925. The comparison of the tax returns for 1928 with those for 1925 are even more striking than are those for 1929, since the amount of income reported in each of the seven brackets between $10,000 and $1,000,000 declined in 1929, evidently as a result of stock market losses suffered in the closing months of that year.

Data presented to the Temporary National Economic Committee show that the highest 1 per cent of income recipients received 13 per cent of the total national income including capital gains in 1923, 14.2 per cent in 1924, and 19.3 and 18.5 per cent respectively in 1928 and 1929. The total amount of income going to these recipients was 8.7 and 9.6 billion dollars in 1923 and 1924, and 15.3 and 15.0 billion dollars respectively in 1928 and 1929.*

Employment in manufacturing establishments, as reported by the Bureau of Labor Statistics, increased in 1922 and 1923, after the drop in 1921, and then declined, not again reaching the 1923 figure until 1929. Pay-rolls in manufacturing followed this same general course, but were practically unchanged for the four years 1925–8. The weekly earnings of factory workers as reported by the National Industrial Conference Board increased from an average of $26.61 per week in 1923 to $28.52 in 1929. The average rate of pay in steel in the Pittsburgh district

* Monograph No. 37, p. 18.

as reported by the United States Steel Corporation remained at 50 cents per hour every month from August 1923 through 1929. Total wages per year paid in manufacturing, according to the United States Census, increased from a little less than 11 billion dollars in 1923 to 11.6 billion in 1929, or by a little more than 600 million dollars, while value added by manufacturing was more than 6 billion dollars higher in 1929 than in 1923, as noted in Chapter v.* Net profits of industrial and mercantile corporations increased from an average of 215 million dollars per month in 1925 to an average of 359 million dollars per month in 1929, as reported by the Federal Reserve Bank of New York.

These data all indicate a condition that would make it increasingly difficult to sell the product from which the total income was derived. The savings of the group that largely received the increase in income, and the speculation by this group in the stock market, did not buy any of the current consumer product.

The single fact, as reported by the Brookings Institution, that the upper 3 per cent of the income-receivers got more than a third of the dollar income in 1929 indicates how impossible it was to avoid a slump. Three per cent of the receivers of money income can take one third of the product for a few years during a capital-building spurt, but obviously, with consumption habits as they are in this country, they cannot continue to buy for consumption and to take as investment one third of the total product when the new capital building begins to augment the total output. An economy built on such a degree of inequality today is verily built on shifting sand. If wages had risen more and if prices had fallen more during the last eight years of the 1920's, less of the national income would have accrued to the upper economic group and prosperity could have been prolonged, but even such voluntary denials of good business could not have saved the situation. The market impasse would have appeared because that is the inevitable result of the com-

* *Statistical Abstract of the United States* (1934), p. 697. These data have since been revised and show slightly larger increases in wages.

pounding of savings, which, whatever the superficial aspects, is the fundamental character of every period of prosperity.

The stock market speculative orgy that climaxed the period of prosperity of the 1920's deserves additional comment. A sizable portion of the total income created in the production of goods and services during the latter part of that decade was used in the purchase of shares of stock rather than in taking consumer goods off the market or in building additional equipment. Our economy had so definitely reached the saturation point in selling goods to people who had cash or credit and desire to buy that there was no place for savings to go except into gambling in stocks. The New York banks at one time had loans in the New York Stock Exchange for the account of others—largely corporations—to the amount of approximately 4 billion dollars. The volume of shares purchased on the New York Stock Exchange, which in the three years, 1922–4, averaged a little less than 260 million shares per year, increased to almost 1 billion in 1928 and to 1.1 billion shares in 1929. The average of the highest price paid for 25 industrial stocks was a little more than $116 per share in 1922 and $118 in 1923. In 1924 the comparable figure was $135, but in 1928 it was over $332 and in 1929 it reached $469.49.* Loans obtained by New York Stock Exchange members (brokers' loans) rose from 3.2 billion and 3.9 billion dollars in September 1926 and September 1927 respectively to 8.55 billion dollars in September 1929.†

The purchase of shares of stock is only part of the story, since purchases mean that sales are made. What did the sellers do with the money that they received for stock sold? In so far as they used it in purchases of consumer goods, such purchases were merely delayed by the stock transaction from what they might have been. Even so, the delay might be significant. Particularly the delay was important when the sellers of certain shares of stock bought other shares with the funds received, for then the goods market was denied the funds until the chain of

---

* *Statistical Abstract of the United States* (1933), p. 275.
† Ibid.

the sale of some stock and the purchase of other was broken. In a speculative mania such as prevailed in 1928 and 1929, particularly in the latter year, the delay in using money funds in the goods market must have been of considerable moment. It is to be noted that the volume of broker loans indicates the amount of money that is being withdrawn from the market. This sum was considerable, as the figure given in the preceding paragraph indicates. Nevertheless, the time involved in withdrawing funds may also have been considerable.

It must be emphasized, too, that business corporations themselves withdrew large sums of money from the stock market in the three years, 1927–9. New capital issues amounted to more than 26 billion dollars for that period, most of which were undoubtedly sold through the New York Stock Exchange. The funds received in this way were presumably held as bank balances or used in plant extension. In either case the situation in respect to the sale of consumer goods and services was made increasingly difficult. In the one case money was held idle and in the other case the volume of consumer goods and services for sale was increased. In short, the entire episode of the stock market in the late 1920's aggravated the problem of disposing of goods.

The collapse of the stock market in the autumn of 1929 was a fatal blow to the continuance of prosperity. It brought to a head the disease that was festering. Demand was at once sharply reduced in luxury lines, employees were dismissed, demand was further reduced by the loss of income to laborers and also as a result of doubt and uncertainty on the part of business men. The economy deteriorated in a cumulative fashion. The train of events that carries a period of prosperity to the slough of depression was accentuated by the speculation and its collapse, but the entire absence of speculation would not have made it possible to prolong the prosperity of the 1920's, as I have demonstrated above.

2

The decline in business that began in the summer of 1929 continued practically without interruption until the summer of 1932. The index of industrial production, compiled by the Federal Reserve Board as a measure of the physical output in manufacturing and mining, fell from a high of 114 (1935–9 = 100) in June, July, and August 1929 to a low of 53 in July of 1932. In each of the three months June, July, and August the index in 1932 was well below half of what it was three years earlier. There were only two cases during these three years in which the output of manufactured and mined products exceeded that of the preceding month. In terms of employment the situation was, of course, roughly the same as in industrial production. The number out of work increased continuously.

An upturn came in August 1932. The index of industrial production advanced to 60 by October and November of that year and then declined until March 1933, when it stood at 54, or within one point of the low of July 1932. The banking crisis in the winter of that year was an important factor in this new decline. This was occasioned in part by uncertainty as to the monetary and fiscal policies of the newly elected administration, but it was perhaps largely the result of the three-year decline in business. Such a course could not but impair outstanding loans throughout the entire economy and weaken all financial institutions. Banks in all parts of the nation closed their doors during the latter part of February and the first few days of March, and by Saturday morning March 4 practically every bank in the country was closed. The unemployed at this time are estimated to have numbered from 15 to 17 million, or one third of the working population. The inauguration of President Roosevelt at noon of that day and his promise of vigorous action stopped the decline, for confidence in the future is of great importance in our economy, however much prosperity may depend on the basic fact of buying power and its distribution.

The business improvement following Roosevelt's inauguration continued at a relatively slow pace considering the period
as a whole, until the outlay for military production beginning
in the summer of 1940 finally gave us full employment. According to the Bureau of the Census, 8.4 million persons were
unemployed in July 1940, out of a labor force of 56.4 million,
or approximately one seventh of the total. This number declined month by month with hardly an exception until it fell
below 1 million in April 1943, which may be accounted as practically full employment.*

The course of business activity was irregular during the
period 1933–40, though the general trend was upward. The enactment of the National Industry Recovery Act in 1933, with
the expectation of an increase in wage rates and a reduction in
working hours, led to a marked increase in industrial output
even before its enactment as business men attempted to "beat
the codes." That is, manufacturers produced for inventory, anticipating that costs would be higher as soon as the "codes" to
be adopted under the Act became effective. The index of industrial production advanced from 54 in March to 86 in July,
a gain of approximately 60 per cent in four months.

This was of course only a spurt, as demand was not adequate
for the enlarged output. Production declined beginning in
August and continued to fall until November, when the index
stood at 69. Then there was a gradual and practically continuous increase for three and one half years, until July and August
1937, when a new peak of 120 was reached in the industrial production index. A very sharp decline began then that carried the
index to 80 in May 1938, a decline of one third in 9 months. The
precipitate character of this recession is indicated by noting that
the decline following the downturn in 1929 did not amount to
one third until the twenty-third month. Following this low in
May 1938, another improvement began that carried the index

* *Survey of Current Business*, February 1945, p. 23.

to 126 in December 1939, or an increase of more than 50 per cent in a year and a half.

The Roosevelt administration was torn between two conflicting purposes throughout this period. It desired to reduce the government outlay of money, to balance the budget, and at the same time to provide relief for the unemployed particularly by work projects. This conflict appeared even during the campaign, as is shown by Roosevelt's speech at Pittsburgh. He deplored the increase in the cost of government, criticized the Hoover administration for creating a deficit, and promised to comply with the Democratic platform which called for a reduction of twenty-five per cent in the operations of the federal government. He then said, however, that "if starvation and dire need" made it necessary to appropriate funds "which would keep the budget out of balance," he would favor doing that.

The President talked much of adding to the purchasing power of the masses, but he was too tightly imprisoned by the idea of "sound finance" to do wholeheartedly what needed to be done. His temporizing course is not to be wondered at when it is recalled how firmly men everywhere held to the notion of the desirability of following "sound" policies. Even professors of economics whom one would expect to be but little trammeled by tradition were on the whole insistent on the need for balancing the budget. Actually, of course, the nation was short of effective buying power, and the one agency capable of supplying it—the national government—should have done so.*

A moderate addition was made to buying power in 1934 and 1935 by government expenditure of newly created funds, which was reflected in the gains in production. A large addition was made in 1936 as a result of the payment of the veterans' bonus, against the wishes of the President, who vetoed the bill in January 1936 as he had vetoed a similar bill in May 1935. This payment was a great stimulus to business. But the recovery that had

---

* Ways by which this could have best been done are noted in Chapter xvi, section 8.

been secured, together with the displeasure caused by the large deficit in 1936, led to strong pressure for a balanced budget. The "net contribution of the federal government to national buying power," which reached a peak of over 600 million dollars a month in 1936, fell to an average of less than 100 million a month in 1937 and to practically nothing in the early months of 1938. This was a most important factor in the severe slump of late 1937 and early 1938. "Net contributions to buying power" by the federal government were then increased again to an average of about 300 million dollars a month in 1939 and early 1940. Business responded accordingly, and, as already noted, the "net contributions" were then sharply increased beginning in the summer of 1940 and the economy responded as it could not help doing.*

The principal error revealed by the record is that the contribution of the federal government to buying power was not more pronounced. Further, given the state of mind of business men during this period, any deficit in the annual financial account of the government was a deterring factor in business revival. This attitude would not have been any more pronounced if the annual deficit had been 7 or 10 billion dollars a year instead of the average figure of less than 3 billion a year for six years. Perhaps when we are again confronted with severe unemployment we shall be more forthright, in part because of having improved our techniques in deficit financing.

3

In this brief review of the past two decades attention may be called again to the recent accumulation of business inventories. The data published in the *Survey of Current Business,* June 1942, show inventories to have stood at a little over 18 billion dollars in December 1938. There was a gradual increase during

---

* Net contributions of the federal government to national buying power are the national expenditures minus the outgo to trust funds or other non-income-creating operations and minus all receipts deemed to be income-reducing, which includes all receipts except: (a) estate and gift taxes, (b) seigniorage, and (c) canal tolls. Sherwood M. Fine: *Public Spending and Postwar Economic Policy* (1944), p. 91.

1939, bringing the total at the end of that year to 19.3 billion dollars. In December 1940 the figure was 21.2 billion dollars and in December 1941, 27.1 billion dollars. The increase continued until May 1942, when inventories amounted to 29.1 billion dollars.* In forty-one months there was an increase of approximately 11 billion dollars, an amount equal to 60 per cent of the volume on hand December 1938. There were only eight months during these forty-one in which inventories showed a decline, and five of these were in 1939. These data reveal a very important factor in the prosperity of the period immediately following 1938. Almost 11 billion dollars' worth of goods, which persons were paid to produce, were kept off the market in a little more than three years. The sale of other goods was thereby facilitated.

This increase in inventories was in part due to the rise in price which took place during that time. This is estimated to have accounted for from one third to one half of the increase for the period from December 1938 to April 1942, but even so "increases have been in record volume in terms of both quantity and value."

While this storing up of goods by business firms contributed to our prosperity during this time, it would undoubtedly have helped to throw us into a bad depression if the defense effort had been relaxed for any reason. The bombs at Pearl Harbor blasted the log-jam that was developing in our markets.

* See also *Domestic Commerce*, August 13, 1942.

CHAPTER XI

A Glance at History

I

THE ARGUMENT of the preceding chapters cannot but raise the question in some minds as to how we could have made the amazing progress that has marked the past hundred years, if our economy has the weakness indicated. To such a question the demurrer must be made that nothing has been said that leads to the conclusion that economic progress is not possible in our economy. The point is simply that progress cannot be continuous—that prosperity must turn into depression. Each succeeding wave of prosperity, however, tends to give the society a higher standard of living than was enjoyed previously, since it permits the full utilization of the improved equipment that was constructed during the preceding period of relatively full employment. As long as inventors and engineers continue to devise equipment that decreases unit costs of production, we shall make progress despite our periodic depressions. We may, however, choose to eliminate depression and treat ourselves to an uninterrupted advance in our level of living.

Certainly the record of the economic advance of the American people since the beginning of our national union is amazing. From the hard, meager living of that time we have advanced to a scale of living in goods, in medical, dental, and other services, and in leisure such as has never been known before by a comparable number of persons. There is still poverty among us—ten million persons one may guess do not have a change of clothing—but the national family is well cared for in terms of any historical standards.

More than 84 per cent of the children of the nation, aged five to seventeen years inclusive, were enrolled in school in 1938. In Ohio the figure for children in school from six to eighteen inclusive runs as high as 95 per cent. We had, as of the first of

1942, one automobile for approximately every four persons, and one telephone for every six. We generate almost 20 billion kilowatt hours of electricity each month, and have a capacity to produce 90 million tons of steel a year. We have a yearly output of about one billion bushels of wheat and 3 billion bushels of corn. These and the multitude of other data that are available show how marvelous are our capacity and our output.

But while we have made progress toward economic well-being, chronic unemployment and periodic mass unemployment have been the rule. We have stood this as a people, as the size of our population today testifies. Our economic institutions have stood it, too, but they have been altered as a result of hard times, especially during the past decade, as witness unemployment insurance, the Surplus Commodity Corporation, the F.H.A., the W.P.A., the guarantee of bank deposits, and the many other devices by which we have collectively sought to prevent and to alleviate economic distress. But essentially our system of private enterprise still stands.

It in no way follows, however, that we shall continue to endure periodic mass unemployment, or even the chronic unemployment of two or three million workers. The reasons, such as those advanced in the first chapter of this book, for our refusing longer to put up with lack of work opportunities may be accentuated if our markets become more congested in the future than they have been in the past. The nineteenth century, or the time from 1800 to the outbreak of the first World War, was a period in which market congestion, as a result of attempting to compound savings, could be somewhat easily overcome. Indeed, several factors contributed especially to this possibility.

The most outstanding of these was the growth of population. From less than four million persons at the time of our first census in 1790, the population of the country by 1900 had increased almost twenty times. For the world as a whole the population was trebled in a century and a half. This stupendous growth was made possible by the great increase in the output of goods per person as a result of scientific advance in agriculture, industry, and commerce, and these economic advances were, in part, made possible by the increase in population.

The steady growth in numbers, to refer especially to this country, made a continuous and somewhat imperative demand for additional goods. Roads, streets, water and sewerage systems, and schools were required, and public credit was provided to supply them. Houses, furniture, and equipment were increasingly demanded. Public utility services, as developed during the century, were required for ever increasing numbers. Capital building was encouraged, and as each wave of building tended to be larger and more efficient than the last, a further growth in numbers both from births and from immigration was encouraged.

Another factor, new in the 1800's, that helped the nation to overcome the constant threats to markets was the progress in techniques requiring huge capital expenditures. Change rode hard all through those roaring decades. Turnpikes gave way to canals, canals to railroads, and after the turn of the century came the automobile. The installation of water systems, the telegraph, the telephone, illuminating gas, and the street car, each in turn called for vast amounts of capital investment. All through this amazing period the new capital was almost always more costly than the old.* Further, most of the capital building resulted in a product that the savers as well as the non-savers bought. When the products were sufficiently durable the funds expended were called savings, but when they were of an ephemeral character the erstwhile savers often frankly regarded themselves as spenders. Some dollars and some men were unemployed and some depressions were very bitter, but circumstances were on the whole so fortuitous that our difficulties were endurable.

It is to be noted in this connection that our extensive capital

* Now the reverse is often true.

building during our national history has occasioned a high degree of obsolescence as observed above. The new life compelled death. It is only by obsolescence that we can find something for our money savings to do, and thus something for the labor to do that the savings represent. Since we save more as the national income rises, if the same pattern of distribution prevails, it follows that the better we do, the better we have to do if the employment situation is not to deteriorate. To paraphrase the Red Queen, we must run faster and faster in order to stay in the same place.

2

The savings problem in the long centuries that preceded the period of industrialism of the past hundred and fifty years was necessarily different from that which we have known. Opportunities for investment were sharply limited. Tools of production were relatively simple in construction, and since there were practically no changes in them from one century to another, and therefore no obsolescence, and since there was almost no increase in population, the use for investment funds in production was limited almost wholly to repairs and maintenance, and because of the durability of goods this was small.

The improvement of the sailing vessel, the development of the keel and of multiple sails, and the invention of the compass and the astrolabe in the period following the year 1000 gave some opportunity for the rich man to take his share of the product in investment goods, not only in the form of ships, but also in goods for export. The growing use of money, the establishment of a higher degree of law and order, and the improvement of roads on land in addition to better facilities at sea increased the volume of trade and gave additional scope for the employment of savings in the business of commerce. But the principal form in which the share of the rich could be taken was in consumption goods and services.

The arts of consumption were highly developed among the rich from the earliest days of recorded history. It is reasonable to believe that the first utilization of a more than average income was in a better than average scale of living. "Conspicuous consumption," as Thorstein Veblen called it, must have been the first result, or the first expression, of a large income. One might well ask what other form an income in excess of the usual income could take in the days when there were no investments to be made. With the coming of a pastoral economy, investment became possible in herds, and perhaps before this some better provision for the future may have been made in implements for hunting, but these were relatively few.

Feasts were evidently not hard to invent. They appeared early. And as the large incomes got larger, the feasts became more elaborate. The many different kinds of meat, the still larger number of vegetables, and a plentiful variety and quantity of drinks helped the man of large income, when we first meet him in history, to take his share from the common storehouse.

Tapestries, spreads, and clothes followed food and drink at an early date as means for utilizing real income and at the same time adding to one's prestige. The palaces of Biblical days were hung with cloths of various colors, and those of the Romans were adorned with tapestries of mythological and other patterns. Pliny records that Scipio Metellus charged that the Stoic Cato paid 800,000 sesterces for some Babylonian table spreads. And in various accounts of the lives of our European ancestors we are told of elaborate dress and cloth. The story of the meeting of the kings of England and France on the Field of the Cloth of Gold in the sixteenth century testifies to the continued use at a much later date of this type of goods as a means of taking one's share of the social income.

Dwellings, too, from an early date served as a means of consuming the income that the top few received. The wide balustrades, high ceilings, floors of marble, and innumerable rooms served this purpose admirably and gratified the vanity of the recipients. In the palace of Ahasuerus the hangings were "white, green, and blue," "fastened with cords of fine linen and purple to silver rings and pillars of marble: the beds were of gold and silver, upon a pavement of red, and blue, and white, and black marble." *

Cicero, we are told, "was far from wealthy," but possessed some eighteen different estates and a town house for which he paid 3,500,000 sesterces. The castles of the Middle Ages were in part for defense, but one object was display. Into these elaborate dwellings went trays, tables, chests, and other forms of furniture that represented in their carvings and inlays the labor of large numbers of persons for a long number of days. The hangings and tapestries with their elaborate designs also added to the labor that was represented in a dwelling and its equipment.

House parties appear very early in the history that we know, and they were sometimes prolonged over an almost incredible number of days. The party, or royal feast, given by Ahasuerus to the nobles and princes of the provinces of his kingdom, and recorded in the Bible, lasted for an "hundred and fourscore days. And when these days were expired, the king made a feast unto all the people that were present in Shushan the palace, both unto great and small, seven days." †

As men's affairs came to take more time, such parties could not be so prolonged, but as late as 1582 the festival in Constantinople on the occasion of the circumcision of the son of Sultan Murad lasted for fifty-one days, with all the various kinds of entertainment with which we are familiar in our present-day vaudeville and circus attractions, such as tight-rope dancing, performances by elephants and lions, trick horseback riding, display of animals, archery, and feats of strength. Along with this entertainment the Sultan distributed one evening "7,000 flat cakes made of cooked rice" and "6,000 large loaves of bread and great quantities of mutton." On another day he gave 600 oxen, 1,000 sheep, and enormous amounts of soup to

* Esther, i, 6.
† Ibid., i, 4–5.

the workers of the arsenal.* Such parties, although on a much smaller scale in western Europe and England, played their part, as did those in the East, in keeping going an economic system in which there was marked inequality of income and practically no opportunity for investment.

Another indication of the consumptive extravagance in the pre-industrial era is found in the gifts made by one rich person to another. The gifts with which Ibrahim Pasha honored the Sultan in the sixteenth century included sixty boys, twenty able to perform on horseback and others trained to produce string music and other entertainments, ten eunuchs, furniture, coverlets, plates of gold set with precious stones, swords, sixty horses, five of which were caparisoned with trappings set with gold and precious stones, an elephant, a giraffe, carpets, flasks, and two dead crocodiles.† The European counterparts of such presents were more modest, but significant nevertheless.

An example of the consumptive display in the nineteenth century, at which time it was somewhat out of place, is reported by John Quincy Adams from what was then St. Petersburg, where he was ambassador for five years beginning in 1809. In a letter to his mother he tells of attending a party given by the French ambassador in the latter's hotel. Adams went to this party in what he described as an "altogether Republican" style, but this involved a carriage, four horses, and four men. The porter who opened the carriages of the guests was dressed in an elaborate uniform, the coat and hat of which were heavily laden with gold braid, and he held in his hand a carved stick on the upper end of which was a silver figure. Within the hotel there was a footman standing on each of the steps of the staircase, twenty in all, dressed in a uniform similar to that of the porter. The function of these footmen was to stand as pieces of statuary until the guests arrived. In the upper rooms there were additional footmen playing the same role as those on the staircase. The description of the dinner, including the cloth and

---

* The *Fugger News Letters*, No. 50.
† Ibid., No. 67.

plate, further indicates the ingenuity with which the rich man of that time devised means of taking his share of goods and services from the market.*

Spiritual and moral leaders inveighed against luxurious consumption from the earliest days. The prophets of the Old Testament were forever denouncing "the women of ease" and the "wearers of fine raiment" and those who "idle on beds of ivory." "It is easier," said Jesus, "for a camel to go through the eye of a needle, than for a rich man to enter into the kingdom of God."

Sir Thomas More was so distressed by the vanity of the rich of the early sixteenth century that in his *Utopia* clothes were very simple and alike for all persons save for differences for the sexes, jewels were scorned, and gold was used only as chains for slaves and chamber pots. Thus, too, for numerous other writers, including the French Socialists of the early nineteenth century, plain living and high thinking were the way to the good life.

Joined with those who have been concerned primarily with luxury as a poison to the soul there has been a goodly company who have protested against display as an economic waste. These groups from time to time secured laws and edicts against luxury. During the period of Mercantilism, which reached its heyday during the reign of Elizabeth but persisted for another hundred years and more, strictures were pronounced against the wastes of display. Men were asked to save their money and thus contribute to the capital and wealth of the realm. Especially was the importation of foreign wines, silks, and laces protested, for instead gold and silver might be imported.

The Mercantilists' demands for thrift were tied to the growing needs of an expanding commercialism. These needs were not sufficiently large, however, to command the use of all the funds that were being saved. This is indicated, for example, by the defense, by William Petty in 1662, of "entertainments, magnificent shews, triumphal arches, etc.," since the costs of these

* James T. Adams: *The Adams Family* (1930), p. 143.

flowed back into the pockets of brewers, bankers, tailors, shoe-makers, and so forth." * Other writers also justified "excess of apparel," proclaimed prodigality an aid to trade, and argued that if everybody spent more, all would obtain larger incomes "and might then live more plentifully." Mandeville's *Fable of the Bees* gave literary popularity to these ideas and was promptly convicted as a nuisance by the grand jury of Middle-sex in 1723. The current was strong against the advocates of spending, but not strong enough to keep them quiet, for there was always danger of unemployment if the receiver of money did not use it promptly. The idea that idle money makes men idle, too, is after all a very simple as well as a profound eco-nomic truth, even if it did escape the economists for a century and a half.

3

As the world moved into the nineteenth century, the doctrine of thrift became enthroned and practically all protests against not spending died away. This was because of the opportunity for the building of industrial equipment. For several hundred years the inventive genius of man had battled unsuccessfully against the confining bonds of handicraft habits, but finally, through the fortunate combination of several factors, the trick was turned in eighteenth-century England, and the human race was off on one of its greatest adventures. Industrial methods that were old at the time of Christ gave way to the new. Inven-tions in rapid succession gave opportunities for the rich to take their portion of the national income in other than luxurious consumption goods. The new goods—the capital goods—thus finally gave strength to the pleas that the moralists had made since men first became rich. At last the economic realities were on the side of the prophets.

It was now possible for men to be rich and to take their share of the total product and yet live like anchorites. But not many of them lived on bread and water. Their living usually proclaimed

* Keynes, op. cit., p. 359.

their wealth, but it was generally so far below what they might have indulged in that their style was accounted to them for righteousness. This was particularly true since their savings went to the construction of equipment that poured out a stream of goods that raised the general standard of living. Avarice and greed were by no means abjured by these new lords, who from their places of business dominated the social and political life of their nations, but they contributed to worthy causes and this together with their constant extension of the railroads and factories won them acclaim from the highest moral authorities.

This mighty splurge of economic activity colored the whole thinking of the nineteenth century. Orthodox economics was its child and its defender. The economists might postulate static conditions, but their thinking was dynamic. Most important of all, for the present purpose, was the bestowal of blessings upon the man of wealth. He was no longer a Dives taking advantage of Lazarus. He was the filler of the nation's horn of plenty. His money made big medicine. It made mass production; it made a high standard of living. Nothing was more important than to preserve and make still larger the incomes of the few. Alvin S. Johnson, later to be president of the American Economic Association, went so far in the early 1900's as to offer in justification of a protective tariff its tendency to siphon income from the poor to the rich and thus make it available for investment.* No one rose in the journals to say him nay. Economists generally were concerned lest estate and inheritance taxes be so heavy that they would be paid from "capital" and not from "revenue."

An occasional tear was shed for the workers who tightened their belts and produced equipment for future use at home and abroad. Hours were long and pay was scant, but since a few men were getting rich, it was held that money would be available for still more investment which would provide employment, whereas if money did not accumulate it was feared that

* *Political Science Quarterly*, XXIII, 221–4 (June 1908).

all would suffer. Typical of this thinking was the succinct appeal of President Coolidge to Congress for a reduction in income taxes in the upper brackets: "We must remember the poor."

The last significant statement against parsimony for almost a century is found in the writings of Malthus, including his letters to Ricardo. As Malthus pointed to the limitations on demand and the danger in savings, Ricardo argued that savings flowed promptly into business. Perhaps neither of these two able men really understood either his own position or that of his opponent. Malthus was thinking of the past, of a society less dynamic than the one he was living in in the early nineteenth century, while Ricardo was concerned with the possibilities that seemed to lie ahead. Malthus underrated the investment possibilities of the day; Ricardo overrated them. Malthus lost, and Ricardo won. The latter's doctrine became the orthodox gospel and the former's suffered the contumely of neglect. As Keynes puts it, "Ricardo conquered England as completely as the Holy Inquisition conquered Spain." *

This did not result, however, as Keynes implies, because the English people were misled in abstract argument, but because the economic realities were on the side of Ricardo. There were abundant opportunities for investment and they constantly expanded as one decade followed another. Depressions occurred, of course, and they led to some very annoying questioning of accepted theories, but presently bigger and better building was under way once more and Ricardo continued as its prophet.

However, as the long hard years of the 1930's drew to a close, increasing doubts were expressed as to the future of investment opportunities. In the learned circles of the social sciences men asked insistently: Has our economy ceased to expand? Has it reached maturity? Is the day of huge capital building over? The concern was, of course, as to whether there would be enough capital building to provide use for our money savings

* Op. cit., p. 32.

and for the labor represented by the money savings. One school of thought expressed faith in the future—insisted that there were new frontiers to be conquered and assumed that these conquests would call for new investments. The other school, of which Professor Hansen has been the principal spokesman, stressed especially the slowing down of the increase in population and emphasized the growing cartelization of American industry as a factor in curtailing such expansion as would otherwise take place. Stress has also been laid on the tendency in some lines of industry for new forms to be much less expensive than were those made obsolete. So far as this is true, it means, of course, that less employment will be furnished in building the new capital goods than was used in constructing the old.

The whole movement of "fair prices," "fair trade," and "industrial co-operation" is anti-competitive and operates to check the demand for the use of savings. There is still competition at the "fair" price, but the attempt is to eliminate the old dog-eat-dog philosophy under which the entry of new firms, whether or not they proved to be successful, increased the demand for capital and thus enhanced the use of savings. The price controls of business also curtail the extension of sales and thus add to the difficulty of making the system work. The new attitudes and the present conduct of business men are on a higher moral plane than those of fifty years ago, but they are less well adapted to the institutional framework of a competitive economy. This growing co-operative attitude is perhaps one of the harbingers of new institutional arrangements that will solve the unemployment problem, even though for a time it intensifies it.

The point is sometimes made that the increase in population is not a vital factor in the maintenance of effective demand, since demand may be enhanced by a given number of persons attempting to raise their standard of living as well as by an increased number attempting to care for their elementary needs. This argument overlooks an essential matter: namely, the degree to which wants are institutionalized. An American city will readily bond itself to build streets, water systems, schools, and so on for an addition to its population, but may refuse to go in debt for swimming pools, parks, or school cafeterias. Families will demand houses and some furniture, but may prefer to save money rather than to live comfortably.

Whatever the future expansibility of our economy may be, it is obvious that the concern in respect to the rate of progress is basically a concern in respect to our ability to use our savings. If they can be used, we can all be employed; if not, some of us will be idle. We have done as well as we have during the past dozen decades because there were very extensive opportunities for capital building. Without these we should have had no escape from serious unemployment unless the lavish consumption of the rich that prevailed before the beginning of the industrial period had been revived.

The frugal living and the savings of the well-to-do have been of inestimable gain to our society. One has but to think of Henry Ford's using almost all of his income to build larger and better plants in which to make more and better automobiles for the people of this and other nations, in contrast to his having used his income to live, surrounded by hundreds of menials, in Oriental splendor, to see the vast social advantage in saving large portions of the large incomes, and using them in capital building. We have had, however, to pay a price in chronic unemployment and in depressions for the gains that have come from the capitalists' using their funds to produce things to sell to the general public. We should contrive to continue to enjoy the advantages of new capital formation and of enlarged consumption by the entire population and at the same time escape the evil of unemployment.

CHAPTER XII

Keynes, Hansen, et al.

I

THE ARGUMENT that has been advanced in the preceding chapters may be further clarified by showing its relationship to the position taken by certain writers who have advanced similar views, and by setting forth also the arguments that economists, almost without exception, have used for one hundred years and more preceding the 1930's to disprove this general line of analysis. The first of these tasks will be undertaken in this chapter, the second in the chapter that follows.

The matter that first concerns us is the relation of the argument here to Keynes, for it is obviously Keynesian. Indeed, the outstanding character of Keynes's work has stamped his name upon all analyses that put the locus of the problem of unemployment in the saving-spending process. The dominant fact about Keynes in relation to this problem is that for the first time since Malthus, who died in 1834, an economist of high professional repute has attacked the doctrine that the economic forces in a private-property economy *tend* to bring about the employment of all who wish to work at the prevailing wage rates. Since the time of Adam Smith the major tenet in economic doctrine, despite Malthus, has been that the economic forces, in a society such as ours, tend to bring about the best possible economic arrangements. The free play of economic forces, so ran the argument, will through the free movement of prices, wages, and rates of interest, and through the free choices of business men and the free mobility of workers, bring about the highest state of economic welfare that is possible, in view of the basic economic resources that are available.

Those economists were not anarchists—they did not cast government out entirely. They had a role for government to play, but this was almost wholly that of a policeman. The government's function was to preserve order, to enforce rules of procedure, and to provide defense. As the 1800's proceeded the economists made a place in their philosophy for public roads, schools, and so forth, and for the regulation of lines of work in which competition was not effective. A place was also made for what was aptly called devices for "raising the plane of competition," such as prohibitions on child labor and minimum-wage legislation. But economic philosophy remained basically one of *laissez faire*—that the government should keep its hands off of economic matters. Competition was the mechanism by which, according to the argument, all was made good within a framework of law and order. Further, it was held that under the rules of competition the basic economic virtues of industry and thrift had full scope to bring well-being to the individual practicing them and through him to the nation.

This doctrine was red meat to business men. It fed their vanity and gave a spiritual blessing to their desire for increased wealth and power. Their sons and daughters in colleges and universities heard gladly that everything *tends* to be good in our economic society even if occasionally "frictions" of one sort or another do interfere. Thus it came about that in press, pulpit, and counting house blessings were placed upon the "free market." Individualism—free enterprise—not only "produced the goods"; it was ethically sound. Economic laws, therefore, should be left alone, for they were immutable. They could not be repealed nor amended.

The application of this doctrine to unemployment was especially delightful. It showed indeed that there is no unemployment and that there cannot be any unemployment—that is, no involuntary unemployment. People may refuse to work, of course; there have always been "sturdy beggars"; but anyone who wants to work can find a job if he will take what he is worth. The crux of the matter, so ran this argument, was that some persons ask more than they are worth. That was the reason for unemployment.

The economists realized, of course, that depressions occur, but they came, so they said, because of such things as lack of rainfall, mistakes of business men, or too high costs of labor. All that was needed when unemployment occurred was that the balance be restored between prices on the one hand and costs, particularly labor costs, on the other. This was difficult to accomplish because the working man was stubborn. But finally when he was starved down sufficiently so that he was willing to take what he was worth, he would be employed and all would be well again.*

Despite minor deflections from the "pure" doctrine, the core of the philosophy of the economists, and of Western society generally, remained unchallenged by any economist of high standing for more than a century. Then Keynes rode in to attack. He had parried the quarry for a quarter of a century, but finally grasped his spear and rode in full tilt. His book, which metaphorically was both his horse and his spear, has been referred to many times in the preceding pages.

His principal argument was that the long-accepted doctrine —the orthodox or classical doctrine—in respect to employment was a *special* theory. Hence he named his book *The General Theory of Employment, Interest, and Money*. According to the older view, economic forces were always tending to put everyone to work. Only when that had happened were the economic forces in "equilibrium"—only then was there no further pull toward more employment. This is an account of a highly *special* situation, said Keynes. Really, he argued, there may be no further "pulls" at various levels of employment. That is, the economic forces may be in equilibrium at other than full employment; something other than a lack of "balance" may be the trouble. Hence we shall need to look to forces other than the "natural" economic ones if we are to keep our-

---

* See the National City Bank *Bulletin,* January 1945, for a present-day statement of the "balance" theorem. The staff of the Brookings Institution currently defends the theory of "balance" by attributing much of our difficulty to the shortsightedness of business men in maintaining prices at too high levels.

selves at work. The plan that had been regarded as God-given will have to be altered, according to Keynes, or supplemented by man-made devices, such as government spending, control of the rate of interest, a reduction in the inequality in incomes, the "euthanasia of the rentier, of the functionless investor," and "a somewhat comprehensive socialisation of investment."

Keynes's argument was disturbing to our whole way of life. It struck at our philosophy of laissez-faire individualism and at our principles of morality that are part of it. Industry and frugality are no longer sufficient, in the new view, to bring economic success to individuals and thus to the society. Indeed, the Keynesian analysis shifts the basis of economic conduct from the individual to the group. For his argument leads to the conclusion that individuals cannot save beyond a rather limited amount, since when some persons attempt to save, the incomes of other persons fall as soon as investments lag, as they must. Since we get our incomes from one another, the failure of one to consume or invest cuts some other person's income. "We are members one of another" in a much more vital sense than we had dreamed of in our philosophy.

Even more disconcerting, because it was more obvious, was the new doctrine when viewed in its more simple relations to economic behavior. For industry and thrift are no longer enough, and indeed thrift may cease to be a virtue and become a sin. Further, the doctrine implies, though it does not so state, that our basic economic institutions will have to be altered sharply to permit the old and solid virtues of industry and thrift to be practiced. For today a premium is placed on waste. It is only through wasteful consumption by the high income groups, or by the nation as a whole as in war, that the lower income groups may have employment.

Keynes's strictures on our age-old virtues as part of our economy are well indicated by what he says in a pamphlet, *The Means to Prosperity*, which appeared in 1933, three years before his *General Theory*. He says scornfully in reference to the poverty of 1932 and 1933:

There are still people who believe that the way out can only be found by hard work, endurance, frugality, improved business methods, more cautious banking, and above all, the avoidance of devices [p. 4].

And his displeasure with the economy as a whole is vigorously stated in an article published also in 1933.

The decadent international but individualistic capitalism, in the hands of which we found ourselves after the war, is not a success. It is not intelligent, it is not beautiful, it is not just, it is not virtuous—and it doesn't deliver the goods. In short, we dislike it, and we are beginning to despise it. But when we wonder what to put in its place, we are extremely perplexed.*

The reaction to Keynes's book was marked. Some of the more orthodox economists sought to dismiss it as a flippant attack upon a sound philosophy, and those who have proposed programs in line with his thinking have been the butt of cartoonists and are brushed aside by some commentators as "zanies." Nevertheless the effect of Keynes's writings on the thinking of economists and on public policy has been pronounced. The ideas of but few men have been more widely extended than have his.

2

Keynes's analysis centers in what he calls three independent variables: the propensity to consume, the marginal efficiency of capital, and the rate of interest (p. 245). The propensity to consume determines the amount that is saved; and the rate that can be earned, or that is expected to be earned, on additional investments in relation to the rate at which savings can be borrowed will determine the volume of investments and hence the volume of employment. Taking as a starting point a propensity to consume that is less than unity—which means

* "National Self-Sufficiency," *Yale Review,* Summer 1933, p. 760.

a propensity to save—the volume of investment determines the level of employment. The level of employment in turn determines the volume of income for the nation as a whole in the next income period and thus the subsequent volume of saving.

Keynes insists, as we have already seen, that the marginal propensity to consume declines relatively as incomes increase. That is, savings increase progressively as income increases, and hence the problem of maintaining employment becomes more difficult as incomes rise. This follows because more investments are then required if all are to have jobs, and since the rate that can be earned on additional investments declines as investments increase, a point is reached at which it does not pay to invest. This point, however, will depend upon the rate of interest. That is, the lower the rate at which money can be borrowed, the further may investments be extended, all other things being equal. Hence, the importance of a low rate of interest in the Keynesian analysis.

Keynes's argument in respect to wages, and particularly in respect to the relation of wage rates to employment, is very complex and subtle and cannot be repeated here.* What it comes to is, essentially, that wage cuts will not increase the effective demand for consumer and investment goods and, in fact, will tend to reduce it because of the decline in workers' incomes. Hence cutting wages is not a means for putting the unemployed to work.

His argument in regard to the nature of the rate of interest is also at the sharpest possible variance with that of classical economics. That view was that the rate of interest correlates the supply of money savings with the demand of borrowers for money funds. The rate had to be what it was at any one time to get people to save what they were then saving. No, said Keynes, the rate of interest is merely the amount paid to get savers to lend rather than to hold their funds idle. It is a means of overcoming their "liquidity preference."

* For a summary of the argument see an article by A. P. Lerner, *International Labor Review*, October 1936.

Attention should be called in this place to Keynes's point that savings and investments are necessarily equal, to which I referred in Chapter iii. Since output and income are equal, and since investment is the amount of the product that is not consumed and since savings is the amount of income that is not consumed, investments and savings are equal, $I = S$. This is very simple looked at in this way, but it may be very confusing when we think in terms of individuals or single firms. For these two quantities rather than *being* equal *become* equal only as a result of an economic process. Indeed, if they become equal by a downward adjustment, this takes place, according to Keynes, as a result of savings having exceeded investments.

For example, suppose that the members of a society have incomes that total 100 during a certain period, and that 80 units are spent in consumption and 20 are saved. If investments to the amount of 20 units are made, the situation will remain unchanged, but if investments amount only to 12 units, then 8 units of the income received will remain unused. Sales and then employment will fall off by this amount, with the result that income will be reduced to 92. Or, since one person's income results from another person's expenditure, the withholdal of 8 units of funds in this case lowers total incomes in the next round by that amount. This fall in incomes will then, let us say, reduce consumption to 75 and savings to 17. If 12 units are invested now, 5 units will be left unused and income will fall to 87. This process will go on until the total amount of income received is used in either consumption or investment. The money incomes of the members of this community will continue to decline until all of them are used, or more specifically until all of the money savings are invested. When this point is reached, savings and investment, obviously, will be equal. A new equilibrium will have been established. Keynes does not use this illustration, but this is clearly what he has in mind. Note, for example, his statement: ". . . when investment changes, income must necessarily change in just that degree which is necessary to make the change in saving equal to the change in investment" (p. 184).

Keynes goes to some pains to correct the confusion that he no doubt felt would come from his reiteration of the point that investments equal savings. He says, for example, that the classical school of economists held, by implication, "that aggregate savings and aggregate investments are necessarily equal," but his next sentence is as follows:

Indeed, most members of the classical school carried the belief much too far; since they believed that every act of increased saving by an individual necessarily brings into existence a corresponding act of increased investment [p. 178].

He also says in reference to Professor Robertson's terminology, which is similar to that used in this book:

When Mr. Robertson says that there is an excess of saving over investment, he means literally the same thing as I mean when I say that income is falling, and the excess of saving in his sense is exactly equal to the decline in income in my sense [p. 78].

In line with the phrasing that savings of individuals and firms may exceed investment, Keynes makes much of the accumulation of sinking funds beyond the immediate need for replacement of plant. Such funds, he says,

. . . are apt to withdraw spending power from the consumer long before the demand for the expenditures on replacements (which such provisions are anticipating) comes into play; i.e. they diminish the current effective demand and only increase it in the year in which the replacement is actually made [p. 100].

Continuing this discussion, he observes:

In the United States, for example, by 1929 the rapid capital expansion of the previous five years had led cumulatively to the setting up of sinking funds and depreciation allowances, in respect to plant which did not need replacement, on so huge a scale that an enormous volume of entirely new investment was required merely to absorb these financial provisions; and it became almost hopeless to find still more new investment on a sufficient scale to provide for such new savings as a wealthy community in full employment was disposed to set aside. This factor alone was probably sufficient to cause a slump. And, furthermore, since "financial prudence" of this kind continued to be exercised through the slump by those great corporations which were still in a position to afford it, it offered a serious obstacle to recovery. [P. 100.]

He makes a similar point in respect to legal provisions for the accumulation of sinking funds by local authorities and public boards in Great Britain. Since these funds are, he says, "entirely disassociated from any corresponding new invest- ment," "it would be a severe task to restore full employment" "even if private individuals were ready to spend the whole of their net incomes" (p. 101). Later in the book he says "there has been a chronic tendency throughout human history for the propensity to save to be stronger than the inducement to in- vest" (p. 347).

Certainly one could not wish for phrasing more in accord with customary usage or with that used in this book. Although the people of a nation cannot save more than they invest, any one person may save more than he invests and thus pull the roof down upon the heads of his fellows, and perhaps also upon his own.

3

The principal difference between the position taken in this book and that taken by Keynes is, in part, a matter of emphasis. He stresses the importance of investing what is not consumed, and here the emphasis is on consuming what is not invested. The difference, however, is more than a matter of emphasis. Keynes holds that the *real* cause of unemployment is lack of investment, while I ascribe it to lack of consumption. He sees a continuous increase in investment as the remedy for unem- ployment, while I regard that as impossible. I believe that the very condition that "makes investment necessary" if we are to have employment—namely, lack of consumption—prevents additional investments from being profitable. And so far as investments are made—so far, that is, as the volume of our equipment is increased—the difficulty is augmented at the following stage because the volume of consumer goods and services offered for sale will be enlarged. An already overcrowded market will be still further crowded with things that cannot be sold.

In other words, the analysis in this book shows, I believe, that periodically the marginal efficiency of capital is necessarily forced below zero. Hence a downward pressure on the rate of interest as urged by Keynes cannot make investment in industrial equipment continuously profitable. Low rates will prolong a period of prosperity beyond the point at which it would otherwise be terminated, but they cannot continue it indefinitely in a market where money is saved rather than used to buy consumption goods and services. Consumption is the head of the problem; investment is its tail.

4

Professor Alvin H. Hansen has become the leading exponent in this country of the Keynesian point of view. He has stressed especially the probable lack of opportunities for the investment of our savings as a result of changes in the character of our economy. The decline in the rate of growth of the population and the general "built up" condition of our industrial plant and of our cities give far less room for growth, he argues, than has been true throughout our national history. Our economy, in his view, is "mature." He, of course, does not mean that there will not be continuous opportunities for investment, but that relatively there will be fewer opportunities than heretofore.

This has led him to emphasize the need for "high consumption" as a means of reducing savings, and also the need for government "investment" as a means of offsetting the savings that are made and not invested. To accomplish this he proposes extensive public works of the usual sort and the placing of railroads and other utilities under government ownership in order that the government may "invest"—build equipment and undertake construction—in these fields. He speaks of this further addition of government ownership as giving us a "dual economy."

This general line of analysis has led him to emphasize the use of government credit—an increase in the government debt —as a means of providing the funds necessary to•carry forward such government investment. Thus he has deprecated the fear that is often expressed of a large public debt. In general he argues for the use of public finance—deficits and taxes—as instruments to achieve economic stability. His book *Fiscal Policy and Business Cycles,* to which references have been made above, is, obviously, devoted to this general topic.

The difference between the position of this book and Hansen is largely the same as in respect to Keynes: namely, that he makes too much of investment as a means of maintaining employment. In addition to this, however, Hansen's early writings show an opposition to the "underconsumption" theory of unemployment that appears to me to be invalid. It is this position that has been the subject of criticism in this book. Despite this fault, Hansen has been of great service to economists and to the public generally in contributing to an understanding of unemployment. Then, too, he is shifting away from his early position in this matter.

Like practically every "well-trained" economist who was a student during the almost one hundred years that fell between Ricardo's *Principles* and Keynes's *General Theory,* Hansen was thoroughly indoctrinated against the contention of the "underconsumptionists." He has had a valiant struggle with his soul during the past few years, and is apparently now within sight of victory.

In his *Business-Cycle Theory,* published in 1927, he says of the "underconsumption" controversy:

The Say-Ricards school [is] fundamentally sound. . . . The Lauderdale-Malthus-Sismondi solution is logically untenable to anyone who will take the pains to think the problem through to the end. [P. 60.]

He did not set forth the argument that he had in mind, but it was obviously the conventional one—Say's Law and its corollaries, which will be reviewed in the next chapter. Hansen gave special place in his thinking to the "balance" theory. Unemployment, he argued, resulted from a lack of balance among the various prices—the prices demanded by laborers and moneylenders and the prices at which products could be sold. Thus "changes" disturbed the harmony of the economic factors and led to unemployment. "The dynamic character of modern industry" causes our difficulties, even in respect to the "maladjustments in the rates of investment and savings." The difficulty is "in no way related to the magnitude of the volume of savings." *

Something of a change in opinion is apparently indicated by an alteration made in his review of Keynes's *General Theory* when he republished it † two years after it first appeared.‡ In the original review he said in criticism of Keynes:

There is one necessary condition, in my view, without which stable underemployment is not possible. It is the condition of cost rigidity (including wage rates) and monopolistic control of supplies. [P. 680.]

But when he reissued the review this statement was omitted. Yet the general idea that the difficulty results from a lack of balance runs through this 1938 book.

In his *Fiscal Policy* he moves further toward the underconsumption view of unemployment, but takes pains to declare that he does not accept it (p. 297 n.). He emphasizes the im-

* *Economic Stabilization in an Unbalanced World* (1932), pp. 154–5. See also *Full Recovery or Stagnation?* (1938), especially the sentence beginning at the bottom of p. 107. Cf. also p. 72 in this book.

† In his book *Full Recovery or Stagnation?* (1938).

‡ *Journal of Political Economy*, October 1936.

portance of consumption, but says that since little can be done about it, "It is necessary, however much one may wish to emphasize consumption, to explore every investment opportunity" (p. 249). He goes on to insist that "a less dynamic" society—one with few investment opportunities—"needs peculiarly to stress consumption if it is to achieve full employment" (p. 299). And analytical economists, it seems to me, need peculiarly to stress consumption, as Hansen is doing increasingly, if they are to achieve full understanding and reveal to their fellows what has heretofore been hid in dark corners.

5

John A. Hobson, a then young British economist, developed an "oversaving" doctrine in the 1880's in connection with a business man, A. F. Mummery. They published their analysis under the title *The Physiology of Industry* in 1889. Keynes speaks of this as "the first and most significant of many volumes in which for nearly fifty years Mr. Hobson has flung himself with unflagging, but almost unavailing, ardour and courage against the ranks of orthodoxy." "The publication of this book," adds Keynes, "marks, in a sense, an epoch in economic thought" (p. 365).

Hobson believed that the excess saving that was practiced led to such a large production of capital goods that general overproduction resulted. But as Keynes observes in regard to this, "the primary evil is a propensity to save in conditions of full employment more than the equivalent of the capital which is required, thus preventing full employment except when there is a mistake of foresight" (p. 368).

In general Hobson saw clearly. He placed consumption as the primary factor in determining production and regarded a more equal distribution of income as an essential step to our permitting ourselves to produce the amount that we would like to consume as a nation. His emphasis on "oversaving," however, indicates that he failed to appreciate that any degree of saving if persisted in will lead to a market impasse except as losses may fortuitously prevent this from happening. Hobson was not able to breach the walls of orthodoxy. Indeed, he was made to suffer because of his "false" and "immoral" ideas.*

6

Two American writers, William T. Foster and Waddill Catchings, published a book, *Profits,* in 1926, which must be considered in this brief discussion of a few items in the "underconsumption" and "oversaving" literature. The point should perhaps be made that neither of these men was a professional economist, in view of what was said above in respect to Keynes and his predecessors. *Profits* received wide attention from economists, not only here but in other countries, in part because the authors offered a prize of five thousand dollars for the best criticism of the book. While the book failed to overthrow the conventional attitude of opposition to "underconsumption" theories, it and other books and articles by these men, both by their argument and by the thinking that they stimulated, undoubtedly contributed to the favorable reception received by Keynes.

The section of the book in which we are interested is Part V, beginning on page 223. The authors begin by asking the question:

Why is it that we cannot long contrive, as consumers, to acquire and enjoy the goods which, as producers, we can readily turn out?

Thus they very properly center attention on the problem of consumption. They argue effectively against the orthodox economic position, which will be considered in the following chapter, that production generates consumption. In our money economy, they insist, production is conditioned by the money demands of consumers. Failure to produce comes from the inability to sell.

* See Keynes: *General Theory,* pp. 364–70 for further information on this point. Also a book by Hobson, published shortly before his death, *Confessions of an Economic Heretic* (1938).

They answer their initial question by arguing that our economic process "fails to provide consumers with enough money to acquire the goods which they are perfectly able and willing to produce" (p. 233). "Inadequate consumer income is the chief obstacle to social progress" (p. 364).

Why is there this deficiency in "consumer buying power"? Their answer centers on the savings of corporations and individuals, with especial attention to the profits of corporations. Hence the name of the book. But they say that even without profits "the problem would remain on a smaller scale . . . as long as individuals saved a part of their income from wages and interest" (p. 306).

The next step in their analysis was an error. They did not distinguish between invested and uninvested savings. Reference was made to the hoarding of money, but rather as if it were a matter of minor consequence. Their principal point was that the use of money in production prevents its being used in consumption. They stressed especially that money is used twice or more in production to once in consumption.

Naturally that argument was not convincing. The building of capital goods and "engaging in production" provide employment, clearly, and the money received becomes buying power. Wages plus interest, profits, and any other return are sufficient to buy the product. Their dictum that the economic process cannot yield the consumers enough money to buy the product "as long as goods are sold at a profit and as long as ten minus one is less than ten" (p. 312) left the inquiry as to why profits were not buying power. The rejoinder that they would not be used to buy consumer goods brought another query as to whether buying of producer goods was not a necessary part of the productive process. The economists returned a verdict, "Not proven."

Foster and Catchings thus failed to establish the point that the investment process is limited, as Keynes has done in his way and I somewhat differently. They got to the correct conclusion, but they got there by jumping. Using money over and over again in production does not induce unemployment—not so long as that process can be continued. Unemployment comes because of limits to that use of money. And these appear, as Foster and Catchings correctly state, because the product cannot be sold.

They were right in their main point—we cannot sell the product that we are able to produce—and they were right that this comes about because the desire to save prevents persons from buying what is, or might be, available. But they failed to trace the consequences of saving, step by step through the economic process. They did not establish the point that savings are almost always on the verge of not being invested and periodically are definitely uninvested. Or, in Keynesian terminology, they did not show that the propensity to save so reduces the profitability of investment that capital building is curtailed, unemployment results, and incomes are reduced. Nevertheless, they deserve a big tally for their assist.

7

By way of emphasizing further that the general doctrine under review has had a tough row to hoe attention may be called to a little book, *Excessive Saving a Cause of Commercial Distress,* by Uriel H. Crocker, an attorney of Boston. It was published in 1884 and is made up of a series of ten items, most of which appeared in newspapers or magazines from 1877 to 1884. The author's argument in support of the thesis which is indicated by the title of the book is thoroughly sound and the illustrations and general style are stimulating. But the reception given to his articles and letters and evidently to the book as well was very cold. The principal article appeared in the *Atlantic Monthly,* December 1878, under the title "Saving versus Spending." The author says, apparently in 1884, that he "can now recall no printed notice of that article, however brief, that treated it with any favor or respect." The belief that saving was always good—that it could never be carried too far—was one of the verities.

Crocker puts the matter of the general limitation on investment well in a letter to a Committee of the United States Senate:

No investment of capital can be *profitable,—i.e.* produce annual returns for the owner,—except so far as the people are spending. If the poor, through their poverty, *can't* spend, and the rich, through their desire to be richer, *won't* spend, the field for the profitable investment of capital must be very small. [P. 29.]

In this same communication he made an interesting though incomplete point in respect to wages:

. . . the larger the wages that the laborer receives, the more he can spend, and the greater consequently will be the field for the profitable investment of capital. On the other hand, the smaller the wages of the laborer, the less he can spend, and the smaller will be the field for the profitable investment of capital. In other words, the more generous capital is to labor, the more will capital itself prosper; and the more niggardly it is, the more it attempts to monopolize the profits, the more likely it will be to find that all profits have disappeared [P. 30.] *

A note in criticism of John Stuart Mill's widely accepted theory of the impossibility of "general overproduction" is especially trenchant, as is Crocker's answer to the subsidiary theory —"misdirected production." †

The *Atlantic Monthly* article deserves especial attention. Its references to the then current situation in this country and abroad are interesting. It also gives support to the ideas that I have developed in the preceding pages, and further, if we keep in mind its unfavorable reception, it helps to indicate the vigor of the orthodox position. I shall accordingly give considerable space to this article. It was published, you will recall, in December 1878.

---

* This statement is not complete as it stands, for what is proposed can be true only within limits.

† These are discussed in the following chapter.

Crocker begins by referring to the belief that the serious and world-wide depression of that time was caused by waste and extravagance. He cites in a footnote an article by Professor Bonamy Price, a distinguished British economist, holding that the cause of the depression "is one and one only,—over-spending, over-consuming, destroying more wealth than is produced; and its necessary consequence, poverty. This is the real *fons mali,* the root of all the disorder and the suffering, the creator of the inevitable sequences of cause and effect." * The view of Crocker, the heretic, was that this generally accepted notion was entirely wrong.

He argues that "the only reasonable object of saving is the acquirement of the means of future spending" (p. 15). "The principal and most effective method" of accomplishing this, he says, is by "productive consumption" or what we now call investment. He then comes to the question of whether there is a limit to "productive consumption" and argues, as in a quotation already given, that this depends on "unproductive consumption," or, as we put it today, on consumption (p. 16). This brings him to the point that the extent to which saving can properly be carried "is limited in a great degree by the extent to which men, and especially the richer classes, *abstain* from saving" (p. 17).

It is very evident that productive consumption is now and for some considerable time has been quite unprofitable; that factories, railroads, steamships, and warehouses bring very small returns to their owners; that the market-rate of interest has been, and still is, unprecedentedly low; and that capital has long been wholly at a loss as to how it should employ itself. These facts surely indicate that the field for profitable productive consumption has been for the time nearly exhausted; that its temporary limit has been nearly reached; and that a larger amount of unproductive consumption is required before that limit can be advanced. The correctness of this conclusion is plainly shown, also, by the surplus stocks of all kinds of products and manufactures which are now, and have long been, waiting for

* *Contemporary Review,* April 1877, p. 787.

consumers, and by the enforced idleness of the thousands of laboring men who have found that their labor was not in demand for the supply of either productive or unproductive consumption. Then, again, the hard times have been felt most seriously in England, America, and Germany, while France has been substantially exempt from them; the explanation being that France, having had its territory devastated by war, and its capital depleted by the subsidy paid to Germany, has had large room for productive consumption, and small capital to devote to it; and hence productive consumption has there been very extensive and very profitable. All available capital has been employed, and the laborers have all been busy; those who have been released from supplying unproductive consumption having been in demand for the supply of a profitable productive consumption. Germany, however, undertook to grow rich by devoting the millions of the French subsidy to productive consumption, which was thereby carried to such an excess that its profit was destroyed. And thus we find a simple explanation of the otherwise inexplicable mystery of the prosperity of the vanquished and the distress of the victorious nation, after their recent tremendous struggle. [Pp. 17–18.]

Crocker then points to the history of the United States during the Civil War—to the "urgent call for every man's labor," to the "marvelous . . . production of the country," to the "immense waste in the war," but yet such "a large surplus of products" as "to enable the great mass of the community to consume much unproductively for their own immediate comfort." When the war ended, the people could have lived still better, and this was required, he said, to replace the consumption of war if the productive facilities were to be kept in use, but those "who by their wealth had the power to act according to their own desires" decided to add to their wealth. "The failure of this attempt of our rich men to become richer lies before us today," Crocker observed. The increased consumption that was necessary to make the added equipment profitable had not taken place. The men of wealth "contributed but little" to this necessary consumption, "and as the poor found but little opportunity or possibility of contributing to it that increase was never brought about," and it was soon evident that investment had been "overdone, and that its profit was for the time ruined and lost." (Pp. 19–20.)

. . . Factories of all kinds [Crocker continues] produced immense stocks of goods which could not be disposed of; their owners competed with each other, and sold their goods at less than cost, and finally, in many cases, shut up their factories and discharged their hands. Then we began to have an actually *diminished* unproductive consumption, where we had needed an increased one. The rich, having lost their "income," felt that they must "economize." The poor, having lost their employment, were forced to do so. This universal economy increased, by its reaction, the original trouble, and thus we went on from bad to worse, until it seemed that we were on a road that led, without any turning, straight to destruction. Today, however, we are hoping, as indeed we have hoped before, that we perceive signs of a change. [P. 20.]

But he, and another one or two like him to whom he refers, were voices crying in the wilderness. David A. Wells in his book *Recent Economic Changes* (1889) makes no mention of Crocker or of his ideas. Indeed, in a long list of alleged causes of the hard times that this country and the world had recently experienced, Wells does not mention "underconsumption" or "oversaving." He does emphasize "overproduction" as a result of improved methods and regards this as the chief cause of the difficulty. Carroll D. Wright, U. S. Labor Commissioner, in his Report (1886), makes a similar point and stresses the decline in investment opportunities. Even such men, however, were not able to bridge the gap from "overproduction," "a plethora of capital," and "lack of investment" to "oversaving" and "underconsumption." Wright even qualifies the term "overproduction" by saying: "or, to be more correct, bad or injudicious production" (p. 89). Certainly neither Crocker's writings nor similar views of other men made the least impression on the thinking of economists of that day, or of any later time until a relatively few years ago.

CHAPTER XIII

The Orthodox Rebuttal

I

THE ANSWERS of the economists to the "overproduction-under-consumption" explanation of chronic and depression unemployment during the past century and a half stem from their general view of the natural harmony and balance of economic forces in a free-enterprise laissez-faire society, which we have already noted. The chief answer all these years to the under-consumptionists has been the argument formulated by J. B. Say, a French economist, in his *Traité d'économie politique,* first published in 1803 and later translated and reissued several times. The quotations in this chapter are from the fifth American edition (1832). His analysis, soon known as Say's Law of Markets, or simply as Say's Law, has been used repeatedly to silence critics of the market process. The term itself has often been sufficient to stifle opposition. Few arguments or few slogans have been more effective, and certainly no argument has been more fallacious. The chapter, number xv, Book I, which contains the famous Law is entitled: "Of the Vent or Demand for Products." Say begins the discussion quite as if he had read the preceding chapters of this book:

It is common to hear adventurers in the different channels of industry assert, that their difficulty lies not in production, but in the disposal of commodities; that produce would always be abundant, if there were but a ready demand, or vent. When the vent for their commodities is slow, difficult, and productive of little advantage, they pronounce money to be scarce. . . .

He then asks why money is scarce, and says that it is because commodities are scarce. Goods are really the demand for goods, he argues. "Sales cannot be said to be dull because money is scarce, but because other products are so."

The basic reason for this relationship, according to Say, is that no one produces goods except to use them or to exchange them for other goods. Supply thus creates demand; supply is demand. The supply of corn is the demand for wool. Even if sales are for money, the money will be promptly used to buy other goods because no one cares for money except to use it. Market gluts are impossible. It is silly, according to Say's argument, to insist, as so many did then and do now, that we can produce more than we can distribute.

This doctrine, obviously, fitted beautifully into the pattern of the eighteenth-century philosophy that natural forces were harmonious and good, and that all would be well if we but gave nature a chance to operate. The doctrine extolled the economic virtues—hard work and frugality. Success was thus a badge of virtue, and failure a penalty for sin. Thus the economically successful could harden their hearts against those who failed and could resist appeals that something be done to prevent or overcome unemployment. All that was ever needed was merely that production should go forward. The way to overcome unemployment was to go to work. "It is the aim of good government," said Say, "to stimulate production, of bad government to encourage consumption."

Say admitted that there might be overproduction in one line relative to other lines, or what Mill later called "ill assorted" or "misdirected" production, but insisted that there was no possibility of general overproduction.

It is evident from this summary that Say considered commerce as barter. His view of money was typical of that long held by economists, which we discussed earlier.* Money was regarded merely as adding one more step to a transaction, but this was a short one. "Money is but the agent for the transfer of values. Its whole utility [in a case cited] has consisted in conveying to your hands the value of the commodities, which your customer has sold, for the purpose of buying again from you."

---

* Chapter iii, section 4.

Observe also a footnote by Say in this same chapter. After arguing that one wants money only to use it he says:

Even when money is obtained with a view to hoard or bury it, the ultimate object is always to employ it in a purchase of some kind. The heir of the lucky finder uses it in that way, if the miser do not; for money, as money, has no other use than to buy with.

What a curious denial of one's own illustration! Although money be acquired for the purpose of hoarding it, thus clearly showing that money has use when buried in a box, Say concludes: "Money, as money, has no other use than to buy with." Then, too, still more curious, the very next chapter in his book is entitled: "Of the Benefits Resulting from the Brisk Circulation of Money and Commodities." This chapter should have shown Say's followers, if it did not indicate to him, the inherent weakness of his Law. But readers were perhaps so overcome by the heady wine of the Law that they were not in a mood for the sobering draughts that followed.

2

Another implication in Say's Law should be stressed: namely, that human wants are insatiable. This was the fundamental reason, as seen by Say and other early economists as well as by later ones, why markets could not be oversupplied. Human beings can never be satisfied; they always want more goods or services. Hence they will never hoard money; they will always exchange their products, or the money received for them, for other products. This, of course, is not so. Consumption wants can be satiated. At least capital goods, savings, are every day preferred by thousands of persons to bigger houses, or more servants, or picnics. People do not always and forever want more jam on their bread.

The men who endlessly say that human wants are insatiable, that supply is demand, could, if they would think of their own conduct for a moment, see that what they say is false. For undoubtedly no one of them uses all his income for consumption. They save; they buy life insurance. They dream occasionally of consuming luxuriously, but the one insatiable desire that they have as shown by their actions is merely to *say* that the desire for consumption goods is insatiable.

Mill in his *Principles of Political Economy,* published in 1848, repeated the essence of Say's Law, and stressed, among other things, another implied feature of it: namely, that human beings are inherently lazy—that they will produce only to consume. After referring to persons, "including some distinguished political economists," who have thought that oversupply is possible, Mill says: "When these writers speak of the supply of commodities as outrunning the demand, it is not clear which of the two elements of demand they have in view—the desire to possess, or the means of purchase." He argues, first, in respect to what he calls the second element of demand, that since one product is a demand for another, there can be no lack of buying *power*. This is sound, contrary to certain critics. Total buying *power* equals the total product.*

In respect to the first element, oversupply arising because of the lack of desire on the part of producers for more goods, Mill admits that this *might* happen, but says "the fact that they go on adding to the production proves that this is not *actually* the case." For, he argues, if a person did not have "an additional desire to consume . . . he would not have troubled himself to produce." †

This is grossly invalid. It is sheer nonsense. Men all through the ages have troubled themselves to produce for reasons other than an "additional desire to consume." It is doubtful if Mill himself troubled to write these lines and the others that make up his huge book in order that he might extend his consumption. It is highly probable that if it had been made clear to him

---

* Though not necessarily at the customary price per unit. See Chapter iii, section 8.
† Book III, Chapter xiv, sections 1, 2, and 3.

that he would never get back the cost of writing and publishing the book, he would have gone ahead with the task if assured only of having some readers. This is not to say that books are not written in the hope of bringing food to the authors, nor that much of the work of the world is not done for a living, but merely that a great deal of economic effort is expended for ends other than consumption goods. Some work is lots of fun. It carries its own reward. If money comes in also, it is welcome, but often not because it is wanted for consumption, but merely because it is desired as security against an uncertain future, or as counters in a game.

Making money is a sign of success just as is a good score in golf, and the one may be as disassociated from a desire for increased consumption as is the other. Henry Ford has surely not wished to have better clothes these many years, but he has wished to make more money. To augment one's bank account, or one's holding of property, gives the same kind of satisfaction to many persons as does the tending of roses to others or the making of speeches to those who like to do that.

There need not be the remotest relation between an act, even if it lies in the field of economic behavior, and the consumption of economic goods. It may be an experience that is vital to life on quite other grounds. But one need not go this far in arguing against Mill, for one may wish to make money with a view either of consuming later, or of being able to consume later if misfortune should destroy other sources of income, and yet have no immediate demand for additional consumption goods. In short, there may be overproduction of consumption goods.

Proponents of Say's Law have admitted this, but they have argued that it comes about only because business men have produced consumption goods when the demand was for additional producer goods. Production has been misdirected. We looked into this matter and noted its absolute invalidity when discussing the limitations on investment in Chapter iv, and need not repeat our argument here.

We may observe, however, that it has been a comforting doctrine all these years. When markets were clogged and producers in every line were running below full time, the priests in the temple of the markets have bowed to the image of J. B. Say and chanted: *Supply is Demand: general overproduction is impossible*. And as they have shriven the business men who have lost their plants, they have had them recount the sin of not having hired more expert analysts to tell them what they should have produced. The priests themselves have never suggested lines of unfilled demand. They have stuck to their specialty.

3

By way of a parting glance at Say's Law and a summary of that argument, let us look at a comment by S. M. Macvane, a member of the Economics Department at Harvard, in the second number of the *Quarterly Journal of Economics* (April 1889). This affords an excellent illustration of the way in which the magic of this law has been able to degrade the thinking of good men. The item under consideration was an answer to a brief comment by Uriel H. Crocker under the title "General Overproduction," which was included in the section "Notes and Memoranda" at the back of the *Journal*. It is perhaps worthy of mention that evidently the Harvard economists who edited the *Journal* did not consider the idea worthy of being developed into an article. Crocker's argument was along the lines of the quotations from him in the preceding chapter. Macvane's answer was short and crisp. He routed Crocker and won a resounding victory by eliminating the overproduction and unemployment that Crocker had talked about. He did this merely by defining the word "demand" in a wholly orthodox manner *à la* Say.

"Supply of one thing is a demand for another," said Macvane. "Demand as a whole can never be less than supply as a whole." Hence there are no goods that cannot be sold and there cannot be any such goods. Men who think they see goods piling up in markets or who believe that they could not sell what they might produce are deluded. *Mirabile dictu.*

Warming to his task, Macvane then defined out of existence any idle money and idle men that less gifted folks might observe during depressions. "In order that the supply of capital shall exceed the demand for it," he said, "there must be more capital offering for labor than the laborers are willing to receive! The mere statement of the case," he concluded triumphantly, "is sufficient to show its absurdity." Verily the statement shows its own absurdity. As well make ducks into horses by definition;* as well follow the professor of physics who opposed trying to investigate the atom because the word means an indivisible particle. Certainly the scholasticism of the Middle Ages never reached more sublime heights than did Macvane and other orthodox economists in making the real ethereal, and the ethereal real. Let us hope that we are about through with the abracadabra of Say's Law of Markets.

4

Another argument that has been used to combat the notion that consumer buying power may not be adequate to clear the market because of the distribution of the national income is that the unused buying power of the rich is transferred to the poor through the payment of wages and that this makes total consumer purchasing power adequate. Mill approaches this question by calling attention to what he considers to be an erroneous doctrine, namely "that the unproductive expenditure of the rich is necessary to the employment of the poor." Suppose, he says, that the consumption of every capitalist and landowner either through desire or by law or opinion is reduced to that of "a well-conducted laborer" and that savings are thereby increased. "It is asked," he says,

how is the increased capital to find employment? Who is to buy the goods which it will produce?. . . there would no longer be any

---

* For an account of how this might come about see Thurman Arnold: *The Folklore of Capitalism* (1937), p. 180.

demand for luxuries, on the part of the capitalists and landowners. But when these classes turn their income into capital, they do not thereby annihilate their power of consumption; they do but transfer it from themselves to the laborers to whom they give employment. . . . The whole of what was previously expended in luxuries, by capitalists and landlords, is distributed among the existing laborers, in the form of additional wages.*

Professor Taussig in the early editions of his *Principles* gives a statement similar to Mill's. After referring to Rodbertus, Marx, and "other socialists," he says:

The well-to-do, it is alleged, are persistently set on investing and increasing production; they are not disposed to spend. The laborers, on the other hand, have not the wherewithal for spending. Hence productive power tends constantly to outrun comsuming power; hence the recurrence of crises. The answer is that the laborers *are* quite able to spend. The process of investment by the well-to-do simply means that the "consuming power" is turned over to the laborers in the form of wages.†

Certainly this is not so. The rich no more transfer their consuming power to the poor than do the poor transfer theirs to the rich. Each gets a certain portion of the money income. If the rich get one fifth and the poor four fifths, each group must take one fifth and four fifths respectively of the total product if continuity in production is to be maintained. There is no transfer, and there can be no transfer other than in the form of a gift, unless by "transference" is meant the process by which money passes from one person to another. But by this definition every exchange becomes a transfer, and the term used by Mill and Taussig becomes meaningless because of lack of special applicability.

Suppose, in line with Mill's illustration that orchids are produced for and consumed by the more well-to-do members of the community but that these persons give up the consumption of orchids and use the money they have been spending for them

---

* Op. cit., Book I, Chapter v, section 3.
† *Principles of Economics,* 3rd edition (1921), Chapter xli, section 2.

to produce capital goods. Mill and Taussig would have us believe that the poor may now consume goods equivalent in cost
to that of the abandoned orchids. Not at all. The only difference will be that the resources of the community will now be
devoted to the production of fewer consumption goods and
more capital goods. There will be no more consuming power
in the hands of laborers as a result of shifting their efforts from
raising orchids for the rich to making steel mills for these same
persons. Not one cent more. Consuming power is not turned
over to a manservant by having him stop mixing cocktails and
assist in repairing a truck.

There is, however, validity to this transfer idea in that in the
long run economic resources may be devoted increasingly to
the poorer groups, as a result of saving by the richer groups.
Thus if well-to-do persons curtail their consumption and with
their savings build factories that will turn out goods for sale
to the poor, this will, although perhaps not until a depression
has intervened, tend to mean that consumption goods have
been transferred from the richer to the poorer group. It is this
aspect of the matter that Taussig discusses in the fifth and final
edition of his *Principles,* wholly omitting the material quoted
above. This, however, is a process extending over a period of
time, and it runs in terms of resources or of goods. It has nothing to do with the immediate transference of money as a result of curtailing consumption and investing as imagined by
Mill and by Taussig as well in his early editions. Hoarded
money could be transferred to unemployed workers in the
fashion suggested, but these men were not talking about hoard-
ings, nor about the unemployed. Their problem was the use of
money by the rich in consumption or investment, and contrary to their view the one or the other can make no immediate
difference in the ability of workers to consume.

Furthermore, it may be noted that if the rich employ the
poor in their purchases, whether of factory buildings or cut
flowers, the poor likewise employ the rich in their purchases.

When a working man buys a ticket to a movie, or gets a gallon of gasoline, or makes a phone call, or pays an insurance premium, or buys anything that has in it an element of pay for railway transportation, steel products, banker's services, and so on, he is surely contributing to the salaries and to the property incomes of the more well-to-do. In the mutual exchange that takes place between the two groups, one or the other may get the better of the bargain, but there is no Lady Bountiful transference. Each must take its share of the total product—an amount corresponding to its share of the total money income—if productive continuity is to be maintained. There is no escape from this through transference, except as money is given away.

Another form in which this transference doctrine appears is in the familiar statement that while, for example, some two or three per cent of the income-receivers get one fifth of the money income, they do not eat one fifth of the food, or wear one fifth of the clothing, or live in one fifth of the houses. The implication is, evidently, that this small group of large income receivers does not really use one fifth of the total product of the nation, but, through some process of transference, gives such a large portion of its share to the remaining income receivers that they have as much food, clothing, housing, and other consumable products as they would have if the upper group did not get one fifth of the money income. This is clearly Mill's view. He asks: "What do these persons do with their savings?" and answers his question as follows: "They invest them productively; that is, expend them in employing labor. In other words, having a purchasing power belonging to them, more than they know what to do with, they make over the surplus of it for the general benefit of the working class." *

This is hopelessly wrong. The one fifth of the money income, or its equivalent in goods and services, that is received by the upper economic group is no more transferred to the poor than is the four fifths received by the other group trans-

* Op. cit., Book III, Chapter xiv, section 3.

ferred to the rich. The funds of the rich do not consist of command over consumables for the poor any more than do the funds of the poor consist of command over factories and yachts for the rich. Each of the two groups, the rich and the poor, wherever the line be drawn, can only command products and services equal in money value to its money income, except by purchases on credit. If either group fails to take from the market, in producer or consumer goods and services or both, the share of the total produce equivalent to its money income, employment cannot be maintained.

5

Another variant of the harmony or balance theorem that has long been used to combat the argument I have advanced is that if prices are flexible a market impasse cannot occur. Difficulties that arise, according to this view, come from price rigidities, including wage rates. This belief has already been shown to be invalid and is referred to here in order to relate it to the general orthodox position. This notion still has such vogue in public prints, however, that it is perhaps permissible to repeat the point that more than eighty per cent of the national product, for example, cannot be exchanged year after year for only eighty per cent of the money income that is generated in producing the national product. Private business enterprise cannot survive by receiving back each year less than it pays out in expenses. Price-cutting medicine has not cured and cannot cure the market congestion to which our savings practices make us heir.

6

Besides these arguments there have been many others directed at the "overproduction-underconsumption" doctrine. Several of these have been noted in the preceding chapters. Indeed, almost every economist who has written in the field of business cycles has considered this doctrine to be fair game. It has always been in such disrepute that writers have added to their respectability by taking a fling at it. Further, each of the many special theories as to why prosperity turns into depression has added to the belief that our economic relations are very complex and that any explanation of them and particularly of their failure to function must be very complex too. Any simple explanation was thus discredited and particularly the simplest one of all.

7

It appears strange, at first glance, that the underconsumption doctrine could have been in such disfavor over such a long period. But as the history of human thought shows abundantly, a belief in any field may exercise power far beyond that to which the test of truth entitles it. The acceptance of a prevailing idea is in the line of least resistance. Further, it is thus that preferment is most probable, for authority and power are usually synonymous. Then, too, of course, the great body of workers in any field are not challengers; they are accepters. In short, if a doctrine is once written down in authoritative books, successive generations of students learn it without questioning it, and, in turn, teach it to those who study with them. It becomes a test of respectability.*

Not only does the acceptance of established doctrine tend to give professional respectability; it also tends to give one standing in the society generally, and especially in the circles of the most eminent group, whether it be of religious, military, or business character. For accepted doctrine tends to justify the behavior of the society in which it prevails. No other condition could well be expected since a society tends to be a unit and the doctrines pertaining to economic behavior, politics, family or-

---

* This is on the whole salutary. Social stability requires that the burden of proof be upon the challenger of the *status quo*. But this means, of course, that many generations may suffer under an error that has respectability because of the inability of the society to discard it and accept a truth with a bad reputation. Countless illustrations could be given of this, but reference to the belief that persons with fever should not be given water is perhaps sufficient. What agony that false notion must have caused for hundreds if not thousands of years. But one does not need to forsake the discussion in hand for an illustration of the suffering that may come from a false doctrine. The victims of Say's Law are legion.

ganization, or any other aspect of life tend to be in harmony with the prevailing practices. Further, any disposition to be critical of the dominant group tends to lead to reprisals of one sort or another—to lack of preferment and to slights of various kinds. Ruling groups have devious ways of making their displeasure felt. Thus the economists have tended to justify the practices of the business group. Indeed, from Smith's *Wealth of Nations* forward there has been a marked tendency for economists to approve of the general plan of the economy. Criticisms have been made, of course, but these have for the most part been very moderate.

Hence there has been strong compulsion to proclaim Say's Law and to belittle any suggestion of underconsumption. Both professional respectability and standing in the community of business men have prompted economists to resist any impulse to develop the idea that there is a fundamental weakness in the free market. Furthermore the analyses that have been advanced —almost wholly by persons who were not economists—were not sufficient to convert the economists. It must be said, however, that the adverse criticisms of the economists were often faulty despite their seeming plausibility, as, for example, the criticism of Foster and Catchings by Hansen, as noted in Chapter vi above. The cards have been stacked against the underconsumptionist. Or, to alter the figure, the judge, jury, and witnesses have been prejudiced against the defendant.

Nothing, however, is more clearly established than that progress can be made. The flatness of the earth finally had to give way to roundness. Authority and respectability could not save it. It went hard, but it went.

APPENDIX TO PART ONE

Stumps to Grub

A DIARY WAS FOUND recently in the attic of an old house in western New York. It bore the date 1827 and stated that the author, V. C. Observer, was then sixty-five years of age and had been a farmer in that region for the preceding forty-six years. The items in the diary that are relevant to our purpose show (1) that the author had been able to grow more corn when he still had stumps in his field, which he had to spend time grubbing, than he was able to raise after he got the field clear of all obstructions; (2) that he had raised more corn in the years when the Indians went on the warpath and he had to take time off to fight them than in the years when they behaved themselves; (3) that he had been able to take better care of his place when his mother-in-law lived with them and he had to spend time entertaining her than either before or after; and (4) that he and his family had had more to eat when he took some of his produce across the river and swapped it with the Indians for wampum which he brought back and buried behind the barn than they had had when he kept all of his produce at home.

This record of the pioneer farmer may appear to be somewhat incredible, but if the word "nation" is substituted for the term "pioneer farmer," and other appropriate changes are made, the statement becomes a matter-of-fact account of our experiences.

We produce more consumption goods when we have stumps to grub and factories to build than when our fields are clear and our factories stand ready to be used. We can have more shoes to wear if we have 100 shoe factories and are building three more than we can have when we get these built and have 103 factories available for use, unless we proceed at once to build four more. We need stumps to grub.

The second and third points are closely similar to each other.

War is only one form of consumption. The forms of consumption suggested in the third point would be as efficacious as war in helping us as a nation to produce more vegetables and build more houses if savers would only indulge in them on a sufficient scale whenever there is a shortage of profitable investment opportunities and unemployment has occurred or is about to occur.

The fourth point, obviously, relates to our gain as a nation in getting rid of goods abroad in exchange for gold or pieces of paper. We can have more cotton clothes to wear if we can sell some of our cotton abroad for gold than if we have to keep all that we raise at home; we can have more automobiles to ride about in if foreigners will take some that we have and give us gold or pieces of paper in exchange, than if we have to keep at home all that we produce.

What makes the tale of the pioneer farmer ridiculous is that such men were never bedeviled by unemployment—they could always work. And what makes it thoroughly applicable to us as a nation is that unemployment, or the likelihood of unemployment, is always with us. By using some of our labor power in ways that do not contribute to welfare at all, and some in ways that do not contribute to welfare immediately, we make it possible to use for purposes of welfare labor that would otherwise be unemployed. By wasting some labor we save still more from being wasted. The fetters of our economic practices impede us in our efforts to make a living for ourselves.

PART TWO

WHAT SHALL WE DO?

"If we would guide by the light of reason we must let our minds be bold."—*Justice Brandeis in The New State Ice Co.* v. *Liebmann, 285 U. S. 262 (March 21, 1932).*

CHAPTER XIV

"Leave Business Alone"

I

Nothing can be much more at variance with what has been said in the preceding chapters than the insistence by certain groups that all that we need do in order to solve the problem of unemployment is to leave business alone. Such an attitude seems pitiful to anyone accepting the analysis that has been given above. The request that business be left alone is usually accompanied by the demand that the political climate be made favorable to business. This means usually that taxes, labor legislation, and government regulations generally be so adjusted that business will be encouraged. Some writers call for rather drastic reforms and insist that if they can be achieved free enterprise will be able to avoid mass unemployment.

This general attitude need not surprise anyone. Conservatism is an essential element in any society. The cohesion of the national group, the economization of energy, and, in fact, the preservation of life itself require that the pattern of behavior should be relatively fixed. We must establish rules of conduct and follow them. We must create habits of attitude as well as of conduct. We cannot each day put on a new set of mental garments. But along with this basic need for stability there is need for progress. The urge to contrive, to invent, to alter human relationships, to devise new rules of behavior is apparently latent in all people. Further, the competition among nations, not only in war but in the arts of peace, is an added spur making for the adoption of new methods and new relationships.

The conflict between these two forces—stability and change —has been unceasing throughout history. But generally conservatism has been in the ascendancy. Established institutions— the state, the church, the economic system—have usually defended the *status quo* and fought down the innovator. Furthermore, the human tendency to remember the experiences that were pleasant and to forget the others has generally led to a glorification of the past and has impeded change. The very richness of our language in words with the prefix "re" indicates the prevalence of this attitude. Whenever a crisis arises and change appears imminent these words are used profusely. Men are called upon to *re*main steadfast, or if change has gone forward, they are asked to *re*turn to the old, to *re*store the past, to *re*claim former methods, to *re*-establish what has been forsaken, to *re*construct and *re*pair the broken ways, to *re*vive dead institutions.*

Men schooled in one type of warfare declare their faith in the old and their contempt of the new. They build Maginot Lines that are outmoded before they are completed, and "dreadnoughts" which have every reason to dread the new wasps of the air and the new adders of the sea. Throughout the ages men have proclaimed their faith in current practices and beliefs—that the earth is flat, that the Roman system of numerals is superior to the Arabic, that bleeding by the barber is efficacious for all ills, that kingship is divine, that human slavery is an expression of God's will—and have crucified the advocates of new attitudes and of new forms of behavior. Perhaps no belief that men ever held and no practice that was ever followed was ever forsaken without strong protests. St. Paul's admonition: "Prove all things; hold fast that which is good," has generally been interpreted as if the final word were omitted.

We of this day and generation are in the strange situation of living in two worlds at the same time—one highly dynamic and revolutionary and the other static and conservative. In the one world, or phase of life, change rides hard. New techniques appear on every hand and are universally applauded. The highest social acclaim is given to him who makes present techniques obsolete. No tears are shed for the old; cheers greet the

* Cf. Carr: *Conditions of Peace*, p. xviii.

new. Engines, seed-corn, egg production per hen, plastics, medicines—everywhere we hail the new and heap honors upon the discoverer. The innovator in the realm of things is king.

But in the field of human relationships we look to the past. We glorify the ways of our ancestors—we denounce the innovator. We extol the social, political, and economic institutions that took shape when the steam engine was in its infancy and the internal-combustion engine and the electric dynamo were not even dreamed of. The economic and political equivalents of "the old-time religion is good enough for me" ring through the land.

There are protests against this attitude and important institutional changes have been made, especially in the past decade, but clearly the dominant attitude in the press, pulpit, school, and public forum is that nothing new can be learned in the field of institutional arrangements. The contrast between the attitudes toward science and engineering and toward human relations is pronounced, even though, as will be argued presently, these two phases of life are essentially one and cannot remain inharmonious.

2

The scientific dynamism that is such a marked feature of this age was not instituted without a long and bitter struggle. Indeed, from the dawn of recorded history until near the close of the 1770's the techniques by which economic goods were produced remained practically unaltered. The work of the American colonists—the way they planted, cared for, and harvested their crops; the way they got materials and made their clothes; the way they built and furnished and heated and lighted their houses; the way they cooked their food—all these were practically the same as in the days of the early Egyptians.

Progress was made during these long years. The compass, astrolabe, microscope, telescope, and printing were gains of a high order, but in the workaday aspect of life practically no changes were made. Inquiry was not encouraged. The hand of the past was heavy. Men of genius were largely concerned with the realm of ideas rather than scientific inquiry. Samuel Johnson, for example, in 1750 extolled Socrates for having drawn "the wits of Greece" away from "the vain pursuits of natural philosophy to moral inquiries"—from "stars and tides, and matter and motion" to "the various modes of virtue and relations of life." *

The fear of unemployment also played its part. By inducing the destruction of machinery, often accompanied by the execution of the inventor, it greatly delayed the Industrial Revolution.† But finally in England in the 1700's the old bonds were broken and inventive genius was stimulated. Man began one of his most amazing adventures, which as yet shows no signs of coming to an end.

The most obvious result of scientific progress in this country since the time of the adoption of our Constitution can be indicated in a simple diagram which divides the working population of the country into two parts: agricultural and non-agricultural workers. The Bureau of the Census has prepared such a diagram for 1820 to 1940, inclusive, as shown below. If this were extended back to 1790 it would undoubtedly show some 85 to 90 per cent of the workers engaged in agriculture. We were almost wholly an agricultural people at the beginning of our national life, but we are almost wholly urbanized today. Decade by decade we have become increasingly interdependent economically. But striking as is the diagram in this particular, it does not tell the whole story. For, on the one hand, the persons now engaged in agriculture are far more dependent than formerly on other portions of the economy for markets in which to sell and buy, and, on the other hand, non-agricultural work has become increasingly large-scale in its operations and this has decreased relatively

* The *Rambler*, No. 24, Saturday, June 9, 1750. Quoted by E. Parmalee Prentice, commencement address, Hiram College, June 9, 1941.
† See Karl Marx: *Capital* (Kerr edition), Vol. I, p. 467 ff.

THE PROPORTION OF THE NATION'S LABOR FORCE
ENGAGED IN AGRICULTURE: 1820–1940

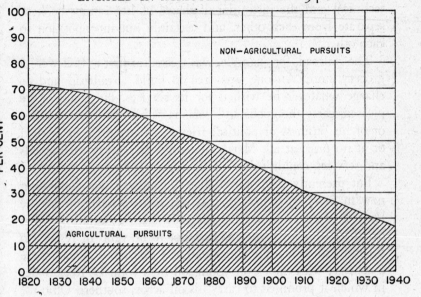

the number of employers and of self-employed persons and has increased the number of employees. Throughout the period under review men have been increasingly divorced from the soil and from ownership of shops and tools. It is this that gives validity to the point made in the opening chapter of this book that while security of property was at one time the basic right, today the security of jobs has become basic. Life and liberty and human dignity depend on jobs today, not on the personal ownership of property as they did in the two hundred years preceding the middle of the 1800's.

The persons who have been in charge of the railroads, steel mills, factories, and the other technical agents that have so completely destroyed the rural America of Washington and Jefferson have found the property concepts and the political ideology of the pre-machine age wholly to their advantage. With themselves in command of the behemoths of the new age of science, they have demanded to be let alone, as Jefferson wished to be let alone on his farm. But life is a unity. The technical and the institutional phases of life cannot be kept separate from each other, and certainly not in opposition to each other.

The railroad, for example, was treated at first as if it were a grocery store. Anyone was free to build a railroad and to charge whatever he wished for its services. He could, if he pleased, carry the goods and persons of his cousins and aunts, or of his business or political friends, at any price he wished or at no price at all. Merchants could give away their goods and services, couldn't they? This was a free country, wasn't it?

But presently it appeared that the railway was something new in more ways than one. It was seen to have altered the basis of moral conduct. The old rule that one could do what he liked with his own was seen not to be valid in respect to the railroad. When the Cincinnati and Marietta Railway made a contract with the clever young oil man John D. Rockefeller in which it promised to carry his oil across southern Ohio for 10 cents a barrel, and to make other shippers pay 35 cents a barrel, and to pay to Rockefeller 25 cents out of every 35 cents collected from the other oil shippers, it became clear to practically everyone that the new technique of shipping goods had so altered human relationships that the old political-economic institutions were no longer adequate. The old bottles would not hold the new wine.

Railway rates could not be left to the forces of the free market as could the prices of groceries. Free enterprise could not be trusted to provide railway services and set the prices for them. Railway men could not be allowed to run their own business in their own way. They could not be allowed to do what they would with their own. A new arrangement was essential.

The Interstate Commerce Commission was established to regulate railway rates. The United States Supreme Court, as anyone might have expected, impeded the work of the new government bureau by limiting its power in one decision after another. The Court was not yet aware of the significance of the new method of transportation. It regarded railway transportation as essentially the same, except for speed, as carriage by wagons, which in the long past had led to the formulation of the law of common carriers. Finally, after a few more decades, judges generally came to see that the new technique of transportation made it imperative that new rules of law be formulated. The bureaucrats of the I.C.C. came to be accepted as a necessary part of the railway era.

Similarly, of course, the automobile brought the need for traffic control, the registration of vehicles, the improving and planning of highways, and the licensing of drivers. The new technique compelled the devising of new laws and new agencies of government. Old rights had to be given up—new rights came into being.

The increase in the purchase of food in stores and the increase in the extent to which people ate in public restaurants also outmoded certain rules of behavior and compelled the creation of new ones. A free-born American citizen could no longer run his own store in his own way, unless that way conformed to the new regulations devised by the new bureau of sanitation.

Countless other illustrations could be given of the fundamental law that as new techniques alter human relationships, new rules of conduct must be devised. These new rules are normally embodied in new legislation by the appropriate legislative body and are administered by a new bureau devised for the purpose.

3

The mass unemployment against which we struggle today is the result, obviously, of modern production and exchange techniques. The almost wholly self-dependent agricultural economy of a century and more ago was not troubled in this way. But as the new techniques have largely divorced us from the soil and put us at work in large-scale, mass-production industries that are intricately geared into a highly sensitive money-exchange, profits-making, savings-accumulating economy, new relationships between men in their work were necessarily created. One of the most important of these is the dependence of an ever increasing portion of the working population on the vagaries of the market for a chance to work. Certainly this cannot but compel us to alter our political-economic relationships so as to prevent mass unemployment. The tail goes with the hide.

The kicks against the pricks of proposed adjustments through the government should be directed against the underlying technical changes. Similarly, of course, current complaints against the numerous boards, commissions, and bureaus of our city, state, and national governments should properly be levied against the railways, automobiles, electric dynamos, telephones, radios, and their like that have destroyed the rural simplicity in which the best government was the government that governed least.

The men who resist institutional change by crying: "America must not be made over" when America has already been made over by the engineers are as impractical as are generals who insist that rules of combat shall not be changed even though weapons have been drastically altered. It is as futile to believe that we can change techniques of production and not alter our laws as it would be to think that the shape, size, and weight of the football could be changed and the rules of the game left unaltered.

4

The relationship between techniques and institutions is strikingly shown by Thomas Carlyle in *The French Revolution*, as he describes the nobles of France as they, with the other two groups in the States-General, formed a processional to Notre Dame in the closing days of the *ancien régime*. Here come the French Nobility, he says:

All in the old pomp of chivalry; and yet, alas, how changed from the old position; drifted far down from their native latitude, like Arctic icebergs got into the Equatorial sea, and fast thawing there! Once these Chivalry *Duces* (Dukes, as they are still named) did actually *lead* the world,—were it only towards battle-spoil, where lay the world's best wages then: moveover, being the ablest Leaders going, they had their lion's share, those *Duces;* which none could grudge them. But now, when so many Looms, improved Ploughshares, Steam-Engines, and Bills of Exchange have been invented; and, for battle-brawling itself, men hire Drill Sergeants at eighteen-pence a-day,—what mean these goldmantled Chivalry Figures, walking there "in black velvet cloaks," in high-plumed "hats of a feudal cut"? Reeds shaken in the wind! *

5

A do-nothing policy has had great support from economists. Their general view of the beneficence of the free market could hardly have led to any other conclusion. Minor proposals have been made, but, generally speaking, the economists have advised that we let nature take her course.

It is interesting to note the close parallel between popular notions in respect to bodily ills and the opinions of many economists in respect to depressions. Three such parallels will be noted. First, there is the implication that there is nothing that we can do to prevent the recurrence of hard times. Certainly this conclusion followed from the writings of W. S. Jevons, an English economist who in the 1870's ascribed the cause of depressions to the cycle of spots on the sun, and from the recent work of H. S. Moore, of Columbia University, who argues that periods of prosperity and depression are correlated with the transit of the planet Venus.

Likewise, emphasis, as by Pigou, a noted English economist of today, on the alternation in moods of optimism and pessimism determining periods of good and bad times, and by Professor Schumpeter, of Harvard University, on the accident of innovations and the resulting imitation thereof accounting

* Part I, Book 4, Ch. 4.

for the periods of prosperity and then, by failing to be continuous, giving us depressions, points to the conclusion that there is nothing that we can do to prevent hard times.

Such analyses may suggest to a growing number of persons today that radical changes should be made in the character of our economy so as to escape the effects of these "natural" forces, but to many persons such arguments during the past decades and even today indicate that hard times are inevitable. This conclusion is strengthened by the popular opinion that rhythm is a characteristic of nature—that the seasons come and go, that shore lines rise and fall, that the weather follows a long-term cyclical pattern—and that therefore a succession of good and bad times is natural. Similarly, men for centuries regarded epidemics as part of God's plan for the world. They were "natural" and therefore inevitable.

Besides the implication that depressions are outside our control, many writers have insisted that nothing should be done toward relieving distress when hard times set in. "The disease must run its course"; prices, wages, and debts must be left free of control, for "a new equilibrium must be established." Such counsel has been heard gladly by those able to weather the storm and likely to profit from the shipwrecks. Furthermore, it has been so closely tied to the naturalistic-fatalistic lore that even the drowning victims have proclaimed it.

Secondly, the attitude of some economists toward unemployment has been comparable to the age-old notion that disease and other ills result from sin. "We had been living too high," some said in 1930. Others have written that the sin of speculation and of going into debt bring their retribution, even as does an alcoholic spree. Some economists, General Leonard Ayres, for example, never fail to connect business adversity with war, and number depressions as the "first postwar," the "second postwar," and so on. Hence to prevent depression, avoid war. But having sinned, the devil must be paid.

Thirdly, the attitude of many economists toward unemployment is comparable with the old notions concerning bodily disease, as well as other calamities, in their emphasis on the good that the evil brings. "A boil is worth five dollars," ran an old legend, "for it gathers and expels the impurities in the blood." Ministers of religion generally have sought to "justify the ways of God to men." Whether disease, untimely death, storms, or other disaster befell, a "purpose" has been declared. "God moves in a mysterious way His wonders to perform," "Whom the Lord loveth He chasteneth," "Sweet are the uses of adversity."

The writings of economists are filled with thoughts that are similar to these. "The old wood is cleared away"; "property passes from weak to strong hands"; "high-cost firms are eliminated"; "wage rates are forced down to labor productivity"; "we learn again that hard work and thrift are fundamental virtues." All is well. Our misfortune is a blessing.

6

Closely similar to the idea of some economists that sin is the cause of depressions is the popular notion that if we will only mix virtue with our economic institutions, all will be well. For example, Max Zaritsky, president of the United Hatters, Cap and Millinery Workers International Union, writes in the *Saturday Evening Post* of January 30, 1943:

> Our economic difficulties are not beyond solution. Unemployment is not a scourge of God but a man-made affliction. It is a disorder that lends itself to treatment. . . . Enlightened leaders of industry and intelligent leaders of labor will have to cope with what is essentially their own special problem.

These two groups, the author goes on to say, "can gear our productive machinery" and "plan our national economy" "to utilize the creative capacity of labor as well as management for the enrichment and the enjoyment of the American way of life." In short, goodwill on the part of management and labor will prevent depressions.

Herbert Agar, in his book *A Time for Greatness* (1942), says similarly, with an eye on the Great Depression:

> The system did not break down of its own defects. It broke down because of the moral defects of all of us, the spiritual thinness of our Western life, which permitted the system first to become an end in itself and then to betray even its own rules in the interest of immediate greed. [P. 173.]

Thus to these and a host of other writers and speakers there is no dichotomy of saving and investment, or of production and consumption; the economic machine will not stall if we will only be good. But certainly good intentions are not enough. Hell itself is paved with them.

Not all business men, however, are content to preach. Some are "doers of the word" and through organization are attempting to *plan* for the elimination of unemployment. The Committee on Economic Development is one such group. It deserves the best wishes and the hearty co-operation of all of us. Nevertheless one cannot expect business men to prevent unemployment so long as they act as capitalists must act. They can by co-operative action reduce or eliminate the unemployment that results from seasonal changes, technological displacements, and shifts in demand—in general, frictional unemployment—but they cannot solve the problem of the unemployment that is the subject matter of this book.

Such planning can do but little, if anything, to prevent savings from being uninvested since it cannot, within the philosophy of business, ask business men and their firms to forgo net income and accumulations. Capitalists cannot plan away the essence of capitalism. Yet efforts at planning are to be commended because they will undoubtedly eliminate some unemployment and, further, because additional light will thereby be thrown upon the problem of unemployment. In particular, the failure of business planning to prevent depressions will help to confirm the analysis presented in this book.

CHAPTER XV

Democracy versus Fascism

I

WE WILL PREVENT mass unemployment. One fifth or more of our working population will no longer endure the humiliation of being outcasts. That is clear. The problem is one of means. The choice is largely between democracy and fascism.

Democracy is the method of making adjustments by compromise, by give-and-take. Its techniques are public debate, the secret ballot, the legislative process. Its base for government is common consent. Fascism is the method of force. It is the rule of a gang that secures power in one way or another and then imposes its will upon the nation. Its base for government is terror. Its methods are secret arrest, torture, and removal without trace.

Fascism is not new except in terms of the past two or three centuries. In the long history of the human race the power of a ruling clique has been a characteristic form of government. Modern fascism is merely a throwback to practices that we thought had been permanently supplanted by democratic methods. The term is new, arising in Italy as the name for Mussolini's dictatorship, but its meaning is as old as human tyranny.

The antiquity of fascism makes it all the more necessary to guard against its appearance. For this means that fascism is latent in human society. It is an easy way out of unrest, distress, and confusion, and hence under such conditions may easily secure a strong base of support in public opinion. For in a period of disturbance—when the methods of debate and election fail to achieve a significant measure of national unity, large numbers of persons usually begin to clamor for a "strong man" to establish order and give direction to the energies of the people. If then a leader of great force and personal ambition arises, he may be able to assume dictatorial power, particularly if he can secure the co-operation of the army. He may, indeed, come to power by constitutional methods as Mussolini did in Italy and Hitler in Germany, and then from the vantage point of that power destroy the legislative branch of the government, bring the judiciary under his control, stamp out all open political opposition, destroy the trade unions, suppress freedom of speech and press, and rule the nation by his own will.

The power of a man and his clique who have taken office is not easily broken. Great advantage comes from having control of the police and the courts, and particularly so when the weapons in the possession of the government are greatly superior to those of the ordinary citizen. The democracy of the past two or three centuries in England and this country, for example, was not unrelated to the firearms of that period. The average citizen a hundred years or more ago was as well armed as a soldier. A man in his own house could defy a squad of soldiers, and citizens at the street barricades could give a good account of themselves. Rulers could not ride rough-shod over the populace. It was this that led to the second item in our bill of rights—"the right of the people to keep and bear arms shall not be infringed." But the development of modern weapons has shifted the balance back to the days when the superior equipment of the king's men gave them easy mastery over any small-scale opposition.

The most important single element in the maintenance of democracy is the prevention of distress or, failing that, a faith that relief can be secured through democratic channels. Men look for new means only when customary ones do not appear to be adequate. And their adequacy depends upon the problems that call for solution. Mass unemployment is the greatest single threat today to democratic processes. The hopelessness engendered as men search fruitlessly for jobs, and the bitterness that develops against minority groups that have jobs, make the way easy for the demagogue. It is upon such meat that would-be Cæsars feed.

2

The distress and confusion that in Italy, Germany, and other European countries led to the establishment of fascist dictatorships had their counterpart in Russia during the first World War and led to the Communist Revolution and the "dictatorship of the proletariat," or, more strictly speaking, to the dictatorship of the Communist Party. Under that regime rule by terror has prevailed as under Hitler in Germany. Political opposition has been ruthlessly crushed and free speech and a free press have not been permitted. Secret arrests, imprisonment, and execution have been used relentlessly against suspected opponents of the group in power.

The bright aspect of the dictatorship in Russia as compared with those in Italy and Germany is that it has always justified itself in terms of the welfare of all the people. Its philosophy has always been one of brotherhood—of universal brotherhood. There has never been any talk there of a master race—never any persecution of minority racial groups. Nor has the expressed philosophy in Russia during the present dictatorship been formulated in terms other than those of democracy and of democratic processes. Practice has fallen far below profession, but the ideal of democracy has been cherished and was formally embodied in a Constitution which was widely discussed while in the process of development during the middle portion of the 1930's. Nor has war been extolled in Russia as it has in the fascist regimes, nor has there been a call for world domination by the Russians.

There was in the early days considerable talk of the importance of extending "communism" throughout the world, and considerable attention was directed to the establishment of Communist groups in other countries. This, however, was something of the sort of thing that prevailed in the United States during the 1800's. We were greatly pleased with our republican form of government and were constantly inviting the people of other nations to overthrow their kings and set up a government like ours. The Russians went further than we did, for they sent out missionaries and controlled them rigorously from Moscow. These persons and their local adherents made supreme nuisances of themselves in this country and elsewhere, but there was no talk of extending the boundaries of the Russian state. The plan was, like all missionary movements, designed to extend the blessings already enjoyed by the focal group and to give it support in case it was attacked. The talk in Rome and Berlin had an altogether different flavor from that in Moscow when it turned to a consideration of other peoples.

Basically the Russian dictatorship came from the industrial workers and from those whom they accepted as leaders, and has been exercised in the name of the masses. Fascism in Italy and Germany, on the contrary, had their bases in the class interests of the upper economic groups, although the programs were adapted to secure support from a considerable portion of the lower economic groups.

Any tendency toward a Communist dictatorship here must be steadfastly opposed, no less than one toward fascism. It is from latent fascists, however, rather than from Communists that the danger lies. The power and influence of the Right rather than of the Left makes any attack on democracy more likely to come from that quarter. But, however this may be, we need to prevent economic distress and political confusion from reaching such proportions that our orderly democratic processes are called in question. To preserve democracy we must keep it so vigorous that adjustments are made before distress has become acute and men have become hopeless of improvements by accustomed processes.

3

Our virile traditions of free speech, free press, freedom of assembly, and of government by officials of our choice will be of great value to us in the days of trial that undoubtedly lie ahead. Our history warrants the hope that we will be able democratically to make the adjustments that need to be made to permit continuous employment. Nevertheless, there are danger signs. The great concentration of wealth—the dominance of our economy by a relatively few big corporations—the power of concentrated finance—the concentration of power over the press and radio—may well give us concern. For these groups may resist the changes that need to be made to permit continuous employment. And they may use the shibboleths of freedom in their resistance.

Indeed, throughout our history, as conditions have so altered that new controls have become necessary in the public interest, the economic groups that were being limited have protested in the name of our most cherished ideals—freedom, liberty, independence. Restrictions on child labor, requirements that laborers be paid in money, limitations on monopoly, legislation to provide compensation for industrial accidents, provisions that laborers be permitted to bargain collectively without intimidation or coercion by employers, minimum-wage legislation, public-school laws and later compulsory school-attendance laws, the prohibition of the shipment of decayed meat as food in interstate commerce—these and practically all other similar attempts to establish controls have been resisted in the name of the freedom of Americans. Often, too, the courts have been an impassable barrier for a decade or two by declaring such legislation unconstitutional on the ground that American liberties were violated. The opposition of economic groups and of the courts has not, obviously, been sufficient to prevent such controls from being established, but it has delayed the establishment of many reforms. Such delay in respect to the prevention of mass unemployment might well be a serious threat to our democracy.

In short, the philosophy of individualism, which was ideal for the time in which it originated, may now do us a great disservice by being used to justify the resistance of Gargantuan corporations to control. In almost every issue of current magazines cleverly drawn advertisements liken the sponsoring corporations to the hardy pioneers who did not like to be "pushed around," and plead with us to "keep America American."

Another variant of the resistance to the political change that is made imperative by economic change runs in terms of the Constitution. Our sacred rights of free government are called upon to prevent the making of orderly changes that alone can preserve free government. The devil can always quote scripture.

Another aspect of this is the frequently expressed opposition to any unusual exercise of leadership or authority by a governor or the President. The dominance of a state legislature or of Congress by a strong executive, or the strict enforcement of law, almost always leads to the charge of dictatorship. But paradoxically, strong leadership tends to prevent dictatorship by bringing about the adjustments that maintain stability. It was the impotence of the government in Russia, Italy, and Germany that made it possible for Lenin, Mussolini, and Hitler, respectively, to acquire the following that led to dictatorship.

There are, we must remember, elements among us that are fascist at heart. That is, there are persons and groups who do not like democracy and who do not trust the democratic process. They oppose minority groups, they dislike trade unions, they fear the citizen voter. Some of these persons have great power over public opinion through the press, radio, and other similar agencies. Such persons in Germany welcomed Hitler and helped to finance his cause; such groups in France said: "Better Hitler than Blum"; * in England persons of this sort encouraged Hitler and hoped for his success; and in this country, too, we had our share of persons who wished Hitler well. Not all persons, however, who have some of the attitudes of fascists may properly be so labeled. Almost everyone, perhaps, has some undemocratic attitudes. This makes it all the more imperative to adjust our economy so that grave economic distress may be avoided and the latent seeds of fascism kept dormant.

* Léon Blum, a Socialist, served as Premier in France from June 1936 to June 1937, and again in 1938.

4

One of the most encouraging elements in our society today is
the trade union movement. The large group of men and women
who compose it—some 12,000,000 in number or about one
fourth of all persons gainfully employed outside of agriculture
—are every day participating in the democratic process. They
are practicing the arts of discussion and adjustment. To be sure,
there are labor leaders who flout the democratic process and
prey upon the workers under their control, but the movement
as a whole is sound. The participation of this group in politics
gives a wide base to the democratic process that cannot but
lessen any tendencies toward fascism.

It is often said that the unions are never satisfied—that they
always want more. This is certainly not an uncommon trait in
an economy whose central principle is that each individual
should attempt constantly to enhance his economic position.
But such aggressiveness on the part of the trade unions need not
be justified on this basis. Its major justification is that any gain
likely to be achieved in the share of the total income going to
labor tends to increase the amount of money used in consumption and to decrease the amount saved and thus makes the
economy more workable.

The trade union movement is part of the rise of the "common
man" that has been under way since the foundation of this
nation. The non-propertied person in England and in this
country as late as the time of the American Revolutionary War
was in a very inferior position. Even the male property-owner,
to whom the right of voting was almost wholly restricted, was
not trusted very far even by the members of our Constitutional
Convention, as witness the indirect method provided for the
election of senators and the still more indirect method by which
the President was to be elected.

The lack of democracy then as compared with today is
strikingly shown also by the way in which men of position
fenced themselves off from the common man by wearing wigs,

knee-breeches, silk stockings, and shoes with silver buckles. Modern leaders do not do that. Even the great philosopher of democracy, Thomas Jefferson, feared the industrial worker in the growing cities of the early 1800's.

The upsurging democratic spirit, however, could not be denied. Inroads were soon made on the privileges of the few, and by the beginning of the second quarter of the new century the general principle of manhood suffrage, with one man one vote, had been secured. This Jacksonian period gave to the common man an increased dignity even beyond that which came with voting. Among other things, public schools were established to which the children of the poor could resort for that start in life which might carry them to the highest positions. The argument of Alexander Hamilton, in his famous Report on Manufactures in 1792, that manufacturing "would make children more early useful," by which he no doubt meant the children of the poor, lost much of its cogency as public schools were provided for all children.

The influence of the public school has been extended since its establishment until today in many states almost every child spends twelve years under its tutelage. The effect of this in giving the members of all economic groups essentially the same cultural pattern can hardly be overestimated. It gives a basis for mutual understanding that has perhaps never before been attained among the members of a large nation, unless in Russia during the past two decades. The motion picture and the radio are also agencies of great importance in removing cultural differences of long standing between the more fortunate and the less fortunate economic groups, and hence in giving a firm basis for democracy.

The mass production of American industry with high quality of goods at low prices is another very important factor in the elimination of class differences and antagonisms. The goods purchased by the rich and the poor are more and more alike. A family of great means cannot get better quality in cooking equipment, refrigerators, or mattresses by having them made to order than by buying the nationally advertised brands. The electric current, gas, and water in a laborer's cottage are identical in quality with those in his employer's house. The man who buys the cheapest automobile on the market gets one that in most respects is equal to the most expensive ones. Formerly only the prosperous could attend the theater and only the rich could sit where the actors could be seen and heard without strain, but now a few cents gives a housemaid access to the best dramatic talent of the age on equal terms with the richest folks in town. Any poor boy with a week's wages, or less, can array himself in garments that make him practically indistinguishable from one who was born with a gold spoon in his mouth. In fact, even children's spoons are more and more alike.

The mechanism of production is, within itself, also a significant element in improving the relative position of the poorer groups and strengthening the basis of democracy. Mastery of the complicated machinery with which he works not only gives the laborer increased respect for himself but also increases the respect of his employer. The employer's regard is heightened, too, by his increased dependence on the skilled employee. The machine tends to make comrades of all who are engaged in the task of using it. Even in the Army, machinery seems to be lessening the age-old barrier between officers and men. The plane and the tank appear to be bringing the officer down off his high horse.

The employee in large-scale industry is regaining something of the status that his ancestor had as the owner of his farm, his business, or at least the tools with which he worked. Perhaps, indeed, the labor group is accomplishing more than this. This group may be making, and by similar methods, a conquest of power today comparable to that made by the business men of England some three hundred years ago.

Class differences are, of course, still pronounced. The marked concentration of income and the still more marked concentration of wealth give social, economic, and political power to a few persons far out of proportion to their numbers, and, as argued above, this is basically anti-democratic. Nevertheless, the many factors just noted are leaven at work in the lump of class interests. The attitudes of superiority and inferiority have less soil in which to flourish than heretofore in our history or in that of our British ancestors. The brotherhood of man and its concomitant democracy have increased virility. The common man is on the march here and everywhere. "The big house on the hill surrounded by mud huts has lost its awesome charm." *

The dynamism of the labor movement added to the dynamism of middle-class liberalism will, we may fervently hope, make the economic-political adjustments that are necessary for the elimination of mass unemployment. Democracy need in no way be sacrificed in accomplishing this; it may be greatly enriched.

5

Finally, in the quest for new orientation that goes forward almost constantly in any society, and which is particularly marked in ours, we need to beware of "fixed ideas." We need to keep steadfastly in mind that there are no absolutes in relationships. There are no definite lines that mark off, for example, capitalism from socialism, as Eric Johnston, president of the United States Chamber of Commerce, so well says in his book, *America Unlimited*.† Doctrines have slain their thousands—in fact, their millions. The absolutes of both Northerners and Southerners brewed the witches' broth of the war between the states, and throughout history such attitudes have substituted bloody conflict for peaceful adjustment.

It is well to emphasize that the sin of doctrinal purity is found no less on the Left than on the Right. Indeed, it is to the everlasting discredit of Marxism that it has charted its course

---

* Wendell Willkie: *One World* (1943), Chapter xiv.
† Page 30.

through the miasmic swamps of hate and has proclaimed piles of corpses as the foundation of a new social order.

In contrast to the beneficent results that we have achieved by the method of accommodation, which we have so splendidly followed throughout almost the whole of our national history, the doctrinaire insistence in Russia on adjusting their economy almost overnight to the Procrustean bed of dialectical materialism brought untold misery. If the New Economic Policy instituted by Lenin in 1921 (private capitalism with the government's retaining ownership and control of large-scale industry, transportation, banking, and foreign trade) could have been left to grow and develop peacefully, the success of this first big attempt at government ownership of the means of production would doubtless have been more pronounced, millions of lives would have been saved, thousands would have been spared the agony of being forcibly transported to strange regions, civil liberties could have been permitted, and the harshness of the GPU could have been avoided.

The whole Marxian either-or approach has been pernicious. Where it has been effective, it has prevented adaptation, accommodation, and compromise, which are essential elements of the democratic process. It was so effective in one place and time as to make it one of the most responsible single factors in producing one of the greatest tragedies of all time—the placing of Hitler in power in Germany in 1933. The doctrine of "no compromise," of "no collaboration with class enemies," of "my way or nothing" as practiced by the Communists under the direction of the Third International in Moscow, prevented the hundred Communists in the Reichstag from co-operating with the Social Democrats, and thus made parliamentary government ineffective. The Communists also by "wild strikes" and other devices harassed German industry. By sabotaging both the economic and the political systems in Germany they contributed to the prevailing turmoil and strengthened the demagogic appeals of the frustrated corporal from Munich. Hitler could not have wished for a more effective ally than he had in the Communists, bitterly opposed to him though they were. Verily, verily they have had their reward.

6

The democratic process is resilient and dynamic. Its action corresponds to need. It fashions tools according to the task that lies at hand. At no time in the history of civilization has its accomplishments been equal to those of today or its promise for the future been brighter. As President Roosevelt said:

The victory of the American people and their Allies in this war will be a victory for democracy. It will constitute such an affirmation of the strength and power and vitality of government by the people as history has never before witnessed. With that affirmation of the vitality of democratic government behind us, that demonstration of its resilience and its capacity for decision and action—with that knowledge of our own strength and power—we move forward with God's help to the greatest epoch of free achievement by freemen the world has ever known or imagined possible.*

* Speech, September 23, 1944.

CHAPTER XVI

Recommendations

I

WE COME NOW to the task of recommending a course of action. I approach this task with considerable misgivings. I have a high degree of confidence as to the general validity of the analysis and the related argument in the preceding chapters. There may be many errors in those pages, but the general view that is presented appears to me to be incontrovertible. It follows from this, of course, that I feel reasonably certain as to the general direction in which we should go in our attempts to meet the problem of unemployment, but doubts arise in respect to specific proposals. A measure cannot but be affected by the particular provisions by which it is implemented and by the manner in which it is administered. Further, the attitude of the persons and groups that are most directly affected by a particular device, or item of legislation, may have a marked effect in determining the degree of success that attends it. Then, too, the extent to which it is desirable to follow any one course of action will be determined by what has been done along other lines. Nevertheless, problems require that positions be taken—that choices be made.

In formulating a program, there is one cardinal principle that we need to keep in mind. It has already been expressed in the preceding pages. This is simply that what we will do—or can do—is limited by what we have done—or are doing. Social change is connected as definitely to experience as are new leaves to the existing branches of a tree. Our course at its best cannot be other than that proclaimed by President Wilson in his first inaugural address:

We shall deal with our economic system as it is and as it may be modified, not as it might be if we had a clean sheet of paper to write upon; and step by step we shall make it what it should be, in the spirit of those who question their own wisdom and seek counsel and knowledge, not shallow self-satisfaction or the excitement of excursions whither they cannot tell.

2

The foremost need is for an increase in the national propensity to consume. Or, to express this same idea in other words, we need to reduce the national propensity to save. There can be no doubt as to the desirability of such a change, our folklore to the contrary notwithstanding. As long as four or five per cent of the income-receivers of the nation get a quarter of the total income after taxes, or anything near this, the relative volumes of consumption and saving will make the problem of maintaining employment difficult if not impossible, except during periods that are especially favored by fortune. In so far as the income stream can be altered toward less inequality, the volume spent in consumption will be increased, and employment will be encouraged.

The means available for lessening the degree of inequality are many. The taxing power can be used to this end. Heavy progressive rates can be imposed, or continued, on the upper brackets, and sales taxes, pay-roll imposts, and property taxes that fall on the low income groups, or that are shifted to them, can be reduced or abolished. Cogent reasons can be advanced for the retention of the gasoline sales tax, for example, and the social security pay-roll tax, but if our object comes to be that of adjusting tax burdens so as to encourage consumption and discourage saving, such considerations might be overcome. It needs to be observed in passing that the portion of the social security pay-roll tax that is levied on the employer is perhaps largely, if not entirely, shifted onto the price of products and thus made a burden on consumption since it falls on marginal firms as well as on others and must be shifted if they are to be able to stay in business. The entire social security program needs to be re-examined. Estate and inheritance taxes would also come in for very special consideration if we resolutely face the problem under consideration.

We need to get it clearly in mind that the constant reiteration by certain newspaper columnists and others that all taxes are really paid by consumers is false. Such statements may not be made with a conscious purpose of misleading the public to the advantage of the denizens of the upper brackets, but they have this effect. Some taxes are very definitely not shifted into prices of products, and this tends to be true of upper-bracket income taxes.

Other means of decreasing inequality and thus stimulating consumption are increases in wages by legislation or by the encouragement of trade unions; decreases in profits by curtailing monopoly and otherwise encouraging price competition; and voluntary curtailment of large salary and bonus payments by corporations. Another line of attack is by way of curtailing the speculative frauds that are too frequently practiced upon the low and middle income groups to the advantage of more well-to-do persons.

It is perhaps pertinent to recall the point made earlier * that equality of incomes as such will not ensure the maintenance of employment. Indeed, equality at a high level would augment the problem, since the volume of savings would be increased thereby. The low incomes of the poorest two thirds or three fourths of the population have been a favorable factor in our economy, for they have been so low that they have had to be spent. The poor have been a blessing to the economy. And their poverty is still such that if a goodly portion of the total income received by the five to ten per cent of the income-receivers at the top was transferred to the low income groups, total consumption would be increased and employment made more secure.

It need not be feared that a shift in the income stream so as to promote consumption would impair our capital building and thus curtail our productivity. Indeed, an increase in consump-

* Chapter iii.

tion might so increase the total national income that capital building would be increased beyond what it was before the change was made in the distribution of income. The extent to which this might happen is limited by the volume of unemployment and of "slow" work that prevails because of the lack of a more vigorous demand. Certainly it is possible for us to have more seed-corn as a result of eating some of what we have.

The propensity to save can also be altered by proceeding directly to reduce the need for individual saving. The extension of insurance of various sorts, particularly those forms included under the general term "social insurance," will help to accomplish this purpose. Obviously, provisions of this kind lessen the compulsion on individuals and families to save for emergencies. Any extension of co-operative ventures of this nature, whether through or outside the government, cannot but assist in the solution of the problem of unemployment. The payment of yearly wages, as recently requested by the steel workers' union, would also increase the propensity to consume by reducing the hazard in the receipt of income.

There is much that we can do along these lines if we will. Individuals and groups whose immediate economic interests would prompt them to oppose such a program need to appreciate that their losses therefrom will tend to be far less than those that might reasonably be expected to result from changes induced by a severe unemployment crisis. Nothing could be much more shortsighted than is a current proposal that a constitutional amendment be adopted limiting the taxing power of Congress to twenty-five per cent of incomes, gifts, and inheritances. It is as if children should seek to prevent their parents from taking matches away from them.

3

We also need to give serious attention to the promotion of investment. Despite all that we may reasonably hope to accomplish in altering the balance between spending and saving, the volume of our savings may be expected to plague us, thus necessitating our finding investments to utilize them. It may be admitted at once that there are contradictions between the elements of the program that have just been recommended and some of the conditions that are practically essential to the stimulation of investment. For certainly one important element in inducing men to invest money is to permit them to make money. Hence a program that looks toward lessening the inequality of incomes, and more especially toward low profits as a result of a double squeeze of high wages and low prices, cannot but discourage the taking of risk. To permit large gains and then tax them heavily comes to the same thing. Similarly, to hold a constant threat of anti-trust prosecution over the heads of business men cannot put them in a mood to expand their undertakings. Nor can demands for patent reform and lower tariffs thrill men who are getting in a mood to try their luck in a new business venture.

The problem, however, is even more confusing than this indicates. The prospect of large profits stimulates investment and thus reduces unemployment, but the securing and retention of large profits (1) increases the need for still more investments if employment is to be maintained, and (2) curtails the ability of business to market its product and hence reduces the profitability of investment and brings about unemployment.

To put this differently, high consumption encourages investment because of the prospect of easy sales, but high consumption comes from high wages and low prices—that is, from low profits—and this discourages investment. Large profits are both a stimulant to and the nemesis of prosperity.

Perhaps neither we nor any other capitalist nation can hold the proper balance between low and high profits. Indeed, as argued earlier,* attempts to augment savings, however small the savings and however low the rate of earnings demanded thereon, will inevitably lead to depression. It was argued, it will

* Chapter iv.

be recalled, that if losses were equal to the accumulation, trouble might be avoided were it not that the fact of losses would curtail investment and precipitate unemployment. Yet we must make the attempt to provide jobs continuously within the framework of our present economy. The better chance appears to lie in increasing the propensity to consume and in accepting the difficulty that will consequently appear in a reduction in the disposition to invest.

Further in respect to the encouragement of investment, attention should be given to the income tax on corporations. This tax is basically faulty. Falling on every corporation with a taxable income of $5,000 or more—the marginal or high-cost ones as well as the most efficient—the base tax rate becomes part of the cost that must be recovered by the least efficient corporations and hence tends to be added to the price of the product and to fall upon consumption.

The imposition of progressive rates as the taxable incomes of corporations increase in size violates the ability-to-pay principle. Such a tax is essentially a levy on the stockholders, but has no relation to their ability to pay, because the resulting rate per share is the same for every stockholder in any one corporation regardless of the total income from this and other sources. This is also true of the lowest rate in so far as it is not shifted to consumers. In no case is this tax apportioned according to ability to pay. The ability-to-pay principle could be realized only by distributing to stockholders—or allocating to them for tax purposes—the net income of the· corporations and then subjecting such sums to the customary progressive rates on individuals.

Our principal concern with the corporation income tax at this place is as a deterrent to investment. It obviously has this effect. But to remove this tax on the ground that the corporate income could more properly be taxed as income to individual stockholders would mean that income retained by a corporation would have to be subjected to a special tax, despite the aversion aroused by such a tax under the revenue law of 1936.

In order to encourage investment it appears at first glance that corporate funds used in new investment—funds used to employ labor to construct productive equipment—should be exempt from taxation, or subject to especially low rates. This is recommended by Eric Johnston, president of the United States Chamber of Commerce.* But if this were done for business corporations, justice would require that the same rule be applied to new residences and other employment-creating investments by individuals and other non-corporate entities. Further, justice requires that the owners of new property should not be favored as against the owners of other property. Thus the proposal for special rates for new business construction, including equipment, comes finally to a proposal for the elimination of all property taxes other than those on land. This would perhaps be a most salutary change in our tax system. It would encourage investment both by increasing the propensity to consume and by lessening the cost—removing the taxes—on investment goods. But we are undoubtedly far from being willing to make such a change.

Robert R. Nathan makes an interesting point in this connection: namely, that the federal government should continue to levy high income taxes and "offer reimbursements to states and localities if they reduce their indirect taxes," such as "property and excise taxes." † Taxes on property are usually defined as direct taxes, but since taxes on business property tend to be shifted, they become indirect taxes on the consumers of the product. The shifting of such taxes means that they are not a burden on the business firm paying them originally, and hence it may appear that investment cannot be encouraged by reducing or removing them. This does tend to be the result in the

* *America Unlimited* (1944), p. 172.
† *Mobilizing for Abundance* (1944), p. 140.

long run, but until sufficient time has elapsed to permit the
forces of competition to shift a tax levied on property, it is a
cost factor. Certainly this is true of taxes on new types of investment property.

Finally, in respect to the encouragement of investment attention needs to be called to the rate of interest. Since this topic
was discussed above,* it will be referred to only briefly in this
place. Certainly low rates rather than high rates on borrowed
funds will encourage borrowing and thus stimulate investment.
Low rates may, however, discourage lending, particularly if
there is a possibility that rates may rise later. Hence a policy of
low rates needs to be made very definite. The Treasury and the
Federal Reserve authorities should take a very forthright position on this matter, making it clear that low rates of interest are
to be maintained. Keeping the rate of interest low not only will
tend to encourage investment but will also tend to reduce the
need for investment, since the volume of savings will be lowered by a reduction of the rate of return on the savings already
made.

4

One cannot expect, however, that we will so encourage investment and so adjust the distribution of income that all of our
money savings will be invested. Our folklore—our belief that
anyone should be allowed to make, to get, all that he can—is
still sufficiently strong to prevent our making these changes in
the near future. We must, accordingly, plan to offset the failure
to use private income promptly. That is, we must extend government spending, including what may properly be called government investment.

We did, as everyone knows, follow a course of government
spending in relief of unemployment during the first seven
years of the Roosevelt administrations, it being discontinued
only when the expenditures for war eliminated unemployment. Indeed, in terms of government deficits the last three

* Chapter iv.

years of Hoover's administration was a period of government spending in relief of business and of the unemployed.

We have developed a considerable body of literature on this subject. The fiscal policy of the government has come to be regarded increasingly as a means of preventing unemployment or of providing jobs to those who have been dismissed from private enterprise. Professor Hansen has devoted an entire book to this topic, as noted earlier, and many other writers have made significant contributions to it. The term "functional finance" has been suggested by Professor A. P. Lerner to designate the effects of fiscal measures or "the way they function." * To be sure, the attitude toward public receipts and expenditures has always been in terms of the functions performed, yet the new and broader view of the use of the fiscal powers of government warrants the term used by Lerner.

There are two features of functional finance. One is concerned with permanent or regular expenditures and the other with those of an emergency character. These are somewhat closely related to what Hansen has designated as "compensatory spending" by the government and "pump priming." We will consider first the extension of regular or permanent expenditures by the government. They may not only "compensate" for a lack of private expenditures but by providing worthwhile services contribute directly to the general welfare.

There is much that can be done. Roads and bridges can be built, river valleys improved according to the plan followed in the Tennessee River Valley, forests planted, public buildings erected, low-cost housing constructed, school lunches and "food stamp" plans provided, university scholarships given, medical and dental care extended, and other similar ventures carried forward.

There can be no doubt that the channeling of a significant portion of the national income through the government will tend to stabilize the entire economy, for to the extent that we

* See his article, "Functional Finance and the Federal Debt," *Social Research,* February 1943, and his book, *The Economics of Control* (1944), Chapter xxiv.

serve our economic wants by co-operative purchases through the government we thereby keep our total purchases more uniform year after year than they would otherwise be. Certainly the cities of the nation in which a large public pay-roll was maintained during the 1930's fared far better than those that did not enjoy such a regular flow of income. Large government budgets would not, however, prevent the main body of the economy from falling into depressions or suffering from chronic unemployment, but they would make such sickness more endurable.

In planning a program of government investment we need to keep in mind constantly the question as to the relative advisability of each line of work that it is proposed to undertake. It is easily possible that labor might be used to build parks when it should be used to make shoes, or to plant forests when there is a greater relative need for new houses. Economic energy has perhaps never been directed ideally in any society. Some things have been done even under the best of conditions that in the eyes of reputedly wise men had better have been left undone and the energy involved devoted to other tasks. Government projects such as have been indicated will make a genuine contribution to welfare, and are immeasurably to be preferred to unemployment. Yet it cannot but be true that if government expenditures are limited to non-commercial projects, such as those enumerated, a considerable volume of public spending would mean that some funds would be used in tasks that were less important than certain commercial enterprises that would be carried forward if business conditions were favorable. In short, any limitation on the range of activity by the government means that extensive expenditures are likely to be in part wasted. Hence, a program of government spending as a permanent feature of our economy and designed to be sufficiently extensive to make a significant contribution to the maintenance of employment should not be limited to non-commercial fields.

Happily, there is a field of enterprise that lends itself splendidly to this purpose: namely, that of public utilities, including the railroads. In this group of industries, we could, under government ownership, find a great outlet for government expenditure in ways that would be self-liquidating and at the same time contribute greatly to the general welfare. The repairs, improvements, and extensions that can profitably be made in these fields over the next several decades make them especially well suited for extensive government investment, and hence would permit them to serve as a balance wheel for our entire economy. Further, the experience with government ownership of electric power, gas, and water and with the regulation of these utilities and the railroads, is especially important in this connection, for it means that the problems in these fields are already well known to us.

An extensive program of investment in the railways and public utilities of the country not only would directly contribute to the maintenance of employment, but would indirectly make the production of steel and a large group of related products much more regular than it has ever been. In short, the increased regularity in railway and public utility construction as a result of government ownership would tend to have a wide influence on the entire economy. Not only would such construction not fall off periodically as it now does, but when a slump occurred in private investment, government investment could easily be extended.

This construction could be financed by the sale of United States bonds at, say, two per cent interest to savers, not to commercial banks. Such bonds would, of course, be self-sustaining, and would in no way be more of a burden on the economy than are bonds now issued against these enterprises by their private owners. Schemes of decentralization could be devised whereby state and local government units could own and operate local utilities, with the securities guaranteed by the national government.

This suggestion, which is similar to one made by Professor

Hansen in his *Fiscal Policy,* would, if put into effect, perhaps almost wholly solve the problem of unemployment. There would, in the private enterprise sector of the economy, still be the difficulty of saving money beyond the opportunities for profitable investment, and hence we should still have depressions, but these would be so reduced in magnitude by the continuous construction at the order of the government that they might be endurable, and hence make unnecessary more extensive government ownership. The business interests of the economy would no doubt be well advised to urge government ownership in limited fields as suggested here, in order to be able to retain private ownership elsewhere.

This line of attack on the dichotomy between savings and investments is not in line with the general spirit of this book, for it stresses investment as a means of making work and permitting us to consume rather than as a means of producing consumption goods and services. It places Secundus in the role of Primus. Yet we are as a nation forced in this direction. If we cannot adjust our income stream and our habits so as to place consumption first, we must then make the best of the situation and invest in order to provide employment and maintain consumption. Government ownership in the field of public utilities and railways would contribute greatly to our ability to do this.

6

Under the program that has just been suggested, we should still need to be prepared for unemployment crises, and we especially need to be so prepared if but little, or nothing, is done to relieve the savings-investment difficulty along the lines already proposed. The need is, obviously, to maintain effective demand —that is, buying power. It is failure here that causes unemployment. Hence government assistance should be provided whenever demand fails as a result of the failure to convert money savings into investments. The extension of public investment as just suggested is one method of overcoming the market impasse. Since the construction of public utility or railway equipment would be self-sustaining, the vexing problem of adding to the public debt would be eliminated. Certainly no one would fear "national bankruptcy" if borrowed funds were used to construct public utility or railway property that will "pay." Taxes would not need to be levied to meet interest charges on bonds if such outlays were recouped from the sale of services.

Although the construction by the government of property that will yield an income has an important advantage over expenditures that do not do so, this is at the same time a disadvantage. For when a market impasse develops—when the consumer goods and services that are available are not purchased in sufficient quantities to permit employment to be maintained—there is a marked gain to the economy in the production of such things as schoolhouses, roads, and parks that do not yield products that must be sold. The outgo of money funds in such cases add to consumer buying power without adding to the supply of consumer goods and services on the market. Nevertheless our penchant for figuring in terms of dollar outlay and return—despite our long experience with roads and schools—will more readily permit government expenditures in self-liquidation projects than in those where the returns are measurable only in terms of general welfare.

Another life-line that should be prepared and kept in readiness for use during unemployment crises is the direct distribution of money funds to potential buyers whenever investments, both private and public, fail to maintain the demand needed to provide employment.

Perhaps the most complete plan of this sort has been developed by J. E. Meade, a prominent economist in England. He proposes that "consumer credits"—in effect, money—be provided by the government and distributed gratis to workers in the low income groups regardless of whether they are unemployed, whenever the ratio of unemployment to employment reaches a certain specified figure.* He expects that this addition to buying power will put the unemployed back at work. There appears to be no reason why this would not be accomplished if enough buying power is provided. How much would be needed would depend in part on the effect of such a program on the persons who were holding their money idle and thus causing the unemployment.

If the well-to-do classes were opposed to the program—if they feared that heavy taxes would later be levied on them to make up for these expenditures—hoarding might increase and a considerable expenditure of consumers' credit—enough to bring about a rise in prices—might be necessary to coax such funds into use. Another difficulty in this scheme is that the largesse would have to be withdrawn later. Much can be said for the distribution of free money income to the low income groups in addition to providing them the services of schools, roads, parks, and so on (for which they may pay heavily in indirect taxes), but it does not appear well to do it intermittently, depending on whether the whole concatenation of circumstances makes it profitable for savers to erect factory buildings.

Meade acknowledges that the variations in income would be unfortunate. He suggests that this difficulty might be overcome by urging the workers to use the extra money received under the scheme in the purchase of durable goods rather than as additions to ordinary expenditures. Here, of course, as in innumerable aspects of life, the use of human intelligence may secure good results from a plan that would not otherwise be advisable.

Meade errs in believing that the injection of extra consuming power will overcome the difficulty that brought on the slump. As our argument in the earlier chapters of this book indicates, the market could be sustained by the creation of extra money, but this would not restore it to a self-functioning condition. It

* *Consumers' Credits and Unemployment* (1938).

is possible, of course, that lucky inventions might appear that would make new investments profitable and thus overcome the hoarding of savings in a relatively short time. Also other accidents might give a fillip to the economy. But one cannot be certain that such events will occur. Nevertheless this method of maintaining buying power and keeping the economy functioning has much to recommend it. Particularly, the persons receiving such extra money would tend to direct economic resources into more wholesome lines of activity than if such sums were expended for "public works."

7

Another proposal designed to improve sales through the aid of government finance has been developed by Mordecai Ezekiel. This was first presented in a book, *$2500 a Year,* published in 1936 and later under the name of "Industrial Expansion" in a book, *Jobs for All,* issued in 1939. This idea was embodied in identical bills introduced into the House of Representatives in 1937 by Allen of Pennsylvania, Amlie of Wisconsin, Maverick of Texas, and Voorhis of California, and in a bill introduced during the following Congress by Voorhis under the title, "The Monopoly Control Act." The general nature of this plan is that the government would contract with industrial firms for the production of a certain number of units, the government promising to buy, at a reduced price, any of these units that the firms were not able to sell. With markets assured, business would go forward, we are told. "Under Industrial Expansion," says Ezekiel, "there will be markets for all that is produced, for buying power will expand as fast as production." *

The argument that has been presented in the foregoing pages indicates that this result would not be realized. Markets cannot be found for all that is produced as long as corporations and individuals desire to accumulate more wealth. If all the work in the nation were in the hands of, say, twenty corporations,

---

* Mordecai Ezekiel: *Jobs for All* (1939), p. 28.

they could not provide markets for one another continuously if the corporations, or their owners or creditors, refused to buy the finished consumer products to which their money incomes entitle them. If they prefer instead to save—to increase their wealth, to accumulate larger holdings, to make a still larger annual profit—there is no escape from a glut in the market. The goose that lays the golden eggs will be killed by suffocation if the eggs accumulate.

The fact, however, that Ezekiel claims too much for his plan does not mean that it is not meritorious. It is, from the side of producers, comparable to Meade's scheme of grants to consumers. It is, again, similar to the plan of purchase by the government during a war, and to the support prices and commodity loans that we provide for agriculture. Employment can be maintained by this method. The difficulty is, as with so many devices, that it does not correct the difficulty that prevents private enterprise from providing continuous employment. It is always possible, however, that if temporary aid is provided, new investments, or other lucky accidents, may restore full employment. At any rate, there are advantages in holding the line against widespread unemployment.

8

Many of the above recommendations carry the implication of the government's disbursing more money than it has received in taxation. That is, there are implications of "budgetary deficits"—of "government debt." This general problem has been the center of a very lively and bitter controversy since the early 1930's. On the one hand, men have argued that a government debt, if it is held internally, should really not be regarded as a debt, since we merely "owe it to ourselves," and that in general finance is a "humbug" since we can always afford financially to do whatever we are able to do physically. On the other hand, it has been insisted that an increasing debt means that we are doing what we cannot afford to do—that national as well as individual debts point toward bankruptcy—that an inflation of prices so high as to make government bonds worthless is the logical outcome of a policy such as we followed in the decade before the beginning of the present war.

The truth appears to be that we need to be more concerned over an interest-bearing debt than the one school apparently feels to be necessary, and also that the fervor of the opposition to the increase of our debt up to 41 billion by June 1940, and but little, if any, concern at the subsequent increase under war conditions to more than six times that amount, indicate that the opponents of the debt policy were thinking largely in terms of traditions or folklore. But what is more important, it is beginning to appear that the debt problem is merely a result of our ineptitude. By the use of elementary intelligence we could accomplish the national purpose of providing employment when private enterprise fails to do so, without involvement in an interest-bearing debt. All that is necessary is that we give up traditional views and think of the problem with an open mind. Here as in many other cases we have to unlearn much before we can learn a little.

What we need to do in the first place is to stop thinking of our nation as a group of separate and independent persons with a government above them, and to think instead of the nation as a social unit that functions in part through a government of its own choosing. From this point of view, if it appears that the national group needs more money than is available, the conclusion will be that the extra money should be created by the government. There need be no borrowing in such a case—no everlasting payment of interest. Then, too, from such a point of view, whenever it appears that the general welfare will be extended by the people's giving up money, taxes will be levied or bonds will be sold to them, as during this war.

It needs to be emphasized, as A. P. Lerner so well says,* that taxes need never be levied so that the government will have

* *The Economics of Control* (1944), p. 307. See also K. E. Boulding: *The Economics of Peace* (1945), Chapter ix.

money to spend. The government can always make the money that it needs. Taxes are justified only when the money in the hands of the people should be reduced in the interest of the general welfare. And let it be emphasized that this is the usual situation when expenditures are undertaken by the government. If, for example, a community wishes to build a schoolhouse and if there is full employment, it is essential that economic resources be diverted from present tasks to the new project. The easy and sensible way to accomplish this is for the residents of the community to give up money and thus decrease present expenditures so that resources can the more readily be diverted to the purpose in hand. The creation and use of additional money would be very confusing in such a case.

Logically, the problem of maintaining the amount of money that the people of a nation need is as simple as controlling the temperature in a room. All that is required is the proper operation of the instruments at hand. This merely calls for the exercise of simple intelligence in turning money valves and tax valves.

This will seem horrendous to some persons. Their general distrust of people and their knowledge of cases of tragic experiences with "easy" money will make them fearful. Some persons were once horrified at the idea of building fires in houses. Men had burned down not only their own but their neighbors' houses by such practices. Yet despite early tragedies and ever present hazards the exercise of simple intelligence permits us to use the fearsome element, fire, to our great advantage.

It needs to be observed that all money systems are made and managed by men. Further, the general movement away from the gold standard during the past two decades has placed in the hands of the financial authorities in the various countries an increased degree of discretion, which on the whole has been exercised excellently. But whether a people handle their money matters well or ill, there is no escape from the task. A money system must be devised and operated. Any proposed change in

the methods used should be carefully considered. The burden
of proof is on the innovator. But this in no way warrants the
assumption that any new proposal is an impious attack upon a
system devised by omnipotence.

Nothing is said or implied here to mean that the administrative officials in Washington should be given power to create
and spend money without limit. Congress alone has the power
to make appropriations—to authorize expenditure. The point
merely is that the expenditure of money beyond tax receipts
may at certain times contribute to the general welfare and that
it is unnecessary that we create an interest-bearing debt in order
to accomplish this.

At least two methods are available. The government could
sell to commercial banks non-interest-bearing notes at a discount
of, say, two per cent, for which the government would be given
bank deposits—that is, checking accounts. The discount would
serve as compensation for the services rendered by the banks.
The notes would be eligible for sale at full value to the Federal
Reserve Banks for reserve purposes or for cash. They would be
redeemable by the government in lawful money. The essential
difference between this plan and the one that we have been following is that interest would be paid for one year, not indefinitely. Thus the paper issued would not be a burden upon
the economy. There would be no debt—nothing to pay off.

A second method of accomplishing the purpose in view
would be to make the twelve Federal Reserve Banks outright
government institutions rather than quasi-government banks
as at present, thus permitting the administrative officials, when
authorized by Congress, to set up checking accounts to be disbursed for specified purposes. The checks issued would be
readily acceptable at any bank, and, of course, receivable by
the Federal banks for the reserve accounts of member banks or
redeemable in money. Again there would be no debt to har-
ass us.

The present method of selling bonds to the banks and taking

a government checking account really differs from the method here proposed only in that we now pledge ourselves as a nation to pay indefinitely for the bank service rendered. Some writers insist that the banks need the money that we now pay them—that the interest that they receive from the government is a subsidy that must be paid to keep them in business.* If it be true that the banking system requires a government subsidy, it would appear to be much better to make forthright public grants for this purpose rather than to do it by a subterfuge.

It needs to be emphasized that what is here proposed is not that there should be a continuous addition to our money supply. Additions should be made only when that is in the public interest. A recommendation that furnace fires be made during the winter does not warrant the conclusion that they be kept going all of the time. Not only do we need to put them out during the summer, we need also to turn on the cooling unit. Money must be withdrawn via taxes as well as added as the readings of the gauges indicate the need for the one or the other. A tax device that would lend itself well to the purpose in hand could be placed in the hands of the Board of Governors of the Federal Reserve System. The Board could be authorized to impose a tax up to a certain limit upon bank deposits, or checks drawn, whenever the index of prices or of employment indicated that to be advisable, and to reduce or remove the tax when that is advisable. This would be only an addition to the wide discretionary powers now exercised by this Board. This entire proposal, indeed, is merely that we take another step in the long and gradual process by which men have sought to make money, which may be a bad master, a good servant.†

9

It deserves to be emphasized that the use of labor that would otherwise be unemployed is costless to the nation. As a com-

* See J. C. Poindexter: "Fallacies of Interest-Free Deficit Financing," *Quarterly Journal of Economics*, May 1944.

† Cf. W. C. Mitchell: *Business Cycles, The Problem and Its Setting* (1927), p. 136 n.

munity not only do we not incur a cost when persons who would have been idle produce goods or services, but we have, in addition to the product, the preservation of skill, morale, and character that would otherwise be lost. If we are all employed, the cost of building a house is the product that we would produce if we did not build the house. Basically this is what we mean when we say that it costs a certain sum of money to build a house; one must pay that amount to get the labor and materials for this use, for that is the amount that they could command in some other employment. But if labor would otherwise be unemployed and the materials not produced, then there is no cost to the nation in producing the house, unless it be the use of materials that otherwise would be preserved for later use, or the extra food that the laborers eat as a result of their activity.

To put the matter another way, if the community provides adequate food, clothing, and shelter as relief to the unemployed, then, setting them to work would mean that the product would not cost anything, and that there would be gains in character and morale besides. Unused labor is lost irretrievably; using what otherwise would be lost is a net gain.

10

A very popular remedy for unemployment is a reduction of hours. This policy, strangely enough, has the support of organized labor and of many of its political friends. In the early days of 1933 a bill to limit hours of work to thirty per week came near to enactment by the Congress. It would perhaps have become law if the National Industrial Recovery proposal had not been brought forward. The various codes under the N.I.R.A. imposed limitations on hours, and after the Act was nullified the Fair Labor Standards Act, which is now in effect, sought to discourage work beyond forty hours per week by providing for the payment of time and a half for work in excess of that number of hours. The American Federation of Labor in its national convention in 1944 adopted a resolution demanding a thirty-hour week.

This policy falls far short of what is advisable as a method of helping workers. It would be logical enough if it were based on the notion that increased leisure rather than an increase in goods is to the interest of laborers, or, what amounts to the same thing, that health would be improved by the short hours, or that a reduction in hours would increase output as it would if workers were not having sufficient leisure to permit recuperation. But as a means of overcoming unemployment it is most inadvisable. It does result in laborers sharing the available work, but this means that they spread their poverty. It does not reduce hours of unemployment, it merely distributes them over larger numbers.

Some trade unionists have been misled by their experience, which appears to have given validity to the jingle:

> Whether you work by the piece or the day,
> Decreasing the hours increases the pay,

and have favored legislation that limits hours on the ground that wages per week would thereby be raised. It may have been true in the case of some unions that, because of peculiar conditions, wages were forced up at the same time that hours were forced down, but this would not make the reduction in hours the cause of the increase in pay. It is certainly clear that a reduction in hours and a raising of pay cannot go forward simultaneously without limit, for this would mean that as hours of work per week tended to approach zero, the output per worker would tend to approach infinity. We cannot as a society produce more and more as a result of working less and less down to the point of not working at all. The shortening of hours cannot solve the problem of welfare except where an increase in leisure is preferable to an increase in economic goods and services, nor can it solve the problem of unemployment.

The advocates of the Townsend Plan have fallen into this

same error. They stress as one of the merits of their plan that pensioners shall not work. Certainly our difficulty is not that we produce too much. When 15 children out of every 100 in a county of 20,000 persons go to school without breakfast,* or when the bottom third of the families of the nation receive a top yearly income of $780 and the second third a top of $1,450 per year,† the difficulty is something other than an oversupply of goods. The overproduction that we suffer relative to our willingness to buy would not be helped by reducing the number of workers, or the hours of work. Such a cure would keep us poorer than we otherwise would be during our best periods and it would make us no better off during hard times and no more likely to escape them.

II

Finally, in this array of proposed devices to facilitate the smooth operation of our economy, attention must be given to proposals to penalize the hoarding, or the "slow" utilization, of money. Since we have found the problem of unemployment to rest on the hoarding of money, a penalty that would overcome this practice would apparently solve the problem. There are difficulties involved, however, in compelling the prompt utilization of money, and, further, it is possible that one of the results that would come from successfully accomplishing it would be unfortunate.

It is certainly incongruous that although the holding of money may paralyze the operations of the economy, yet money is practically the only form of wealth that it costs nothing to hold. Goods generally require protection from the elements and deteriorate with time, but money can be held at practically no cost and may appreciate greatly in value while it is being held. Indeed, if enough persons hoard money so as to induce a depression, the resulting fall in prices will make the holding of the money anything but costly to the holders thereof. It is also

---

* In 1940, *Consumers' Guide,* September 1942.
† For twelve months 1935–6, The National Resources Committee.

incongruous that the earnings from economic activity that is beneficial to the nation, such as producing wealth and rendering services, are subject to taxation, while money that is held idle to the disadvantage of the nation in normal times is tax-free.

A great deal of attention has been given to this matter. Various forms of tax-stamp money have been proposed as well as devices for the periodic depreciation of the face value of currency as means of penalizing the holding of bills beyond certain periods of time. But since it is increasingly appreciated that our principal form of money consists of bank checks, attention has turned to a consideration of the taxation of bank deposits. More particularly, the ability to substitute currency or bank deposits for each other makes it advisable to tax both in order to accomplish the purpose in view.

The imposing of penalties on the slow utilization of money is, however, easier talked about than done. The various devices that have been proposed in respect to currency would be so inconvenient in operation that it is doubtful if they would be tolerated. And the difficulties of enforcement in the case of bank deposits might make such schemes unworkable. The taxing of deposits according to their volume would not, as some persons seem to think, accomplish the purpose intended. The problem is the rate of turnover. The bank balance of X may be ever so large, but if he turns it over frequently in legitimate transactions there can be no complaint against him in terms of hoarding, while a person with a small deposit might by not checking against it contribute along with other like depositors to a considerable volume of unemployment. The writing of checks in itself, however, is not a sufficient criterion for the purpose in view, since depositors might draw checks against each other merely in order to evade the tax.*

Assuming that a practical plan of securing the prompt utilization of money were devised and applied, goods would not go

---

* The difficulties involved in such a program are discussed, and articles dealing with the problem are cited, by Arthur Dahlberg in *Recovery Plans,* Monograph No. 25, Temporary National Economic Committee, Part I, 1940.

unsold and laborers would not be out of work because of the lack of a market. Further, according to the proponents of these schemes even more than this would be accomplished. The rate of interest would be lowered, investment extended, production increased, monopolies broken, and arbitrary prices reduced. Many birds are expected to be killed with the one stone. These results, it should be noted, are expected to be in part the steps leading to full employment, and in part additional benefits from quick-moving money.

The advocates of these proposals do not usually stress the effect which such penalties, if they were effective, would have on the consumption of the persons who would otherwise hoard their money. We should expect the penalties to increase their consumption as well as their investment. This would, generally speaking, be unfortunate. For although additional consumption on the part of those already well cared for may be preferable to unemployment, it is certainly not justifiable to titillate the jaded senses of those who have already consumed almost to surfeit when the economic energy utilized might be used to improve the scale of living of those at the foot of the economic pyramid. Hiring laborers to blow soap bubbles for the edification of large income receivers may enable such laborers to eat, but they could eat still more if their energies could be directed with proper pay to an increase of the amount of food available.

It is to be noted, too, that we cannot expect to prevent depressions by the prompt utilization of money income, except in consumption, for investments cannot be made continuously. The finite nature of the world imposes limits on compounding. A market impasse cannot be avoided. Nevertheless, experiments along these lines should be made if we do not otherwise make it possible to distribute what we produce or could produce.

12

Any plans for meeting the economic problems that lie ahead must almost necessarily include an item looking toward a reform of the structure of our national government. Our system of an elected President to serve for four years, of a House of Representatives to serve for two years, and of a Senate wherein the members serve for six years, with one third elected every two years, is most unfortunate. Certainly no student of affairs would recommend this arrangement today in view of our experience and in view of the experience in Great Britain and Canada with a system of parliamentary responsibility. Our legislative and administrative branches are, as anyone would expect, jealous of their prerogatives and suspicious of each other under the most favorable of conditions, and, as so frequently happens during the last half of a Presidential term, if the House and a large group in the Senate are not in sympathy with the President, the machinery of government functions very badly. If grave emergencies induced by mass unemployment or other catastrophe occur during such a period of political stalemate, and economic difficulty during the first part of a Presidential administration tends to create just such a stalemate during the second part, we are in a very unfortunate position. Such a condition might easily lead to chaos and revolution.*

The essence of the parliamentary system of government, which has been found to function so well in Great Britain for hundreds of years, is that the executive and the legislative branches of government are combined. The legislative branch, in effect, selects the executive, and if the executive takes a course of action that is not approved of by the House, either the executive must resign or the House must be dissolved and an election held. When the latter course is followed, if a House of the same opinion as the one dissolved is elected, the "government" must

---

* Professor F. L. Paxson, a noted student of the history of our institutions, has said recently that within our recollection ". . . four presidents, Cleveland and Taft, Hoover and Wilson, have come to political disaster through the partisanship of a Congress on 'dead center,' with one or both houses controlled by the party of the opposition. This is a mechanical check, built into the Constitution to be a check, invariably bringing about a shading of duty for the sake of politics, and capable one day of wrecking the United States." (*Political Science Quarterly*, December 1944, p. 638.)

resign and a new one is appointed that is in sympathy with the House. The government machinery cannot be stalled because of party differences between the legislative and the administrative branches of the government.

Our constitutional fathers, as everyone knows, wished to limit government. They felt with Jefferson that the best government is the government that governs least. This was a thoroughly reasonable attitude in this country in the latter part of the eighteenth century. Almost all of the less than four million persons in the thirteen colonies lived on small independent farms and produced almost wholly for the consumption of their own families. The economy was agrarian. Manufacturing still meant, as the word itself indicates, "made by hand," and was largely confined to the farms. Not a single man in the constitutional convention had ever seen a complicated piece of machinery, and only a few of them at the most had seen the crude steam engine of that period. Certainly no one of them, not even the imaginative Franklin, foresaw the changes in our life and in our economy that were implicit in the steam engine.

In addition to the framework of the simple economy of that time, the constitutional fathers were mindful of the jealousies of the existing states and also disinclined to follow British patterns. At any rate, they provided for a "separation of powers" in the government which they devised; they set up a plan of "checkes and balances" by which each arm of the government would be restrained by the others. This arrangement was inadvisable even at that time and is fatally weak now with the nation a group of 138 million persons, largely divorced from the soil, engaged in highly interdependent, large-scale, mass-production enterprises of all sorts, and subject to widespread unemployment. Further, even when we shall have eliminated unemployment, our present governmental machinery would still be inadequate to the proper performance of the tasks that would confront us. If we did no more than provide that the members of the two houses of Congress and the President should be elected at the same time for the same term, we would greatly improve the workability of the government. We need, however, to go further than that. "If we would rule by the light of reason we must let our minds be bold."

CHAPTER XVII

Government Ownership of Large Enterprise

I

IF WE ARE UNWILLING or unable to prevent chronic and depression unemployment along the lines recommended in the preceding chapter, are we likely to attempt to solve the problem by government ownership? An affirmative answer appears to be called for. Perhaps the best support for this conclusion is found in the persistently repeated statements by business men of the merits of free enterprise.

The leading magazines have been filled with advertisements during the past few years proclaiming the virtues of private ownership, committees of business men devote themselves to "educational" programs to this end, and business leaders deliver countless addresses in defense of the American traditions of business. Candidates for political office declare their faith in private enterprise and ask for an opportunity to be placed in positions where they may be able to help in the preservation of capitalism.

This defense of private ownership is new in our thinking. Heretofore we have taken it for granted. There has always been a small band of opponents of the present system, but no one in power or authority has taken them seriously. Business men have not taken time off to defend private ownership and operation, and political leaders have no more troubled to declare their faith in private business than their acceptance of monogamic marriage or Christianity.

The current declarations of faith in our economy are especially noteworthy because of the lack of any organized movement against private ownership. Aside from small groups such as the People's Lobby, the few thousand members of the Socialist Party, and still fewer members of other Left-wing parties, there is nothing in the way of a campaign to extend gov-

[223]

ernment ownership. Further, Left-wing voters are much less numerous relatively and absolutely than they were forty years ago.

Perhaps the declarations by business leaders of their faith in private ownership in the absence of any concerted attack is an indication that they are losing faith. Doubts often lead to public avowals that there is no basis for doubt. We may have here evidence of a decline in the spiritual significance of capitalism to which Professor Schumpeter, among others, has called attention.

The votaries of private enterprise, says Schumpeter in his *Capitalism, Socialism, and Democracy* (1942) no longer appear to regard it as an indispensable way of life. Large-scale industry, he believes, has undermined the individualism of an earlier day. It has, he contends, routinized business affairs and lessened the importance of any one person, thus weakening the prestige and the spiritual significance of the business man. Further, he insists that the process of substituting "mere parcels of shares for the walls of and machines in a factory, takes the life out of the idea of property. . . . Eventually there will be *nobody* left who really cares [to defend] dematerialized, defunctionalized and absentee ownership" (p. 142). "The true pacemakers of socialism," he says, "were not the intellectuals or agitators who preached it but the Vanderbilts, Carnegies, and Rockefellers" (p. 134).

However much business men may be suffering from spiritual qualms and however free the scene may be of a government-ownership campaign of serious proportions, there can be no doubt that the scent of government ownership is in the air. The spirit of the times is increasingly one of co-operation through the government in economic affairs. The social security program and indeed the whole body of New Deal legislation, which was approved almost in its entirety by the Republican platform in 1944, indicates this trend. Another serious unemployment crisis such as in 1932–3 might lead to urgent demands that the government assume charge of our major industries, and this might be done regardless of which one of our political parties was in power. We must accordingly consider this method of solving the problem of unemployment.

We are not concerned here with the war of ideologies. We are not concerned with Socialism and with all of the notions of religion, family life, and equality that have been mixed up with economics under that term. Nor are we concerned with any extension of government ownership beyond a relatively few major enterprises. Our problem is merely that of employment, and our inquiry will be limited to a consideration of whether collective ownership of major business units through the government would solve this problem without creating still worse ones.

This method of preventing unemployment should be considered in terms of minimum changes. There need be no confiscation of property. In taking over any corporation the government could, and one may expect would, assume the obligations of the corporation to its stock- and bond-holders and other claimants. The government could also, and should, assume the obligations of the corporations to the officers and other employees in respect to tenure and rates of pay. And it could, and of course would, continue for some time anyway the prevailing practices as to selecting and paying employees, keeping records, conducting the work of the enterprise, and pricing and marketing the product. The only essential change would be that the purpose of the enterprise would be altered from that of making money to that of serving the public, and since these two purposes are not in conflict in most enterprises except during periods of unemployment, the change even in this aspect would be less than one might suppose. In general the visible change from private to government ownership, other than when there are large numbers of persons out of work who are given jobs, might be as little as when the government took over the railroads in December 1943. The visible change then consisted of five executives wearing uniforms of the United States Army.

2

Would government ownership of the major enterprises of the country solve the problem of unemployment? The answer is yes. The problem would simply disappear. The case would be essentially like that of a pioneer, self-sufficient farm family, which never created unemployment for itself. If two of the sons were engaged in clearing land while the others and their father cultivated the land that had been cleared, all were not thrown into idleness and misery when the job of clearing was completed. Nor was it necessary to hunt up some other capital-building task for the two sons. All of them could work at cultivation. If they raised too much they could merely take more leisure.

A system of government ownership would be a pioneer farm on a big scale. The work to be done could always be divided among the available workers. There would never be any lack of work as long as additional goods were preferred to more leisure, nor any need to work beyond that point.

Today steel mills and factories are closed, or partly closed, when the management believes that less will be lost by curtailing output and dismissing employees than by continuing to produce at capacity. In fact, plants are never closed, nor put on short time, except when the prospect of loss is greater if full production is continued than if work is curtailed. The firm loses whenever it reduces output, but it loses less than if it continues full production.

Such a condition could not arise under government ownership. The nation could never lose less by having workers and plants idle rather than at work producing the necessities and comforts of life. House rent may fall so low during a period of hard times that a landlord may decide that he will lose less by evicting the tenant and letting the house stand empty, but rents never fall so low that one who is living in his own house abandons it and sleeps in the park.

More particularly, what of the savings-investment problem? Let us assume government ownership, with salaries and wages as today, and also with savings by individuals and loans by them for the construction of plant and equipment. In short, let us assume that conditions are identical with those with which we are familiar except that the people collectively own and operate industrial equipment.as they now own and operate post offices. If savers hoard under such conditions, what will happen? Will goods go unsold and workers be dismissed? Not at all. Prices will be cut so that the entire product can be purchased by the persons willing to use their money for this purpose, and production and employment will continue.

The hoarded money will be by-passed as the early economists apparently assumed would be done in our present economy. But that cannot be done in a private-property economy because of the money losses that firms would experience. Or when it is done losses and disorganization occur. The nation as a whole, however, is not concerned with money losses, but only with real losses. The people would lose collectively if one line of goods was produced when another should be produced, or if there was waste of materials or labor, or, of course, if some of them stand around idle. But they would not.lose as a nation if they paid out 100 units of money in producing a certain quantity of goods and if 20 units of the money burned up and the entire batch of goods had to be sold for 80. Similarly, of course, if 20 units of money were hoarded and sales were made for the 80 that were kept in use, there would be no loss to the nation as a whole. Further, if we assume that the hoarding of savings would throw construction workers out of employment, it would be easy enough to absorb them in the production of consumer goods, if the government owned the facilities of production.

These cases in which it is assumed that savings are hoarded under government ownership and that construction workers are dismissed make the worst possible situations so far as government ownership is concerned, but even these lead to no great difficulty. Actually, one can hardly conceive of a cessation of new investment, or construction, under a regime of government ownership. Plans would certainly be made for continuous construction of factories, mills, and so forth. There is no reason why these would need to be built by spurts, as has always been true under capitalism. Hence, borrowing for such purposes could be continuous at given rates of interest, if such work were not financed by taxation or other public receipts. There appears to be no reason under government ownership for a decline in investment opportunities every few years and a consequent hoarding of savings. But even if spells of hoarding occurred, the economy would continue on its even course.

If it should appear after considerable additions to productive plant that there was no need to continue so much work of that kind, workers could be released and offered jobs in consumer-goods industries. If the supply of consumer goods should finally outrun the need for such goods, all that would be required would be a general reduction in hours of work.

This analysis shows the invalidity of the point that is frequently made to the effect that since progress—change—is the cause of unemployment, an economy of government ownership would be subject to unemployment if it were progressive. Progress in manufacturing under government ownership would be no more disturbing to the economy than is the familiar case of an improvement in our government-owned highways. The closing of outmoded plants under government ownership would lead to no more difficulty than does the closing of an old schoolhouse when it is no longer needed. An additional batch of consumer goods under government ownership could never result in "retrenchment," in getting in "a liquid position," in dismissing employees, and in otherwise spreading a plague.

There does not appear to be any way in which unemployment could persist in a government-ownership economy; nor any way in which there could be periodic unemployment, or any manifestations of the "business cycle." Whether one accepts the theory of depressions that is advanced here or some one of the many other explanations offered during the past sixty years, it is equally true that government ownership would eliminate the ups and downs of business. Collective controls are adequate to correct any of the maladjustments that have been alleged to be causes of the familiar cyclical pattern of business.

How extensive government ownership would need to be in order to eliminate chronic and depression unemployment cannot be readily ascertained. At least I do not feel competent to draw the line as between what would need to be owned by the government and what might be left under private control. The present purpose is served by the conclusion that the government ownership of major enterprises would solve the problem of unemployment, even though the term "major" is not defined precisely. A corollary of this is, of course, that small-scale manufacturing and distribution units, repair and service enterprises, and the entire farming industry could be left in private hands. The significant point is that the government-ownership sector need only be sufficient to eliminate unemployment. This can be accomplished with relatively less government ownership as various items noted in the preceding chapter are put into execution.

3

Soviet Russia, it may be noted, has not experienced any of the usual indicia of chronic or depression unemployment. Although no capitalist country escaped the depression of the 1930's, the Soviet Union did not catch the disease. It suffered in having the prices of its exports fall more in the world markets than did the prices of the things which it wished to import, but this did not cause any unemployment. Nor is there now, as the war draws to a close, any fear among any groups in Russia that jobs will not continue to be available.

Failure to appreciate the significance of the Russian plan of economic organization in respect to the savings-consumption problem has led many able analysts astray. Thus Professor Carr of the University College of Wales, in his book *Conditions of Peace* (1942), says:

The Soviet regime introduced at an early date a system of production which in some quarters encouraged the belief that planned production might by itself provide a cure for our economic ills. In attempting to apply the precedent to Western Europe, it was, however, commonly forgotten that Russia was in a primitive stage of economic development, having a vast territory not yet fully exploited, a still rapidly expanding population, a low standard of living, no important exports other than raw materials, and a home market capable, even in staple commodities, of almost indefinite expansion—a combination of circumstances in which the possibility of over-production scarcely existed. [P. 97.]

All of these things that Carr mentions are but trimmings on the façade of an economy. The degree of regularity in employment will depend on whether the foundation of the economy is or is not one in which the savings-consumption relationship has been harmonized. Carr is certainly the last man, in view of other things in his book, who ought to say that "a low standard of living" and "a home market capable, even in staple commodities, of almost indefinite expansion" give conditions "in which the possibility of over-production scarcely exists." The whole history of capitalism is replete with periods in which production was stalled in the midst of poverty.

The various items that Carr lists in respect to Russia have been true of this country throughout our entire history until recently, at least, and yet we have reached a condition of over-production every decade or so and have had to suffer the agony of unemployment while the investment-consumption relationship was readjusted. The fact that our economy was expanding during the past one hundred years did facilitate recovery after a market impasse had been created and a depression had occurred, but it did not prevent the recurrence of the market-impasse and depression sequence. It is to the removal of the dichotomy between investment and consumption that one must look for an understanding of continuous employment in the U.S.S.R.

4

Many persons will say at once that even if government ownership of certain major industries would eliminate unemployment, the cure would be worse than the disease because of the sharp reduction that would occur in the general efficiency of the economy. It will be contended that the removal of the opportunity to make profits from private ownership will greatly lessen the incentive to work effectively and to make improvements. This raises two questions: First, what change in this respect would be made by the transference of large industries to government ownership? And, second, are other economic and non-economic rewards as effective in stimulating effort as are profits?

In respect to the first question it is interesting to note that profits as an incentive have already practically disappeared in our large business units. There is perhaps not a single person among the several millions who work for the two hundred largest corporations who is influenced by the thought that if he does his work well, the profits of the firm will be increased and his income will automatically be enlarged. But few of these millions of workers own any stock in the companies that employ them, and of those that do the holdings of any one are so limited in respect to the total that his share of increased dividends out of increased earnings as a result of better service by him would be insignificant. It is perhaps no more to be expected that profits stimulate efforts in such companies than that the desire to reduce their taxes causes men to drink frugally from a public fountain. To be sure, the efforts of managers in these companies are sometimes encouraged by making an increase in profits the basis for a bonus or an increase in salary, but this makes profit of significance only as a criterion for wage payment. Physical output under government ownership would serve equally well.

Abundant statistical confirmation of this point can be found in a recent book by R. A. Gordon.* He gives an array of data to show the separation of management and "control" from ownership. He shows, for example, that the 264 top-flight executives in 149 "very large corporations" received as compensation an average (median) salary of $61,200 in 1935, but that their income in dividends from stock owned in the employing company was only $500. The 52 public utility executives who were included in the study received an average (median) dividend payment of only $90 from their employing companies, and the 51 railway executives received no dividends at all (p. 301). Certainly the oft quoted statement by Arthur Young in reference to agricultural England, long before the Industrial Revolution: "The magic of private property turns sand into gold," has no relevance today in our giant corporations. The loving husbandry that brings in the gold is performed by hired hands—not by owners.

Not only do large-scale operations remove the profit incentive from the executives but private ownership in such cases appears to act as a positive drag on the efforts of large numbers of wage-earning employees. The size of operations, the impersonal relationships that almost necessarily prevail, and the well-known inequality in income that exists between the wage-workers on the one hand and the managers and owners on the other develop a resentment that in many cases cannot but retard effort. "Take it easy" is the whispered rule in many plants.

Government ownership would tend to change this attitude. For by making the plant "ours" rather than "his" or "theirs" co-operative efforts would be encouraged. Perhaps such a change in attitude as a result of turning to the production of war goods is an important factor (plus the matter of ready

* *Business Leadership in the Large Corporation* (The Brookings Institution, 1945).

markets for output) in the stupendous records that we have achieved during the war. This matter of feeling that the product of one's efforts is "ours" is repeatedly emphasized as an element in the rapid industrial progress made in Russia during the past two decades. Perhaps today the magic of public property turns sand into gold.

Secondly, what is to be said about motives other than that of making profit? The removal of profit as a source of income does not abolish economic gain as a motive to effort. Differentials in wage scales, with promotion dependent on merit, prevail all through our government employment, as in private enterprise, and are presumably as effective in securing good service in the one field as in the other.

Particularly it is significant that research and invention have long been almost entirely removed from the profit incentive. The men and women who engage in this work for the big corporations are employees—they work for wages—and they are almost invariably under a contract to sell to the employing corporation for one dollar any discovery or patentable knowledge that is developed.

There can be no reason why such work would not go forward equally well under government ownership and, indeed, there are cogent reasons why the results achieved in research under government ownership would be superior to those with which we are familiar. The consciousness of working for the common good may inspire one far more than does the knowledge that one is working for the profit of a private corporation and that any findings may be suppressed in the interest of profits.

The remarkable discoveries in the field of agriculture during the past several decades have been carried on almost wholly under government auspices. Far from there being any attempt at private profit, the various discoverers have publicized their findings as widely as possible. The thrill of discovery has been enriched by the knowledge that the public interest is being widely served.

It is reasonable to believe that the number of persons engaged in research work under government ownership might be considerably in excess of those so engaged under private enterprise. It is said that before the war one per cent of the national income in the Soviet Union was devoted to research as compared with one tenth of one per cent in Britain, and six tenths of one per cent in this country.*

The success of the Russian people against the armies of Germany in this day of highly developed mechanized warfare, when equipment requires the greatest possible skill and ingenuity in its construction and operation, is striking evidence of the scientific advance that is possible under government ownership. For the Germans have been one of the leading nations of the world in all branches of science for some seven decades, while the Russian people were largely a heterogeneous mass of superstitious, illiterate peasants as recently as twenty years ago. Their cultural, scientific, and industrial transformation since the substitution of government ownership for private enterprise is, unquestionably, one of the most dramatic episodes in all history.

Further, in respect to the general efficiency of government ownership it is commonly contended that the government cannot attract the most able men because of the failure to pay high salaries. The government could afford to pay whatever was requisite, but the enormous salaries to which we are accustomed in private business would disappear under government ownership, after allowing for a transition period. The removal of competition among the giants for executive talent and of the opportunity for the officer group to set their own salaries would drastically alter personal rewards without affecting talent, unless to improve it. The Army and Navy offer excellent illustrations of the ability of the nation to get men of top-rank ability at yearly salaries below the sums that the leading business men allot to themselves for one week's work or less.

---

* J. D. Bernal: *The Social Function of Science* (1939).

Men are not the cold, grasping, self-seeking creatures that some of them profess to be. Even those who draw enormous salaries perhaps regard most of what they get merely as a symbol. The well-known scientific genius of General Motors, Charles Kettering, in testimony before the Temporary National Economic Committee, when asked whether the inventions that he had made had been prompted by the hope of financial reward, answered in the negative and added that an inventor is like a poet—he works because he cannot help it. Almost all of us, and especially organizers and managers, are artists of a sort and get from the sense of accomplishment a major part of our reward, whatever the money income may be.

In general, we need to keep in mind that the human drives to accomplish and to excel are found everywhere—in religious orders, parliaments, armies, courts of law, research groups, and kindergartens, as well as in business groups. Government ownership of economic establishments not only would not suppress these drives but would tend to give them an outlet that is denied them in modern large-scale enterprise with its tendency to monopoly and cartelization.

Within each industry and among the various industries owned and operated by the government full utilization could be made of what the Russians call "socialist competition," which is comparable to the competition among the schools of a city. In furtherance of this, a high degree of autonomy could, and should, be allowed for each industry. There need be no over-all, minutely detailed plan. There could be as much divergence as there is now among agencies of the federal government. The Post Office, the T.V.A., the Geodetic Survey, the Panama railroad, the Interstate Commerce Commission, and the Board of Governors of the Federal Reserve System, to cite a few examples, each goes its own way under rules that are largely of its own making, but mindful always of the public interest and of the controlling power of Congress. "Politics," too, can be kept out of government-owned and operated industry as effectively as it has been out of these agencies, with the exception of the Post Office. We have tolerated "politics" in the Post Office because the character of the work was such that political appointees could, in most cases, soon learn to perform it effectively. Even this political concession, however, has recently been greatly curtailed.

Government enterprise is often subject to unfair comparisons with private operations because some of its undertakings, particularly the publicized ones, are created hurriedly during an emergency and function poorly in the early period. They are perhaps abandoned before sufficient time has elapsed to perfect an efficient organization. No smoothly functioning enterprise involving thousands of persons, or only hundreds, can be built in a day. The General Motors organization as now constituted did not spring full-blown one fine morning from the brain of some godlike private enterpriser. It takes time to perfect a social organization as well as to grow an oak.

The common notion that government activity is infested with graft and corruption is likewise weakened by analysis. An important point here is that the affairs of a government agency are subject to public scrutiny—the records are public property—and the members of the political party that is out of office are usually on the alert for evidence of corruption. The fact that but relatively few cases are ever mentioned indicates a degree of rectitude on the part of government officials that should give us pride. The affairs of business, on the contrary, are private and such graft and corruption as prevail there are generally not revealed. Occasionally an investigator unearths some seamy tales and publishes them, as John Flynn did a few years ago in a book entitled *Graft in Business*. But for the most part such conduct does not become the subject of public discussion. Further, the adding of relatives to pay-rolls and the retention of persons after they have ceased to be useful, as is often charged in respect to government agencies, also prevail in private enterprise where the size of the corporation and the number of the stockholders mean that the money involved does not come from the pockets of those responsible for its disbursement. Certainly the increase of one's own salary, or of a group of salaries by the management, may be accomplished far more easily in private corporations than in government enterprise.

Another very significant point here is that such graft and corruption as do take place in government are almost wholly related to private business. It is the sale of goods to the government or the performance of work for the government by private enterprise that furnishes opportunity for a government official to take a bribe. The constructing of public highways, for example, has sometimes led to public scandal, but if the government got out its own raw material and fabricated it in its own plants, how could there be any opportunity for graft in constructing a road? Government ownership instead of increasing graft by government officials would greatly reduce or eliminate the small amount that now prevails by lessening the opportunity for its exercise.

Another point in relation to the general conditions of efficiency under government ownership is that restrictions upon improvements would be eliminated. Everyone knows that marked improvements have been made in the techniques of production and the quality of products by private enterprise during the past several decades, but the significant question for the present purpose is whether there has been deliberate retardation in improvements. Trade secrets and patent control, including patent suppression, have undoubtedly restricted economic progress, and perhaps also discoveries have been made that have been kept secret—not patented—in the interest of profits. While competition tends to compel improvements, as in the durability of automobile tires, this usually calls for only minor improvements in any one season. We would not expect one of our tire companies to announce an everlasting tire, assuming that one could be made. That would be poor business. We have been told that the formula for a permanent match is known and also the formula for an everlasting razor blade, but whether true or not we can understand why a private enterprise company would withhold such information and especially such a product. To be sure, a new firm or a firm not engaged in a given line of endeavor might produce a vastly improved product. It would be to its interest to do so. But in the first place, the formula for such a product is not likely to be developed except in the research departments of firms already in that line of business, and, secondly, if such a discovery were made outside the established firms, it is likely that patents already held by them would prevent the interloper from proceeding. The threat of prosecution for infringement might be enough to stop the adventurer, or at least might make it appear advantageous to sell out to the firm claiming a patent, thus permitting it to suppress the discovery. The newspapers recently reported that the formula for making a permanent paint has been discovered.* This news came from Russia, and could hardly have come from any other country.

Not only would we expect the dictates of "good business" in some instances to retard developments under private enterprise, but it is to be expected that quality will be deliberately made inferior when that appears profitable. Some years ago it was reliably reported that a company manufacturing razor blades instructed its scientists to make a blade that could not be used more than three times. The anti-trust division of the Department of Justice has records of many attempts to impair the quality of products. Wendell Berge, head of that division, in his book *Cartels* (1944), cites certain of these cases.† Among these are the case of a company manufacturing flashlight lamps that sought to reduce the quality of a bulb so that instead of lasting three times as long as the accompanying battery it would not outlast the battery; the case of a company that sought for a formula that would make its commercial product, sold at 85 cents a pound, unfit for use in dentistry, where the product

* *New York Times,* April 29, 1945.
† Chapter iii.

was sold for $45 a pound; and that of a manufacturer of paint that developed an improved pigment and then sought to make it unfit for use with textiles. Such cases need not, of course, surprise anyone. When conditions of monopolization—and a patent may give that—make it to the interest of a private enterprise firm to lessen the quality of its product, it is to be expected that that will be done as a matter of course.

Government-owned industry is under no such compulsion. Scientists need not be degraded under government ownership by being asked to thwart the public welfare. Further, under government ownership any gains in quality or in techniques of production would be introduced at once and would be promptly communicated throughout the economy. Each unit of industry would operate in a glass house. There would be no secrets. The gains from this might be considerable. Perhaps here is to be found an important reason for the amazing industrial progress of the Russians during the past twenty years.

Finally, in respect to efficiency under government ownership it may be noted that the avoidance of depressions would contribute far more to output than could possibly be lost by any conceivable decline in managerial efficiency. It is estimated that the loss to us as a nation in goods and services not produced during the 1930's amounted to 200 billion dollars. To this we should properly add the loss in morale, character, skill, and child health and training that the nation suffered. There are many reasons to believe that succeeding depressions, if we allow them to occur, may be even more severe than was that of the 1930's. The gain to us as an economy and as a nation from continuous production is almost incalculable.

5

Today the principal argument of the opponents of government ownership, however, lies in the non-economic field. The matters that we have just considered are in many cases admitted, or passed over, and attention is directed to the question of freedom. Instead of insisting, as for the past one hundred years or more, that "capitalism works—it produces the goods," the dominant point now is that capitalism is democratic while government ownership is necessarily authoritarian. William Röpke said a few years ago: "Economic collectivism means economic dictatorship and . . . economic dictatorship cannot be had without a political dictatorship." * Walter Lippmann observed: "It is impossible for the people to control the plan . . . the planners must control the people . . . [and] there can be no plan to find the planners: the selection of the despots . . . has to be left to the insecurity of irrational choice." † W. W. Aldrich, president of the Chase National Bank, says: "A democratically 'planned economy' is an impossibility." Judge Jerome Frank, when chairman of the Securities and Exchange Commission, said that private enterprise and democracy will stand or fall together, and Professor F. A. Hayek in a recent book, *The Road to Serfdom* (1944), elaborates this general view.

It may be noted first that democracy is not a necessary adjunct of privately owned industry and for that reason may be less antithetical to government ownership than the writings of the men who have been quoted indicate. A system of private enterprise in no way requires freedom of religion, freedom of speech and of the press, freedom to choose the officers of government, freedom to be secure against arbitrary search and seizure, or the right to trial by a jury of one's peers if accused of a crime. These Anglo-Saxon civil rights came along with capitalism, but are not a necessary part of it. The historical relationship has obscured the real relationship.

All of the freedom that capitalism—private enterprise—requires is that business men be free to make business decisions. What shall be produced? What wages shall be paid? What prices shall be charged? Shall production be continued or dis-

---

* *Harper's Magazine*, July 1939.
† *The Good Society* (1936), pp. 104–5. In his syndicated column, December 17, 1937, he said: "In so far as any nation attempts, by its government, to plan and manage the labor of its people, it must, as in Russia, make itself the master of their lives and of their conscience as well."

continued? Shall men be hired or fired? It is in the free determination of these and other similar questions that the essence of private enterprise lies. Absolutism in other matters may be ever so extreme—there may be a hereditary kingship, the absence of a parliament, the prohibition of political activity, a single state church—and yet enterprise be free. Indeed, business men may own their laborers as some did for a short time in the North and for a long time in the South without violating the principle of free enterprise. That system does not depend on any group other than business men being free, and their freedom need be only in the field of business.

To be sure, an absolute government would be likely to interfere with business. It was to escape this that the rising business men in England many years ago insisted on having control over the king. But so far as they were concerned, it was not necessary to go beyond this. Manhood suffrage, the secret ballot, pay for members of Parliament, and other present-day provisions of political democracy came long after the business men had achieved political control, and, in fact, these extensions of democracy were secured in the face of the violent opposition of the business group.

If the people of the United States should decide that the major industries of the country ought to be owned and operated by the government, and if the terms of purchase were agreeable to the present owners, there is no apparent reason why our democracy should be impaired in the slightest degree. This might be inadvisable for many reasons, but an adverse effect on democracy would not be one of them. The addition of the large-scale factories, mills, and mines to our already extensive public property would not mean "the loss of the last vestige of human liberty." If the managers of industries should be chosen by the directors of government corporations instead of by the present boards of directors, officials would not thereby become masters of "the lives and consciences" of the people of the nation.

Nor is the co-operation of citizens through the government "the road to serfdom," as Professor Hayek would have us believe in his book of that title. We do not move from democracy to totalitarianism as a result of first regulating our economic affairs and then taking up government ownership or "planning," as Hayek calls it. His "proof" that we do consists in denouncing what is bad and in approving what is good in government control, the test being whether competition is restricted or facilitated by the control. Practically no examples are given in his book, thus leaving to the unwary reader the task of supplying illustrations from what he happens to like or dislike. This clever device confirms the reader in his prejudices and strengthens his opposition to any further controls that he does not like.

Hayek is greatly disturbed by the grant of power by legislative bodies to administrative boards. They point, he thinks, to the disappearance of democratic legislative control and the exercise of power by administrators who find no stopping place short of extreme totalitarianism. The road is easy, but the yoke will be heavy. There are no illustrations, however. Does he mean that the granting of power to a sanitary inspector to determine whether a bake-shop is clean puts us on "the road to serfdom"?

Discretion is a necessary part of government, however simple and primitive the society may be, but the more complicated it becomes, the more the legislative body must delegate discretion. Congress could not legislate railway freight rates nor channels for radio stations. Nor could it legislate minute-by-minute orders to troops in battle. And how absurd it is to imply that the delegation of power in such cases destroys the "rule of law" and subjects an otherwise free people to an administrative despot!

Hayek not only implies that even one step toward control over our economic affairs will be fatal, despite an occasional declaration in favor of "social security" and "monopoly control"; he distinctly states his case in terms of complete control.

Thus he speaks of the direction of "all of our activities according to a central plan" (p. 57). This, he warns, would call for "a complete ethical code in which all different human values are allotted their due place" (p. 57). This code would be made, of course, by the absolute dictator whom we should have brought on ourselves by giving government officials a little control over some of our actions, such as, one may suppose, regulating public utility rates or setting up traffic lights. "*All* of our activities" must be meant to include all economic matters such as the growing of potatoes and the manufacture of women's hats; strictly speaking, the words cover even the brushing of the individual's teeth. The need for "a *complete* ethical code" comes from the dictator's having to decide for us what is to be produced and in what quantities, and how it is to be divided among the population. Hayek's "all or nothing" position is as absurd as would be the position of a boy who resists a request that he take off his cap on the ground that compliance would lead to a demand that he take off all of his clothes.

Mr. Lippmann's argument is similar to Hayek's:

There is, in short, no way by which the objectives of a planned economy can be made to depend upon popular decision. They must be imposed by an oligarchy of some sort, and that oligarchy must, if the plan is to be carried through, be irresponsible in matters of policy. [For] a plan subject to change from month to month or even from year to year is not a plan; if the decision has been taken to make ten million cars at $500 and one million suburban houses at $3000, the people cannot change their minds a year later, scrap the machinery to make the cars, abandon the houses when they are partially built, and decide to produce instead skyscraper apartment houses and underground railroads.*

One should expect from this that public roads, schoolhouses, county jails, and the like, which are provided democratically often through bond issues approved by popular ballot, are quite universally left half completed all over the country. Mr. Lipp-

---

* *The Good Society* (1936), p. 103.

mann cites no cases of this. But anyway he proves too much. For if it is the way of wisdom to guard against a change of mind before a task is completed, then it follows that collectivism is preferable to private enterprise, since an entire community is much less likely to change its mind than is a single individual.

Lippmann's version of Hayek's "complete ethical code" for the planners is that as between proposals to make cars or build houses, "The planners would have to consult an oracle; they could have no objective criterion by which to determine whether freedom of movement or stability of residence was more conductive to an abundant life" (p. 100).

This contention of these and other critics of planning has been thoroughly discredited by Taylor, Lange,* and other economists. They show that the market forces under government ownership could, as now, be allowed to decide as between cars and houses, or snoods and lipstick. Certainly the postal authorities do not, as Lippmann must believe that they do, consult oracles to determine how many one-cent or three-cent stamps to order day by day, nor do merchants need such assistance in deciding what goods to procure. The customers determine what will be produced next, and so they could however extensive was government ownership. No despot need hover about with a "complete ethical code" to determine what is to be done. The market can decide that.

Why need anyone suppose that a decision to own and operate certain of our industries collectively or to otherwise control them would cause us to relinquish principles and practices of freedom that we and our political ancestors, the British, have cherished for hundreds and hundreds of years? Does not our experience with public schools, parks, libraries, roads, the Post Office, and T.V.A. furnish a clue to our behavior under still more government ownership? Why suppose that we would lose all balance, common sense, and poise if the boards of the

* Oscar Lange: *On the Economic Theory of Socialism* (1938). The address by Taylor referred to is included in Lange's book.

big corporations became government officials? Certainly the fact that other peoples with far different traditions have submitted to tyrants is no reason to believe that we will. At any rate, the cases of despotism in the last thirty years have come from inefficient and impotent government, not from strong and powerful government. And in almost every case this came out of the failure to prevent or to alleviate unemployment. This was unquestionably true in the case of Italy and Germany.

If we are on "the road to serfdom," it is because Hayek and men like him in books, newspaper columns, editorials, cartoons, public speeches, and radio comment are instilling into the public mind such a fear of "omnipotent government," of "dictatorship," of "state socialism," that we will deny ourselves the privilege of democratically putting our house in order against the evils of unemployment. This indoctrination is encouraged by selfish interests that fear further regulation and by political opponents of the party in power.

An additional reason for the belief that democracy would disappear under government ownership stems from the notion that if a group is powerful enough to assume control of the machinery of government and to impose its will upon business men to the extent of depriving them of their properties, it will be powerful enough to suppress all opposition and, furthermore, will find it necessary to do so in order to maintain its control. This line of argument means only that if adjustments are established by force they must be maintained by force, for a time at least. But if changes are accomplished democratically, they could by a parity of reasoning be operated democratically.

Lack of political democracy in Russia has been the result, in part at least, of a belief by the group in power that Socialism was not sufficiently secure to warrant their trusting opposition parties, particularly since they might be under foreign influence. This has made it appear that collectivism and democracy are incompatible. Suppose, however, as many observers insist is the case, that democratic practices are being extended in Russia as the fear of opposition declines, and that in the postwar period, with the fear of attack by Germany and Japan removed and the need for speed in economic progress lessened, democracy as complete as we have known should come to prevail there. If then a revolutionary party should seize power by destroying the democratic processes and suppressing the opposition, and then establish capitalism and maintain it by force, democracy and capitalism would appear to be incompatible.

To have democracy, it is really only necessary to want it. This means that what we do together must be limited to public desires; that all activities shall be subject to debate and shall be abandoned when no longer desired. If we attempt to do only what we wish to do, there is no need for firing squads.

6

Perhaps the principal reason for fearing that our liberties will be jeopardized under an extension of government is the basic fear of what is new. Monsters can easily be seen in the dark, by those of little faith. The significant faith here is a faith in mankind—a faith in democracy. Such faith will remove mountains of doubt as to the future course of society.

A splendid antidote for the lack of such faith is the history of the development of our institutions. As observed earlier in this book, practically every attempt to correct the faults that have appeared as our economic life has changed has been denounced as an interference with our "liberties." Each item was to be another rivet in our self-imposed chains of slavery. Yet no one today would propose abolishing the pure-food laws, compulsory school attendance, quarantine and vaccination regulations, accident-compensation legislation, or almost any one of the items that were once bitterly denounced as infringements of "freedom." Particularly significant is the support given by the opposing political party in the campaign of 1944 to practically every item of legislation enacted during the first three terms of President Roosevelt. What was anticipated as tyranny was soon seen to be merely additional incidents of democracy at work.

Equally significant in retrospect are the dire forebodings that were made as to the effect on our liberty if we went to war. The *American Mercury,* for example, in its issue of July 1938 featured an article which declared that on the outbreak of war

> . . . all wages will be fixed by Presidential proclamation; all business will be licensed . . . the press, radio and movies censored, and personal liberty destroyed . . . you and I will become obedient robots of a giant machine. Our minds, as well as our bodies, will be at the service of an overpowering dictatorship. . . . Within twenty-four hours, we would not have a duly-elected chief executive—we would have a super-*Führer*.

All such predictions have proved to have been woefully false. We have had far fewer limitations on our usual liberties than during the first World War or the Civil War. Furthermore, in the midst of the war and at its most crucial stage we went through a political campaign in which the President and Commander in Chief was vilified and denounced as but few men have been in the history of our country, and not an administrative finger was raised against such conduct. The government through its well-organized control over war and civilian supplies saw to it that an adequate amount of paper was provided for the opposition press,* and adequate radio time was provided for every opposition orator.

Fears are commonly expressed as to the effect of government ownership on labor. The trade union movement we are told would be destroyed and the right to strike abolished. But why need there be any change? Why could not laborers bargain through their unions as they do now? And why should a change from private to government ownership alter the right to strike? There is a saying that one has no right to strike against the government, but what is its validity? Policemen and

---

* One of Hayek's few specific points concerns "the supply of paper" being controlled by "the planning authority" and thus not available to the opposition (p. 85).

soldiers must not strike because of the peculiar character of their work, but there does not appear to be any more reason for not tolerating strikes on the railroads, for example, if they were owned by the government than if they are owned privately. We should, of course, avoid strikes regardless of the form of ownership. They are a primitive and sometimes ruthless method of bargaining, and as faith in people would lead one to expect, the extension of democracy and experience with its methods tend to weaken the reliance on strikes as a means of effecting economic adjustments.

In respect to fear as to what lies ahead, it is interesting to consider the probable reaction if it were now proposed for the first time to establish state universities. Those of little faith would be apprehensive of the success of a school with a legislative appropriation of some three million dollars per year and a staff of two thousand or more employees. It would be insisted that it would be dominated by politics, that its personnel would be tools of the politicians, and that freedom in teaching and research would be denied except to those who happened to think as did the politicians who were in power at any one time.

Certainly, the almost total lack of any interference by legislatures or governors in the affairs of the state universities during the past fifty years, and the vigorous and capable teaching and research that go forward in all of them, unmolested except in rare cases by special groups or interests, would be a cause for wonder to many persons if they were not so familiar with the situation that they take it for granted. It is often said that there is no genuine freedom in the universities today, but on the basis of twenty-five years' service in one I am proud to say that I cannot imagine anyone having a greater degree of freedom than I have had. And my field is at the focal point of modern controversy.

The condition of freedom in state universities is not due, as is often said when the point is raised, to the high caliber of the men who are on the faculties, but rather to the high qualities of the citizens, including the politicians. They appreciate that the universities must be free to choose their own personnel and develop their own programs. If the men of the university staffs are of high caliber, it is because the basic attitude of the people of the states attracts such persons to the universities. The high traditions that prevail are not unique. Such traditions are developed wherever work calls for persons of more than mediocre ability. Faith in democracy could not lead one to expect any other result.

7

Finally, in respect to government ownership it may be noted that the many absurdities that we experience in our economy would disappear if we eliminated unemployment in this way. We could then be prosperous with a given stock of equipment. We would no longer be under the curse of building, building, building when we already were adequately supplied. We would not need stumps to grub. This means, of course, that we could under government ownership always adjust the volume of work done to the relative need for producer and consumer goods. We could keep our eye on consumption and construct equipment only as it was needed. We could, in short, act like rational economic men.

There would be no need under government ownership to engage in leaf-raking, or in "boondoggling" of any kind. We could at last stop "making work," whether in the production of unneeded equipment or in relief. There would be no need to use tools like those used in building the pyramids while twentieth-century machines stood idle in order to provide employment as under the W.P.A. Nor would we need to suffer derision as from the Young Pioneers in Moscow during the 1930's who, according to Walter Duranty, when told that we were using hand shovels rather than snowplows to remove snow from city streets in order to "make work," shouted: "Why don't the Americans use spoons to remove the snow?"

Government ownership would also, it seems, greatly decrease

the trade union practice of creating featherbed jobs. Such jobs are degrading to personality and it is hard to believe that they are often desired except as an escape from possible unemployment. Some persons will always want soft jobs, but certainly with the fear of unemployment removed, all such practices would lose much of their appeal and certainly would lose any justification that they may now have.

In general, policies of restriction would not need to be followed any longer. Food would not need to be destroyed or only one blade of grass let grow where two would like to grow; and industrial plants would no longer need to stand idle as long as men wished the goods that might be produced. Nor would there be any suppression of good ideas as there is here today through the control of patents and trade secrets.

The absurdities that now arise in our foreign trade relations would likewise disappear under government ownership. We would no longer desire to have our exports exceed our imports. We would stop the silly practice of swapping goods that we might use for gold that we proceed to bury. If goods were sold on credit to underdeveloped countries, it would be for the purpose of later getting imports in payment, not for the purpose of permitting ourselves to work. Also under government ownership, if we found ourselves in the position that we were in at the close of the first World War, when foreign nations owed us large sums of money, we would tell them to bring on goods to that value and we would be very happy about it. We would, furthermore, not have to refuse indemnities from a nation that forced us to war, nor refuse repayments from allies.

Nor under government ownership would we be embarrassed by having goods on hand at the close of a war or at any other time. Nor would it ever be necessary for us to go to war, or to threaten war, in order to acquire markets for the disposal of our goods, nor to build armaments and incite to war in order to create employment and stifle unrest. In short, solving the problem of unemployment by government ownership would permit us to achieve more fully that degree of rational conduct in our daily affairs and that measure of brotherhood in international relations that the better part of our natures has always urged us to attain.

CHAPTER XVIII

The Area of Choice

I

WHAT WE WILL DO in respect to the problem of unemployment will be largely what we must do. Our area of choice will prove to be far more limited than most persons may believe it to be. In the field of social conduct we are sharply limited as intelligent beings. The alternatives are usually of such widely varying degrees of satisfaction that only one is practicable, or at most only a very few. We have really no alternative to the use of traffic lights at the more congested street intersections of our cities. Given the automobile and the prevailing density of traffic, there is no other practicable method of traffic control.

Similarly no American city is really free in respect to whether public schools shall be provided, entirely aside from any statutory compulsion. Intelligent citizens cannot but arrange for public education today. Likewise as sensible persons there is no escape from a centralized water supply, whether public or private, in our modern cities. The same point can be made in respect to fire protection, garbage and sewage disposal, control of epidemics, and other items. If we are to act intelligently it is as imperative that certain procedures be followed by the group as it is that as individuals we observe certain rules of diet.

Looking at a broader area of social interest, we cannot escape the conclusion that the area of choice was sharply limited in regard to whether railroads should be subjected to government control of some sort or left unregulated. The early notion that railroads were essentially like grocery stores in their operations, and hence that they could be left subject to the discipline of competition and only to that, was found to be grossly invalid. While men were and long had been free to establish grocery stores anywhere, free to charge whatever prices they wished, free to sell to some persons at lower prices than to others, and free, indeed, to give groceries to favorite customers, it soon became evident that such practices could not be tolerated in respect to railroads. There was no alternative but to prevent discrimination among users of railroad services and to subject the entire agency to control. The method to be followed, however, was problematical. Various forms of regulation or outright ownership and operation by the government were all possibilities, but there could be no debate as between doing something and doing nothing, if we were to act intelligently. Laissez-faire in relation to railroads was not the part of wisdom in late nineteenth-century America.

Countless other illustrations could be given. Pure food and drug legislation, workmen's accident compensation, regulations in respect to safety in factories, supervision of life-insurance companies, and almost innumerable additions that might be made to this list illustrate the compelling force of circumstances. Sensible men have had to make provisions such as these.

This is not to say that there is a "historical necessity" that carries us along regardless of our will. Far from it. Rather this argument emphasizes the "moral necessity" of changing our behavior and our institutions as new techniques make it inadvisable to continue as before. The steam engine did not make us automatons in a historical trend, but it did make it advisable for us to create new political institutions to deal with the new economic conditions that appeared because of the steam engine. We may as persons of free will fail to act rationally. We may let our national house leak and crumble at the foundations. We are not compelled to act wisely. But if we do act intelligently, we are likely to find the area of choice narrowly circumscribed. If we are to eliminate depression unemployment we shall undoubtedly find that the alternative courses of action are few rather than many.

2

Another way of putting this is that the totality of life tends to be consistent. The economic, political, social, and religious aspects of life tend to be harmonious. Changes in any one of these realms tend to compel changes in the others. For the past two hundred years the economic aspect of life has been the one most subject to primary change, whatever may have been true earlier. And as changes have come in the methods of making a living, other changes have been added to them. To paraphrase Carlyle, steam engines, improved plowshares, and bank checks transformed the feudal lords from social pillars into reeds in the wind. They then adjusted themselves to the new social forces as in England or were consumed in the fire of revolution as in France.

Modern technology with its agglomeration of workers in interdependent large-scale urban enterprises has compelled new attitudes and new practices in all phases of life. There can be no escape over any considerable period of time from the oneness of life.

3

Adjustments may come tardily and they may come violently, but they may not be prevented when changes have created stresses and strains in social institutions. Government ownership, for example, may be extended by purchase or by confiscation. The slaves were freed by a war that was ruinous to a generation of Southern leaders, but only a few years earlier the owners of slaves could not only have received compensation for freeing them but have spared themselves, their families, and their Southern compatriots the agonies of an unsuccessful and devastating war.

The methods of adjustment that have been followed in the past have depended, obviously, largely on the quality of leadership. If those in the positions that have become vulnerable have been sufficiently wise, they have been able to maintain their social eminence by bringing about a reorientation of institutions in harmony with the needs and demands of the new conditions and with but little, if any, jeopardy to themselves.

Particularly the problem of unemployment today offers an opportunity to business men to assume leadership in overcoming this modern scourge. Unenlightened business men may keep their eyes on the past, but those of understanding know that the past is dead. They know, to quote Sandburg, that the past is but a bucket of ashes, a wind died down, a sun sunk in the west.

We need as a nation, in Lowell's words, to understand our

> . . . own age and the next,
> And make the present ready to fulfill
> Its prophecy, and with the future merge
> Gently and peacefully, as wave with wave.

Index

THE TEXT OF THIS BOOK IS SET IN GRANJON

a type named in compliment to Robert Granjon, type-cutter and printer—Antwerp, Lyons, Rome, Paris—active from 1523 to 1590. The boldest and most original designer of his time, he was one of the first to practise the trade of type-founder apart from that of printer.

This type face was designed by George W. Jones, who based his drawings upon a type used by Claude Garamond (1510–61) in his beautiful French books, and more closely resembles Garamond's own than do any of the various modern types that bear his name.

This book was composed, printed, and bound by Kingsport Press, Kingsport, Tenn. The typography is by James Hendrickson.